B.C.

Works by the
Rev. Principal A. E. GARVIE, M.A., D.D.

STUDIES IN THE INNER LIFE OF JESUS
THE CHRISTIAN CERTAINTY AND THE
    MODERN PERPLEXITY
STUDIES OF PAUL AND HIS GOSPEL
THE PURPOSE OF GOD IN CHRIST
THE MISSIONARY OBLIGATION IN THE
    LIGHT OF MODERN THOUGHT

HODDER AND STOUGHTON LTD.
PUBLISHERS   LONDON, E.C. 4

THE
BELOVED DISCIPLE

STUDIES OF THE FOURTH GOSPEL

BY

ALFRED E. GARVIE

M.A. (Oxon.), D.D. (Glas.)

PRINCIPAL OF HACKNEY AND NEW COLLEGES, LONDON

HODDER AND STOUGHTON
LIMITED   LONDON

Printed in Great Britain by T. and A. CONSTABLE LTD.
at the Edinburgh University Press

TO THE SACRED MEMORY

AND BLESSED PRESENCE

OF

A WIFE BELOVED

PREFACE

IN dealing with the subject of Christology the writer has been forced again and again to face the Problem of the Fourth Gospel. Tentative solutions have been accepted, but at last a solution has been reached which for the writer at least is as satisfactory as probably the difficulties of the problem will allow. This he ventures now to submit to the judgment of readers, as he has read enough and thought enough on the subject to entitle him at least to offer an opinion, however modestly and diffidently, and not to be content with saying Yea or Nay to the views of others. While other theories are referred to when necessary, the main endeavour is to gather from the Gospel itself the indications it offers regarding the mode of composition, the characteristics, the purpose and the authorship of the Gospel. Two series of articles in *The Expositor* form the basis of this volume, and the writer is grateful to the editor for permission to use this material. But the whole volume has been rewritten.

ALFRED E. GARVIE.

NEW COLLEGE,
LONDON, *June 30th*, 1922.

TABLE OF CONTENTS

III

IV

V

TABLE OF CONTENTS

X

INTRODUCTION

(1) A COMPARISON of Bishop B. F. Westcott's Commentary [1] and Dr. E. F. Scott's exposition of the teaching of the Fourth Gospel [2] at once forces on us the question : how can two so fully qualified scholars be led to so different conclusions regarding the same book ? Each is weak in that he does not give heed to what in the Gospel gives strength to the position of the other. The book is a Janus-like reality ; it is history and doctrine, fact and idea, reminiscence and reflexion. There are signs of an eye-witness in the familiarity shown with local and temporal details ; there is a personal response of human faith to the divine grace as revealed in Jesus Christ ; Christian experience finds itself more at home in the Fourth Gospel than in any other. These are all supports of Bishop Westcott's position. The Prologue shows a speculative rather than a historical interest ; the peculiarities of the Johannine Epistles are reproduced in thought as well as language ; the manner and method of teaching assigned in the Fourth Gospel to Jesus is very unlike the presentation in the Synoptic Gospels. These features of the Gospel lend countenance to the contention of Dr. Scott.

(2) A solution of the problem has been sought in ' partition ' theories in which a more or less historical source has been separated from additions or modifica-

[1] *The Gospel according to St. John.*
[2] *The Fourth Gospel : its Purpose and Theology.*

tions made by an editor, influenced more or less by a
doctrinal interest. The main difference in these theories
is in regard to the comparative historical value to be
assigned to the discourses or the narratives.

(i) H. H. Wendt [1] uses as his clue ' the difference
between the point of view of the Evangelist and that
of the discourses of Jesus ' in respect of the purpose of
the miracles ; and reaches the conclusion that ' the
source contained discourses and conversations of Jesus,'
and ' does not seem to have included any piece of
purely narrative character.' Such a principle of
partition seems to be arbitrarily imposed on the Gospel.
From this standpoint he offers a detailed analysis of
the *source-components* of the Gospel.

(ii) Mr. J. M. Thompson, in an article on ' The structure of the Fourth Gospel,' [2] calls for ' a recognition of the
dual nature of the Gospel, a reconsideration of internal
rather than external marks of different points of view,
and an attempt to distinguish in broad outline the parts
of the Gospel which express each of these divergent
tendencies.' The two standpoints are represented by
the Prologue (i. 1-18) and the two passages (xii. 36-43
and xx. 30-31) which may originally have formed one
conclusion. ' The conclusion assumes that the chief
work of Jesus was to do miracles ($\sigma\eta\mu\varepsilon\hat{\iota}\alpha$, signs), and
that the main object of the Gospel was to describe
them : that the miracles were meant to rouse belief
in Jesus as the Jewish Messiah : and that those who
believed in Him would obtain that eternal life which
was the goal of their apocalyptic hopes.' The difference
from the Prologue is evident. ' The dual point of view
regards the Prologue as the Preface to the discourses

---

[1] *The Gospel according to St. John: an Inquiry into its Genesis
and Historical Value*, p. 166.

[2] *The Expositor*, 8th series, vol. x. pp. 512- 14.

the way of comment and background by the Evangelist himself. That the Gospel is divinely inspired I strongly hold, and especially inspired in being adapted to further high Christian thought in ways which the writer only dimly foresaw. But inspiration does not work by giving the inspired man a direct knowledge of events which have happened in the world ; that is not the character of inspiration. He may be careless of fact, or misled by incorrect information, nor is he in any way infallible ; but he is an exponent of the life of the Spirit under the forms of his own age.' [1] While, as the sequel will show, not agreeing with Dr. Gardner in details, the writer heartily welcomes his testimony to the value of the Gospel for Christian thought and life and his recognition of the complexity of the structure of the Gospel.

(vii) Dr. V. N. Stanton [2] distinguishes the evangelist who wrote the Gospel from the witness on whose teaching he depended for most of his material. He still, but not very confidently, identifies the witness with John the son of Zebedee ; the evangelist, he maintains, may also have been a Jew of Palestine who as a boy had seen and heard Jesus, and who removed to Asia as a lad or young man before John did. ' For the fact that John the son of Zebedee lived and taught in Asia in his latter years the reminiscences of Irenaeus of what he had heard in his youth from his elders, and the general tradition of the Church in the latter part of the second century may be thoroughly trusted, because this would be matter of common knowledge, about which it would have been exceedingly difficult for an error to arise and to hold its ground ; all the more

---

[1] *Op. cit.* pp. 122-23.
[2] *The Gospels as Historical Documents*, part iii., *The Fourth Gospel.*

so in this case because there were those whose interest it would have served to have cast doubt upon it in a bitter controversy at a time when it would not have been too late to call it in question. But the authorship of the Fourth Gospel by the Apostle John, though included in the second-century tradition about him, cannot be regarded as therefore established.' [1] He does not think it probable that the Apostle, coming to Asia in mature life, could have undergone the intellectual development which must be presupposed in the evangelist, who may be assumed to have gone to Asia ' at an age when his mind was more supple ' [2] than the Apostles can have been. The assumption that the evangelist had also seen and heard Jesus he regards as necessary because of the claim in i. 14 of eye-witness, also 1 John i. ' These expressions cannot be interpreted of spiritual sight and touch and hearing because these would not have been referred to merely as experiences in the past ; this meaning is also inconsistent with the general tenor of the contexts. One can, however, understand that the claim in question might be made by a youth or boy, younger by some years than the Apostle John even if the latter was the youngest of the Twelve, but who could remember having sometimes himself seen and heard Jesus, and who had derived a sense of knowledge which was at least almost immediate of the Divine revelation made in the Lord, by intimate association with His personal disciples very soon after His departure.' [3] The writer does not accept either of these arguments as conclusive, but the question of authorship will be later discussed. What has here to be noted is that, although Dr. Stanton makes no

---

[1] *The Gospels as Historical Documents*, part iii., *The Fourth Gospel*, pp. 279-80.
[2] *Op. cit.* p. 281.   [3] *Op. cit.* p. 281.

attempt at an analysis, he recognizes in the Gospel the contributions of the witness and the evangelist. The only encouragement he gives to ' partition ' is the acknowledgment that the Appendix is by a different hand from the rest of the Gospel, ' although there appears to be no ground for interposing a long interval between the composition of the one and the other.' [1]

(3) Only an indication can now be given of the hypotheses of the composition of the Gospel which will be presented in this volume. The *Appendix* on the one hand and the *Prologue* on the other afford us justification for distinguishing the contribution of a later editor, whom we may call the Redactor (R), and of the Evangelist (E) from the matter provided by the Witness (W) although his matter has passed through the hands of the Evangelist. The *Appendix* shows an ecclesiastical interest in the Synoptic tradition, which affords us a clue to other portions of the Gospel which we may ascribe to R. In this analysis the writer finds himself in very close agreement with Dr. Bacon, although he retains for the witness some passages which Dr. Bacon assigns to the redactor. The *Prologue* proves a theological interest of the evangelist's which we can also trace elsewhere in the Gospel. Even in the contribution of the witness we can distinguish, if we cannot always separate, two strands. (Here John iii. is of special value.) The *reminiscences* of the witness, which include words and deeds of Jesus as well as his comments which cannot always be detected, very often pass over into *reflexions*, in which the results of his religious experience and the effects of his intellectual environment are blended together in one stream. These *reminiscences and reflexions* are reproduced by the evangelist, himself

[1] *Op. cit.* p. 27.

a disciple of the witness, to whose affection possibly
is due the description of the witness as ' the disciple
whom Jesus loved,' if it was not already current in
a circle of disciples in Ephesus.   It is not often possible
to separate the reflexions from the reminiscences, nor
even to distinguish the report of the evangelist apart
from his own comments from the teaching as it was
given by the witness.   Even as regards the utterances
of Jesus we cannot be always sure that we have the
ipsissima verba, and not a paraphrase from the evangelist's standpoint.

While this solution of the problem may at first sight
appear too complicated, yet with the data in our hands
can any simple solution be expected ?   To treat the
Gospel as a unity on the one hand, or to resolve it
verse by verse into its different elements, is a solution
that the character of its composition forbids.   What is
here suggested is not a mechanical invention but a
vital development, which has greater probability of
truth.   The Gospel grew rather than was made.   The
view here offered involves also a conclusion regarding
authorship ; but that conclusion can be reserved until
the analysis of the Gospel has been completed, as
that analysis will itself offer the data, on which the
conclusion rests.

BIBLIOGRAPHY

A. BOOKS REFERRED TO IN THIS VOLUME

(I) THE FOURTH GOSPEL

1. *The Gospel according to St. John,* with Introduction and Notes, by B. F. WESTCOTT. John Murray, 1890.

2. *The Gospel of St. John,* by MARCUS DODS. *The Expositor's Greek Testament,* i. Hodder and Stoughton, 1897.

3. *The Gospel according to St. John : an Inquiry into its Genesis and Historical Value,* by H. H. WENDT. Eng. tr. T. and T. Clark, 1902.

4. *The Character and Authorship of the Fourth Gospel,* by JAS. DRUMMOND. Williams and Norgate, 1903.

5. *The Criticism of the Fourth Gospel,* by WM. SANDAY. Clarendon Press, 1905.

6. *The Fourth Gospel : its Purpose and Theology,* by E. F. SCOTT. T. and T. Clark, 1906.

7. *The Ephesian Gospel,* by PERCY GARDNER. Williams and Norgate, 1915.

8. *The Origin of the Prologue to St. John's Gospel,* by RENDEL HARRIS. Cambridge, 1917.

9. *The Fourth Gospel : its Significance and Environment,* by ROBERT HARVEY STRACHAN. Student Christian Movement, 1917.

10. *The Fourth Gospel in Research and Debate,* by B. W. BACON. Yale, 1918.

11. *The Gospels as Historical Documents.* Part. iii., *The Fourth Gospel,* by V. N. STANTON. Cambridge, 1920.

12. *The Aramaic Origin of the Fourth Gospel,* by C. F. BURNEY. The Clarendon Press, 1922.

(II) NEW TESTAMENT

1. *The Miraculous Element in the Gospels*, by A. B. BRUCE. Hodder and Stoughton, 1890.

2. *The Theology of the New Testament*, by G. B. STEVENS. T. and T. Clark, 1899.

3. *The Gospel History and its Transmission*, by F. C. BURKITT. T. and T. Clark, 1906.

4. *A Critical Introduction to the New Testament*, by A. S. PEAKE. Duckworth, 1909.

5. *An Introduction to the Literature of the New Testament*, by JAMES MOFFATT. T. and T. Clark, 1911.

6. *The New Testament : a New Translation*, by JAS. MOFFATT. Hodder and Stoughton, 1913.

7. *Gospel Origins*, by W. W. HOLDSWORTH. Duckworth, 1913.

(III) CHURCH HISTORY

1. *Ante-Nicene Library. The Writings of Irenaeus.* 2 vols. T. and T. Clark, 1884.

2. *Nicene and Post-Nicene Fathers : The Church History of Eusebius.* Parker and Co., 1890.

3. *The History of Dogma*, by HARNACK. Eng. tr., vol. i. Williams and Norgate, 1894.

(IV) THEOLOGY

1. *Eschatology, Hebrew, Jewish and Christian*, by R. H. CHARLES. Black, 1899.

2. *The Other Side of Death*, by R. G. MACINTYRE. Macmillan and Co., 1920.

B. ARTICLES REFERRED TO IN THIS VOLUME

1. The Appendix to the Fourth Gospel, by R. H. STRACHAN. *The Expositor*, 8th series, vol. vii. pp. 255 ff.

2. Is the Fourth Gospel a Literary Unity ? by R. H. STRACHAN. *The Expository Times*, vol. xxvii. pp. 22 ff., 232 ff., 280 ff., 330 ff.

3. Accidental Disarrangements in the Fourth Gospel, by J. M. THOMPSON. *The Expositor*, 8th series, vol. ix. pp. 421 ff.

4. Is John xxi. an Appendix ? by J. M. THOMPSON. *The Expositor*, 8th series, vol. x. pp. 139 ff.

5. The Structure of the Fourth Gospel, by J. M. THOMPSON. *The Expositor*, 8th series, vol. x. pp. 512 ff.

6. The Composition of the Fourth Gospel, by J. M. THOMPSON. *The Expositor*, 8th series, vol. xi. pp. 34 ff.

7. The Interpretation of John vi., by J. M. THOMPSON. *The Expositor*, 8th series, vol. xi. pp. 337 ff.

8. Some Editorial Elements in the Fourth Gospel, by J. M. THOMPSON. *The Expositor*, 8th series, vol. xiv. pp. 214 ff.

9. The Beloved Disciple, by SWETE. *Journal of Theological Studies*, July 1916, mentioned in *The Expository Times*, vol. xxviii. p. 97.

10. The Festival of Lives given for the Nation in Jewish and Christian Faith, by B. W. BACON. *The Hibbert Journal*, vol. xv. pp. 256 ff.

11. The Fourth Gospel in the Light of Modern Scholarship, by A. T. ROBERTSON. *The Constructive Quarterly*, vol. v. pp. 671 ff.

12. Irenaeus and the Fourth Gospel, by H. A. A. KENNEDY. *The Expository Times*, vol. xxix. pp. 103 ff., 168 ff., 235 ff., 312 ff.

13. Jesus' ' Native Place ' in John, by B. W. BACON. *The Expositor*, 8th series, vol. xxiii. pp. 41 ff.

14. The Fourth Gospel and the Sacraments, by J. P. NAISH. *The Expositor*, 8th series, vol. xxiii. pp. 53 ff.

15. The Disciple whom Jesus loved, by B. GREY GRIFFITH. *Expository Times*, vol. xxxii. pp. 379 ff.

16. The Disciple whom Jesus loved, by F. WARBURTON LEWIS. *Expository Times*, vol. xxxiii. p. 42.

17. Was Lazarus ' the beloved Disciple ' ? by H. RIGG. *Expository Times*, vol. xxxiii. pp. 232 ff.

18. The Rearrangement of John vii. and viii., by G. H. C. MACGREGOR. *Expository Times*, vol. xxxiii. pp. 74 ff.

19. The Raising of Lazarus, by EDWARD GRUBB. *Expository Times*, vol. xxxiii. pp. 404 ff.

20. A Sometimes Neglected Factor Illustrated, by INNES LOGAN. *The Expositor*, 8th series, vol. xxiv. pp. 75 ff.

21. Our Lord's Discourses with His Apostles after His Resurrection, by Rev. G. HENSLOW (pamphlet reprinted from *The Interpreter*).

As the titles of books and articles have been so fully given, they will not be always repeated in the footnotes.

ANALYSIS OF THE FOURTH GOSPEL

1. THE EVANGELIST.

   i. 1-18, 48 ; ii. 17, 21-22, 24-25 ; iii. 31-36 ; iv. 18, 44 ; v. 18 (?), 19-29 ; vii. 39 ; viii. 27 ; xi. 42, 51-52 ; xii. 33, 38-41 ; xiii. 1-3, 18-19 ; xiv. 29 ; xv. 25 ; xvii. 3, 12 ; xviii. 4, 9, 32 ; xix. 24, 28, 36, 37 ; xx. 30, 31.

   Some of the comments of the Evangelist may come from the Witness.

2. THE REDACTOR.

   iv. 43-54 (?) ; vi. ; xii. 20-36 ; xiii. 36-38 ; xviii. 17-18, 25-27 ; xix. 35 ; xxi. .

   Some of the matter in vi. and xii. 20-36 is probably reminiscence of the Witness.

3. THE WITNESS.

   (a) Reminiscences probably out of their proper context : iii. 14-15 ; vi. 62 ; iii. 13, 11, 12 ; vi. 51c-57 ; xiv. 16-20, 26 ; xv. 26-27 ; xvi. 7-15.

   (b) Reminiscences in proper context : i. 19-34 (except 30 = i. 15), 35-51 (vv. 41, 42, 45, 48, 49 contain doubtful elements) ; ii. 1-12 ; iii. 22-30 ; ii. 13-25 (except 17, 21-22, 24-25) ; iii. 1-10, 16-21 (reflexions on reminiscences) ; iv. 1-42 (except 18 doubtful and 24 a reflexion), 43-45 (except 44), 46-54 (doubtful) ; v. 1-18 (18c doubtful), 24, 30-47 ; vii. 15-24 ; vii. 1-14, 25-36 (possibly viii. 12-20 may follow here), 37-44, 45-52 (possibly 37-44 should follow 45-52) ; viii. 12-20 (if not after vii. 36), 21-59 (except 27) ; ix. 1-41 ; x. 19-29, 1-18, 30-39, 40-42 ; xi. 1-16 (doubtful), 17-46 (except 39 and 42), 47-53 (except 51 and 52), 54-57 ; xii. 1-11, 12-19, 44-50, 37-43 (except 38-40) ; xiii. 1-17 (except 1-3), 18-31a (except 18b, 19, 20), possibly 34-35 ; xv. 1-25 (except 25) ; xvi. 1-6,

16-24 (possibly followed by x. 1-10), 25-33 ; xiii. 31*b*-33 ; xiv. 1-25, 28-31 (except 29) ; xvii. 1-26 (except 3 and 12*c*) ; xviii. 1-14 or 16 (except 4 and 9), 24, 19-23, 28-40 ; xix. 1-34 (except parts of 24, 28) ; xix. 38-42 ; xx. 1-29.

The displacements, for which reason is given in the discussion, have been assumed in the order given above ; where possible comments, whether of evangelist or witness, have also been indicated as exceptions to the reminiscences. Any such analysis must be tentative.

I

THE PROLOGUE

(1) THE Prologue has a twofold interest, (*a*) to assert the identity of the Word with Jesus, and (*b*) to deny the superiority of John the Baptist to Jesus. With reference to the second and subordinate interest a note from Dr. Peake's *A Critical Introduction to the New Testament* may be quoted, as although the writer read the work referred to on its appearance, he has not now access to it for the verification of his remembrance of it. 'This has been argued with great originality and acuteness, but also with much violent exegesis by Baldensperger in his *Der Prolog des vierten Evangeliums*, 1898. His views have met with little acceptance, though the brilliance and suggestiveness of his discussions have been amply recognized. Pfleiderer and E. F. Scott think that he has made out his point for the first three chapters of the Gospel. On the other hand see Jülicher and Loisy, also an article in the *Journal of Biblical Literature*, vol. xx., 1901, Part i., by Prof. C. W. Rishell.' [1]

Without discussing Baldensperger's view, as it is not relevant to the main purpose of this volume we may ask, assuming for the moment the present order of verses as correct, why should the Gospel throw into the very forefront and interrupt the presentation of the primary and dominant purpose by the denial that John is not to be identified with the Logos as Jesus is, if there was no party or school which exalted John

[1] P. 224.

A

above Jesus ? The report of John's witness to Jesus, and of the abandonment of John for Jesus by the first disciples gains greater significance, if such a contention had to be met.

(2) The possibility must, however, be admitted that there are displacements in the Prologue, *i.e.* that the passages dealing with the Baptist, *vv.* 6-8 and *v.* 15 are insertions. Certainly *vv.* 1-5 and 9-14 would form a compact and continuous exposition of the doctrine of the Logos. On *v.* 14, *vv.* 16-18 would form an appropriate commentary. Verses 6-8 and 15 (of which *v.* 30 is a repetition which interrupts the sequence of *vv.* 29 and 31) would seem also to belong to the Prologue as *v.* 7 refers to *v.* 5, and *v.* 15 if it teaches as Westcott argues it does, that it is Christ's eternal nature that gave Him necessarily (historical) priority to John,[1] puts on John's lips the metaphysical doctrine of the Prologue.[2] Only if these verses about John do not belong to the Prologue does the above statement need modification. We may assume that these verses do belong to the Prologue, that they followed *v.* 18, and formed a suitable transition to the record of John in *v.* 19.

(3) Was this twofold interest characteristic of the teacher (the witness) or the scholar (the evangelist) ? If the witness was, as is probable, one of the earliest disciples (*v.* 37) he would have a personal interest in justifying his preference for Jesus. But if he was an early disciple, is it likely that he would himself have so identified John with the Logos, as to be expressing a personal interest, a result of personal

[1] 'The argument . . . points to a present consequence of an eternal truth.' (*The Gospel according to St. John*, p. 13.)
[2] It is not likely that the Baptist was led by the Apocalyptic books as Dods suggests (*Expositor's Greek Testament*, i. 696) to affirm the Messiah's pre-existence.

experience, in a denial of the identity ? Does not the Prologue gain a living power if it is the confession of the experience of the evangelist ? He had been influenced by Philo's teaching ; he had for a time sought in what he had learned about the Baptist the realization of the ideal. What the witness had done for him was by the presentation of the life and teaching of Jesus to convince him that the Word had become flesh not in the Baptist but in the Christ. As doubtless in his former view he had not stood alone, so in reporting the witness's teaching, which had so changed all things for him, he was not merely confessing his own personal experience, but was making his personal appeal to his former associates to follow in the path into which he had been led. Apollos, who knew only the baptism of John, came from Alexandria (Acts xviii. 24-25) ; and Alexandria was Philo's home. The disciples who had been baptized only ' into John's baptism ' (xix. 1-3) were met with in Ephesus. Do not these two facts suggest a possible connexion of the teaching of Philo and the baptism of John in a school or party, which was at a later date still represented in Ephesus ? If the evangelist was won by the teaching of the witness from this party the Prologue gains in personal interest.

(4) It must be admitted, however, that this is conjecture ; and that against the conjecture that the evangelist came by the way of Philo as well as the Baptist to Christ is that the theology of the Gospel, as we shall soon see, is not dominated by the philosophy of Philo, neither is the theology of the Johannine Epistles, of which the evangelist may still be regarded as the author. (*a*) As regards this last point—the identity of the authorship of the Gospel and the Epistle—the words of Dr. Stanton may be quoted as

the writer himself is in this volume concerned only
with the identity of the witness, and not of the evangelist—for his present purpose only a subordinate
consideration : ' My conclusion is that the First
Epistle of St. John is from the same hand as the
Gospel, and that it was written earlier. Difficulties
connected with the supposition that the author is the
same appear only when the Gospel is held to be the
earlier writing. And there is nothing to constrain
us to assign this order to them. Indeed the differences
between them in the main point to the opposite one.' [1]
(b) As regards the theology of this First Epistle in
relation to that of the Prologue especially Stanton
says : ' The thought in the opening verses of the
Epistle is logically prior to that in the Prologue to the
Gospel.' [2] Had the evangelist been a disciple of Philo
that difference would have been at least improbable.
(c) Stanton thinks it unlikely that a man of fully
matured mind, as we must assume the witness to have
been, would have been so ready to assimilate the
teaching of Philo even to the extent that the teaching of the Gospel shows, as a younger man—the
evangelist—might have been. ' Although the composition of the Fourth Gospel did not require the
Alexandrian training on the part of its author which
some have held that it did, and although there need
not have been any fundamental difference between
the conception of the Person and Work of Jesus in
the mind of a primitive apostle, and that which we
meet with in this Gospel, yet it would be strange that
one who had come among the Greek or Hellenised
population of western Asia Minor in the last two or
three decades of a long life should have been able in

[1] *The Gospels as Historical Documents,* part iii. pp. 102-103.
[2] P. 97.

his presentation of the truth to adapt himself to his hearers and readers, laying aside earlier habits of speech and points of view, and should show also that in his own thought he has undergone development to the extent that we find here.' [1] With this judgment the writer entirely agrees, and has only to add these modifications : (i) that, as he will try to show, the Christology of the evangelist is not identical with that of the witness, who stands even in his reflexions nearer the primitive tradition ; and (ii) that the Christology of the evangelist is not so entirely dominated by the Logos philosophy as has been assumed. To this consideration we next pass.

(5) Dr. Scott affirms while Harnack denies that the identification of Jesus with the Logos dominates the whole of the Fourth Gospel.[2] The writer's own study has led him to agree entirely with Harnack. What impressed the witness in the early life of Jesus was ' the glory as of the only begotten of the Father, full of grace and truth ' (v. 14). It is this glory which shines in every page of the record. The interest of the Gospel is not cosmic, but ethical and spiritual ; and so the Son expresses the meaning he finds in Jesus, and not the Word. Doubtless it was the testimony of the witness which persuaded the evangelist that Jesus was the Word ; but the interest in the Logos was, to begin with, the latter's and not the former's. This explanation removes the difficulty of the otiose introduction of the idea of the Logos which the current view involves. That the Christology of the evangelist himself was influenced by the Logos philosophy cannot be denied ; but no less was it influenced by the

---

[1] *Op. cit.* pp. 280-281.
[2] Compare Scott's *The Fourth Gospel*, pp. 163-175; and Harnack's *The History of Dogma*, vol. i. p. 329.

doctrine of the Son, which he had learned from the witness.

(6) If the evangelist has contributed this conception we need not ask whether a Palestinian origin of it can be proved, as we might have some reason to do if the conception were characteristic of the witness. (a) Bishop Westcott's view that ' the sources of the Logos doctrine in the Gospel were Palestinian and Biblical ' Dr. Stanton sets aside on the ground that this derivation does not as adequately account for the teaching of the Prologue as does a Philonic source.[1] Dr. Stanton also dissents from the view advanced by Dr. Rendel Harris in his book, *The Origin of the Prologue to St. John's Gospel* : ' Our hypothesis that the Logos of the Fourth Gospel is a substitute for a previously existing Sophia involves (or almost involves) the consequence that the Prologue is a hymn in honour of Sophia, and that it need not be in that sense due to the same authorship as the Gospel itself.' [2] The writer has himself found Dr. Harris's argument more ingenious than convincing.   But even were his hypothesis proved, the argument here would be in no way affected—that the Prologue is due to the evangelist and not to the witness.   (b) We may still maintain the assumption that the doctrine of the Prologue depends on Philo.   The reasons for adhering to this position are well stated by Dr. Stanton.   ' Since in the writings of Philo, composed sixty or more years before the Fourth Gospel, we find a doctrine of the Logos, which in certain of its broad features (to say at present no more) resembles that of the Prologue ; since in Philo the Logos appears under a twofold aspect, the one

[1] *Op. cit.* p. 162, note pp. 185-186.
[2] *Op. cit.* p. 6.   Dr. Burney's view is discussed at the end of this volume.

interior to the life of God, the other as conditioning God's relation to the universe ; since there too it is through the Logos that God created and that He sustains and guides all things, and even the title Son of God is there given Him ; since through the Logos He reveals Himself to man, and only in the Logos that He can be known, it is surely unreasonable to suppose that the thought of the Prologue is wholly independent of that of the Alexandrian school, of the doctrines of which the writings of Philo are the representatives to us.' [1] As the case of Apollos shows, a teacher from Alexandria might carry the teaching of Philo to Ephesus. (c) We need not assume that the evangelist had a first-hand knowledge of Philo's teaching, nor that when he was led to identify the Logos with the man Jesus he transferred even the conception of the Logos unmodified by the new associations. The witness's presentation of Jesus was dominated by the conception *Son of God*, and this is the characteristic feature of the Gospel as a whole. Whether the evangelist had, before coming under the influence of the witness, adopted the idea of the Logos as the solution of his own intellectual problem, or after he had already been convinced by that teaching, had borrowed it for his apologetic purpose, it was the evangelist, and not the witness who identified Jesus with the Word. Just as the more cosmic side of the work of Christ expounded in the *Epistle to the Colossians* was not native to the mind of Paul, but was forced upon him by the incipient Gnosticism of the heresy he was combating, so this new cosmic idea of the Logos was not congenial to the witness; but it found its way into the Fourth Gospel through the evangelist for the one or the other of the reasons above suggested.

[1] *Op. cit.* p. 186.

(7) The Logos doctrine of the Prologue has been influenced by the Christology of the Gospel ; and in the Prologue we may already detect the contrast of the two doctrines—the Philonic and the Johannine. Even if Dr. Harris's conclusions were accepted, the comparison [1] with the fully developed Philonic doctrine of the Logos would retain its interest and value.

(i) The contrast which has been most insisted on is this, that for Philo the Logos, while more than a personification, is not yet a person, while in the Fourth Gospel the Logos is personal : and this difference is regarded as a proof of the greater theological genius of the evangelist ; but this way of dealing with the matter seems to the writer quite erroneous, and to ignore two very important considerations. (a) It is not by any greater speculative insight that the evangelist advances beyond Philo. It would have been no merit in Philo, had he conceived the Logos as a person distinct from God, but a defect, as he would have thereby abandoned his monotheism, and have moved towards polytheism. There was nothing in the revelation of God, so far as he as a pious Jew had received it, to warrant any such step. Until the Incarnation there was no necessity for thought to raise the problem of the personality of the Logos. What led the evangelist to go beyond Philo was ' the fact of Christ.' How could the historical personality find a place within the Godhead ? The doctrine of the Logos seemed to offer a bridge for thought from history to theology. We must try to reproduce the mental process as accurately as we can. It was not any speculative genius which led to the discovery of

---

[1] *The Origin of the Prologue to St. John's Gospel.* He finds in the Prologue ' a hymn in honour of Sophia ' (p. 6) and derives it from the Jewish Wisdom literature (p. 43).

the necessity of personal distinctions within the Godhead ; Christian faith has not usually felt itself much
at home in these speculative constructions. What
was present to the evangelist's mind through the
teaching of the witness was the concrete individuality
of Jesus ; this he identifies with the Logos, without
considering the metaphysical difficulties which such
an identification involved, difficulties from which
Christology in its subsequent developments made
ineffectual attempts to escape. Paul's procedure in
Phil. ii. 1-11 is similar.[1] The historical personality
is transferred to the eternal reality ; the Logos is
conceived as personal because identified with the
person of Jesus. That Christian faith saw God in
Christ is assuredly an immeasurably great advance
for the religious thought and life of mankind ; but
that is not the same as regarding the doctrine of the
Prologue as speculatively an advance on Philo's idea.
(b) We must not conceal from ourselves the fact that
the identification of Jesus with the Logos was rather
a problem than a solution for speculative theological
thought. If we invest the Son or the Logos in the
Godhead with the concrete individuality of Jesus,
regard Him not only as personal, but as a person in
the modern sense of the word, we make the Godhead
incomprehensible or sacrifice the divine unity to
tritheism. Subsequently Christological thought showed
that where the equality of Father and Son and the unity
of the Godhead were emphasized, the doctrines of a
distinct personal Logos fell into the background ;
wherever, on the contrary, the Logos doctrine pre-
vailed, and the difference from God was asserted, the
divine monarchy was safeguarded by an insistence
on the subordination of the Logos. We must regard

---

[1] See *Studies of Paul and his Gospel*, by the writer, pp. 117-118.

the Logos doctrine as an ally of very doubtful value
to Christian theology ; and the greater emphasis on
the distinct personality of the Logos only increases the
difficulties for thought.

(ii) The problem which Philo sought to solve by
his Logos doctrine was primarily a *cosmic* one, the
relation of the finite world to an Infinite God. The
Prologue to the Fourth Gospel does (*v.* 3) refer to the
making of the world by the Word ; but immediately
passes from the cosmic to the moral and religious
interest. That the physical images of light and darkness are used does not involve a physical dualism as
the basis of the moral and religious contrast in human
history on which such stress is laid. It is with unbelief and unrighteousness and faith and goodness
that the Gospel and the Prologue are alone concerned.
The writer cannot see any warrant for the assertion
that the Logos doctrine has influenced the Fourth
Gospel as regards the choice of the miracles recorded.
The feeding of the five thousand and the walking on
the water (vi. 1-21) are derived from the Synoptic
tradition. The miraculous draught of fishes (xxi. 6)
has a parallel in Luke's Gospel (v. 4-7). If the writer
is correct in his theory regarding the additions by the
redactor, neither of these narratives belongs to the
Gospel in its earliest form. The relation of the
witness (the beloved disciple) to Mary the mother of
Jesus and his own presence adequately account for
the report of the turning of the water into wine at
Cana (ii. 1-11). The record shows no trace of the
evangelist's interest in the cosmic functions of the
Logos. Here there is a marked contrast between the
Fourth Gospel and Philo's teaching.

(iii) In Philo the Logos is a necessity for thought as
mediating between the transcendent, incomprehensible,

and indefinable deity and the world. The divine
transcendence is the dominating consideration ; but
even in the Prologue God is brought very near to man.
It is the glory of the only begotten from the Father
which men behold. The invisible God has been declared by the Son in the bosom of the Father. Men
through Him may gain the right to become the children
of God (*vv.* 12-14, 18). Throughout the Gospel immanence is the key-word. The Father dwells in the
Son, and the Son in the Father : the believer dwells
in Christ, and Christ in him; and the Father in the Son
dwells in men, and men in Him.[1] The dualism of which
the Philonic doctrine of the Logos is a result, is foreign
to the Gospel. In this, as in other respects, the Logos
doctrine is no clue to the interpretation of the Gospel.

(8) The teaching about pre-existence peculiar to the
Gospel is not necessarily only a deduction from the
Logos-idea, but may be brought into relation with
Jesus' religious consciousness. It may be convenient
to deal with the passages presenting this conception
at this stage. In i. 30, John the Baptist is represented
as already testifying to the pre-existence of the man
who was to come after him, ὅτι πρῶτός μου ἦν, the
personal superiority is based on temporal priority.
Was John the Baptist likely to know of the pre-existence of Christ ; and was he the man to express himself
in such subtle language ? As this verse almost
verbatim reproduces the statement in *v.* 15, it is probably a later gloss, for which neither the witness nor
the evangelist is responsible. When in iii. 13 it is
stated that ' no man hath ascended into heaven, but
He that descended out of heaven, even the Son of
man which is in heaven,' it is more probable that we
have before us a comment of the evangelist to explain

---

[1] Chaps. xiv.-xv.

the phrase ' heavenly things ' than a saying of Jesus.
If it fell from the lips of Jesus it was certainly not in
the interview with Nicodemus that it was spoken, but
at a later date in the ministry. ' Many ancient
authorities omit *which is in heaven* ' (R.V. *marg.*).
The allusions to descent from heaven in the discourse
in Capernaum (vi. 33, 38, 50, 58, 62) are entirely improbable in the historical conditions, and in this discourse we must recognize the development in the mind
of the witness of pregnant sayings of Jesus (even if
they are not comments of the evangelist). The
challenge to opponents in viii. 14, ' I know whence I
am, and whither I go,' does not explicitly assert pre-
existence. But the words in viii. 58 do, ' Verily,
verily, I say unto you, Before Abraham was, I am.'
Westcott's comment on the last words is : ' The
phrase marks a timeless existence. In this connexion
" I was " would have expressed simple priority.' [1]
As Jesus' claim was challenged, His certainty of His
relation as Son to God as Father grew ; and this
certainty might include a distinct intuition that this
relation was not, and could not be temporal, but
must be eternal as God Himself. While for reasons
to be afterwards shown, we cannot accept the seven-
teenth chapter of the Gospel as the *ipsissima verba* of
Jesus, yet the dominant conception of His death as a
return to the glory that He had before the world was
(*v.* 5) is not improbably a reminiscence of what Jesus
did say to a disciple who could understand His deeper
thoughts as the Twelve, according to the Synoptic
testimony itself, could not.[2] This inward certainty

---

[1] Westcott's *St. John,* p. 140.
[2] ' The confidence with which John lets him speak to the Father,
" Thou lovedst me before the foundation of the world," is surely
overheard from Jesus' own certainty.' (Harnack, *Das Wesen des
Christentums,* p. 81.)

need not and cannot be represented, as by Tholuck, in an extreme metaphysical form as ' a continuity of the consciousness of the historical Christ with the Logos.' [1] A developing human consciousness that carried the remembrance of the previous state of existence is unintelligible and incredible. The word *pre-existence* is itself a contradiction in terms, for it describes the eternal reality of the relation of Father and Son in the Godhead in temporal terms. The explanation given above of a certain intuition of eternal relation to God, which may have emerged in Jesus' consciousness only when to meet the challenge of men He needed and gained such assurance from God, is both credible and intelligible. Such an intuition can also be harmonized with the Christology which is based on history, and not on speculation, and recognizes a progressive Incarnation under the conditions of human development.

[1] Quoted by Dods *in loco*, *The Expositor's Greek Testament*, i. p. 841.

II

COMMENTS BY THE EVANGELIST

WHILE it is the evangelist who has reproduced the
teaching of the witness in the Gospel; while it is in
his language that the report is given, except where
there may be the *ipsissima verba* of the reminiscences
and reflexions of the witness, and while we cannot
now with certainty separate what is due to the one
or to the other throughout the Gospel; yet there are
comments which we may ascribe to him rather than
to his teacher. His adoption of the Logos doctrine
in the Prologue on the one hand, and the indications
given in the First Epistle of his own theology on the
other, may serve as a clue. It is true that that theology
had been formed under the influence of the teaching
of the witness, but that does not involve that the
scholar cannot have developed the teaching he had
received : and evidence can now be offered that his
tendency was to emphasize the supernaturalness of
the person of Jesus in putting on His words and works
a construction which the report which he himself
gives does not itself demand. We can get nearer to
the historical reality as presented by the witness when
we have set aside the comments of the evangelist.
It is possible that some of the comments may go back
to the witness himself, if we assume that he too had
undergone a theological development similar to the
evangelist's ; but to distinguish the one from the other

14

possible source is an impossible task, and our purpose
does not require it.

(1) The first kind of comment places the Fourth
Gospel alongside of the Synoptic Gospels. The interest
in the fulfilment of prophecy was common to all the
writers of the New Testament. In Jesus' zeal in
cleansing the Temple the disciples are represented as
recognizing the fulfilment of the words, ' The zeal of
thine house shall eat me up ' (ii. 17, Ps. lxix. 9). In
Jesus' riding into Jerusalem on an ass (xii. 14, 15)
is found a fulfilment of the prophecy of Zechariah
regarding the peaceableness of the Messiah (ix. 9).
In the unbelief of the people the statement of the
prophet regarding the servant of Yahveh, and Isaiah's
own experience are seen to have a counterpart (xii. 37-
41, Is. liii. 1, vi. 10). The Psalmist's complaint anticipates the causeless hate directed against Jesus
according to His own utterance (xv. 25, Ps. xxxv. 19)
as also the betrayal by Judas (xiii. 18, Ps. xli. 9).
The fulfilment of prophecy is found also in the three
details of the Crucifixion—the dividing of the Garments,
the leaving of the Body unbroken, and the piercing
of the side (xix. 24, Ps. xxii. 18, v. 36, Ps. xxxiv. 20,
v. 37, Zech. xii. 10). Jesus Himself is represented as
assigning the fulfilment of scripture as the reason
why only the son of perdition has perished (xvii. 12,
Ps. cix. 8). It is possible that in xix. 28, the evangelist
gives as the motive of Jesus' cry, ' I thirst,' the desire
to accomplish the scriptures as he elsewhere ventures
to interpret the inner life of Jesus, but it is more
probable that he himself sees in the word the fulfilment
of prophecy. ' Jesus did not feel thirsty and proclaim
it with the intention of fulfilling scripture—which
would be a spurious fulfilment — but in His complaint and the response to it, John sees a fulfilment of

Ps. lxix. 22.' [1] This kind of comment, however, throws
no special light on the theology either of evangelist
or witness.

(2) The second kind of comment seeks to show the
meaning that was, not at the time, but only afterwards
seen in utterances of Jesus. In Jesus' challenge,
'Destroy this temple, and in three days I will raise
it up' (ii. 19), a reference is found to the temple of the
body, but it is admitted that the saying was remembered, and so understood only after the Resurrection
(vv. 21-22). An explicit reference to the Resurrection we may be sure was not intended by Jesus at
the time, although it is just possible that He did in
His own mind connect the spiritual restoration that
He anticipated with His own experience. Jesus'
reference to the streams of living water that should
flow from believers (vii. 38) probably indicates
abundance of spiritual life, and is not intended as an
express promise of the Spirit, as it is taken to be (v. 39).
The teaching of Jesus regarding Him that sent Him,
misunderstood by the people, is quite properly referred
to the Father (viii. 27). These two kinds of comments
may be just as fitly referred to the witness as to the
evangelist.

(3) It is in the third kind of comment that the
evangelist in offering reasons for the words or the
works of Jesus betrays his own conception of the
person of the Incarnate Word. These comments are
not to be regarded as merely applications of the Logos
doctrine to the person of Christ, as on the one hand
we have already indicated that the Logos doctrine
does not dominate the Gospel, and on the other the
comments can be regarded as hyperbolic statements
of supernatural features which we must recognize as

---

[1] Marcus Dods in *Expositor's Greek Testament*, i. p. 858.

belonging to the person of Christ according to His own self-witness, although, as exaggerations, out of harmony with the conception of the person which we may derive from that witness.

(i) It is doubtful whether in the words in v. 18c, ' making himself equal with God,' the evangelist is simply repeating the inference of the Jewish opponents from the words of Jesus : ' My Father worketh even until now, and I work ' (v. 17), or is himself presenting that view.   If he does, then he contradicts the assertion of the entire dependence of the Son on God as Father (v. 19) and the argument (x. 34-36) from the use of the word *gods* in the Psalms (lxxxii. 6), as well as the express declaration that the Father is greater (xiv. 28).

(ii) The general statement regarding the knowledge of men by Jesus (ii. 24, 25) gives the impression that the evangelist desires to ascribe omniscience to Jesus ; and yet the verbs γινώσκειν and ἐγίνωσκεν, if the distinction usually made is to hold good, point to an acquired knowledge, and not an innate. We may affirm a tendency to lay emphasis on the supernaturalness of Jesus' knowledge. In Jesus' answer to Nathanael (i. 48) and the surprise it evokes he intends to represent the knowledge of Jesus as more than the moral and spiritual insight into the inner life of others which the Synoptists also assign to Him (Mark ii. 8). The mention to the woman of Samaria of the number of her husbands (iv. 18) may be explained as a mistake on her part in reporting the conversation, as it was easy for her in her excited condition to transfer the contents of her own guilty conscience to the speech of Jesus (a conjecture which the hyperbole of v. 29 confirms) ; but the evangelist's intention in his record is clearly to emphasise this supernatural knowledge. A supernatural insight, moral and religious, into the

inner life of others with a view to His ' cure of souls '
we may ascribe to Jesus consistently with the necessary
conditions of Incarnation, but the evangelist evidently
thinks of something more.

(iii) In one set of explanations the evangelist aims
at exhibiting the accuracy of Jesus' fore-knowledge,
and the infallibility of His judgment in regard to all
His deeds. It is doubtful whether in the phrase ' his
own country ' the reference is to Judaea or to Galilee
(iv. 44).[1] Whichever it may be, the evangelist desires
to make clear that Jesus was guided, not by circumstances, but by His own convictions. His view of
the intention of Jesus to retire from the excitement
His ministry had caused in Judaea to quieter labours
in Galilee, however, approves itself. For the simple
act recorded in xviii. 4, there seems to be no necessity
of seeking a motive as the evangelist does. It is
uncertain whether the evangelist sees in Jesus' plea
for the safety of His disciples a fulfilment of His own
utterance (xviii. 8, 9), or would have us believe that
the prediction was the reason why Jesus spoke as He
did. If the latter be his intention, it introduces an
element of unreality into the life of Jesus that we
may be sure was always absent from it. Conscious of
the humility of Jesus in washing the disciples' feet,
the evangelist ' protests too much ' (xiii. 1-3) Jesus'
sense of His own dignity, and so invests that act
with an excess of condescension which would rob
it of its grace. It is his own theology that he here
transfers to Jesus' inner life.

(4) In the fourth kind of comment the evangelist
puts on the lips of Jesus Himself explanations of
words and works, which show rather his own conception than the consciousness of Jesus as revealed

[1] Cf. Matt. xiii. 57.

to us even in the evidence the Gospel itself offers of
His ' inner life.'   An impression of unreality, of something spectacular, in the ministry of Jesus is made by
the explanation given of Jesus' ejaculation, ' Father,
I thank thee that thou heardest me ' (xi. 41) which
is itself quite credible.   Would Jesus, addressing the
Father in such an hour, be thinking of the impression
to be made on the multitude (v. 42) ?   One cannot
avoid the suspicion that the apologetic use of His
foresight in warning (xiii. 19, ' From henceforth I
tell you before it come to pass, that, when it is come
to pass, ye may believe that I am He ') or promise
(xiv. 29, ' And now I have told you before it came to
pass, that, when it is come to pass, ye may believe that
I am He '), would be artificial and unnatural on the
part of Jesus Himself.   The difficulty of the assumption that the evangelist put his own words on the lips
of Jesus might be removed by the conjecture that
it was a comment of the witness that was transformed
in his memory into words of Jesus.

(5) Several other comments there are which cannot
be classified.   Can we doubt that it is the witness's
own confession of faith which has slipped into the
prayer of Jesus (xvii. 3) ?   Would Jesus Himself in
prayer have defined eternal life, or described Himself
as Jesus Christ ?   It is his own view of the death of
Christ that he imposes on the utterance of the High
Priest (xi. 51, 52), for even had the High Priest possessed the prophetic endowment, its exercise would
not have given him such insight into Christian doctrine.
Again, the reason for the Jews' reply, ' It is not lawful
for us to put any man to death,' is found in the necessity
of the fulfilment of Jesus' own prediction regarding
the manner of His death (xviii. 31-33).   The discussion of these comments is not only relevant to the

literary and historical criticism of the Gospel, but
necessary also for our understanding of the theology.
They modify, and not advantageously, the doctrine
of the Person of Christ which the Gospel as historical
testimony offers for our consideration.

(6) There are some longer passages which are more
probably comments of the evangelist than reflexions
on his reminiscences of the witness. (i) The first of
these passages is iii. 31-36. If, as is not improbable,
the preceding passage, *vv.* 22-30, only is displaced and
should follow ii. 12, then this passage is a comment
on the witness's reflexions in *vv.* 16-21. If, however,
vv. 31-36 have also been displaced with *vv.* 22-30, then
the passage is the evangelist's explanation of the
superiority of Jesus as Bridegroom Himself to the
friend of the bridegroom (*v.* 29). Even the Baptist,
great as he is as sent before the Christ, is still of the
earth, and can speak only of the earth, whereas the
Christ as from heaven can bear direct personal testimony to the heavenly reality. While his testimony
is generally disbelieved, the believer can confirm that
testimony as the very truth of God. The thought
here offers several points of resemblance to that of
the Prologue. The reason for the trustworthiness of
the heavenly witness is further developed. He who
has come from heaven is the Son of God, loved, sent
endued with the Spirit without measure either as
His own possession or as the channel of its communication, and given all things of God. If in the clause in
v. 34, οὐ γὰρ ἐκ μέτρου δίδωσιν τὸ πνεῦμα, the subject
is Jesus as in the preceding clause, and the recipients
are believers, then the fulness of the Spirit in the
Christian Church is offered as confirmation of the
truth of the message from God received through Him.
If God is the subject (as in A.V.) and Christ the

recipient, then the clause offers an interesting contribution to the Christology of the Gospel, which shows
a point of contact with the Synoptic account of the
Baptism. Christ Himself receives the Spirit which
He afterwards imparts. But the interpretations are
not mutually exclusive : for communication implies
possession. The explicit statement of the truth would
have an added interest ; as it would show that the
evangelist did expressly conceive the relation of the
Father to the Son as mediated by the Spirit. This is
not a valueless theological subtlety ; but thereby the
inner life of Jesus is brought into closer likeness to
that of His disciples. The Reformed Christology
afterwards made fuller use of the idea of the mediation
of the Spirit than did the Lutheran. Verses 35-36
draw the practical conclusion from the doctrinal
statement. Since testimony of such authority demands
acceptance, belief results in eternal life, and disobedience in the divine displeasure.

(ii) As has already been indicated, the evangelist
appears to regard the saying of v. 17 as a claim by
Jesus of an equality with God. This equality he then
expounds in the passage *vv.* 19-29, which cannot be
regarded as belonging to the witness's reminiscences
or even reflexions. (*a*) What at once strikes us in
reading the passage is the twofold mode of Jesus'
reference to Himself. In *vv.* 30-47 and in vii. 15-24
(which we shall afterwards see is to be treated as the
continuation of the discourse) He speaks of Himself
in the first person, and there is nothing in these passages
altogether incongruous with the occasion. But in
v. 19-29, apart from the introductory formula, ' Verily,
verily, I say unto you ' (*vv.* 19, 24, 25) He refers to
Himself in the third person, except in *v.* 24, which, as
faith is set forth as the condition of eternal life, presents

no difficulty, and may be at once accepted as a saying
suitable to the occasion. But its proper place would
seem to be after v. 38. But is the exposition in those
other verses of the intimate and absolute relation of
the Father and the Son, with its reference to the future
judgment and the future resurrection, at all likely to
have been given by Jesus to His opponents ? Even
if less reserved in Jerusalem than in Galilee, is it
credible that at this stage He so entirely cast off
reserve, especially when such language would provoke
only deeper misunderstanding and keener hostility ?
So apposite is Jesus' speech in the Synoptics, that we
must suspect in the Fourth Gospel utterances which
do not seem necessary or relevant to the occasion.
Does not the use of the third person throughout in
the balancing of Father and Son in their mutual
relations appear much more credible as a later doctrinal development ? The eschatology of this passage
is also in contrast to the teaching of Jesus, as reported
in the Gospel, of a present judgment, a spiritual resurrection, and an eternal life here and now. Verse
24 affirms all these modifications of the current
eschatology as stated in vv. 25-29. Regarding this
passage Dr. Strachan's statement may be heartily
accepted : ' After his fashion the evangelist suddenly
moves from the actual historical situation to the
contemporary situation. They are no longer the
Jews of Jerusalem who are disputing about the Divinity
of Jesus, but the Jews of Asia Minor, disputing with
the Christian Church of the day.' [1] (b) The development of the thought is as follows. The absolute
dependence of the Son on the Father is shown in the
entire resemblance of the Son's work to the Father's.
As the dependence is one of love, it involves a complete

[1] *The Fourth Gospel*, p. 116.

knowledge by the Son of the Father's purpose, and
a fulfilment of that purpose through the Son in a still
more wonderful way than that already witnessed in
the healing miracles. The power to raise the dead,
and the authority to judge, both divine prerogatives,
are entrusted to the Son in order that He may receive
equal honour with the Father. So far the argument
is plain ; but two meanings can be assigned to the
raising from the dead and the judgment. Is it a
present inward experience or a future outward occurrence ? Verses 25, 28, 29, except the clause in *v.* 25,
' and now is,' which is not repeated in *vv.* 28 and 29,
refer to the general physical resurrection and the
final universal judgment. The evangelist believed as
the whole Christian Church then believed ; and we
can understand how he would regard these events
as Christ's greater works. But Jesus would not have
so referred to these in controversy with His opponents,
and *vv.* 21-23 and the clause in *v.* 25 point to a present
inward experience, as does *v.* 24, which, however, does
not seem to belong to this context. For our thought
there is some incongruity between the future event
as it was anticipated in its outward form in the Apostolic Age and the present experience, although the
evangelist may have been able to combine the two,
the future event being the necessary and appropriate
completion of the present experience. We may share
the latter, but the former has fallen into the background, if it has not vanished altogether from the
range of our spiritual vision. The theological statement here has an experimental value, and not merely
a speculative, as it touches experience very closely.
The Christian experience has an absolute validity, for,
as Christ's work now or hereafter, it is God's own
work, because of the relation of the Father to the Son

which is here set forth. The passage does go beyond what Jesus is likely Himself to have said on this occasion ; it does not go beyond a reasonable interpretation of Christian experience, even although while according equal honour to the Father and the Son in our worship, we may be constrained, as was Paul (1 Cor. viii. 6, Col. i. 19, Phil. ii. 9, 1 Cor. iii. 23, xv. 28) to recognize in our theology a necessary subordination of the Son to the Father, as the first two verses here do. (c) To vv. 28-29 exception can be taken on another ground. ' This is,' says Dr. R. G. Macintyre, ' the only passage in any of the Gospels which speaks of a resurrection of others than the righteous, and therefore based on another principle than faith—union with Christ. . . . What are we to make of this passage which seems to be in direct contradiction to the whole trend of the Fourth Gospel ? . . . The only method of interpretation which would permit us to retain verses 28-29 as a genuine part of Johannine teaching would be to take them as an exceedingly bold piece of symbolism and interpret them spiritually in harmony with the preceding verses. This view has attractions for the present writer, but the language used and the way it comes in compels him, somewhat reluctantly, to put it aside.' [1] Canon Charles is quoted by this writer as remarking on the passage : ' The scene is depicted in a most materialistic form, in fact it would be hard to find a more unspiritual description of the resurrection in the whole literature of the first century A.D.' [2] ' Following Wendt,' says Macintyre, ' he would excise it from the Gospel as an intrusion by a less spiritual mind.' These opinions give confirmation to the conclusion here stated regarding the whole passage

[1] The Other Side of Death, pp. 173-175.
[2] Eschatology, p. 371.

(*vv.* 19-29). It must be added that the evangelist
has not inserted this addition at what would appear
to us the most appropriate place, as it is incongruous
with the context. A more suitable occasion would
be, as Mr. Thompson suggests, after the raising of
Lazarus in chapter xi.

(7) The recognition of this distinct theological
tendency first of all to exaggerate the supernaturalness
of the person of Jesus, and then to represent Jesus as
seeking to make an impression by His display of His
supernatural powers, cannot be confined to the passages
which bear so distinct evidence of being comments
by the evangelist. It must affect, and does affect,
his representation of the words and works of Jesus,
even when we cannot separate comments from the
report of the witness's teaching. While it is entirely
probable that on the one hand Jesus revealed His
inner life more freely to a disciple who could understand Him so much better than the others could, and
on the other that in controversy with the rulers and
the teachers of the nation who challenged His claim,
He asserted His dignity and authority more confidently
and constantly than was necessary, or even desirable,
with the multitude in Galilee ; yet one cannot suppress
the conviction that the evangelist has not only at
times transferred to the lips of Jesus his own inferences
from the relation of the Father to the Son as he conceived it, but has given to Jesus a certain artificial
pose of the debater and controversialist, which places
Him in a less attractive light than do the Synoptists.
We cannot conjecture how far the witness in his teaching had already given this colour to the teaching of
Jesus, or how far it is entirely due to the evangelist.
As the zeal of the one or the other to vindicate the
claims of Jesus, it has a different moral value than

when it is presented under the guise of Jesus' anxiety
to assert Himself.

(8) As in his Comments the evangelist most directly
expresses his own theology, this seems the appropriate
place at which to refer to the resemblance between
the teaching of the Johannine Epistles and that of the
Fourth Gospel. As his teaching was influenced by
what he had heard from the witness, even if the
Gospel be later than the Epistles, that resemblance
is not confined to his comments. (a) The style of
both has much in common with the parallelism of the
Psalms and other poetical writings of the Old Testament. The truth is stated in co-ordinated sentences,
complementary in thought. Common to both are
such key-words as κόσμος, ζωή, θάνατος, ἀλήθεια,
ψεῦδος, φῶς σκοτία, σκότος, ἀληθινός, ἀγαπᾶν, ἀγάπη,
φιλεῖν, μισεῖν. In both the contrasts of life and
death, truth and falsehood, light and darkness, love
and hate, faith and unbelief, are vividly presented.
There is very little use made of the Old Testament.
Where the First Epistle uses terms unknown to the
Gospel, the special circumstances and the polemical
purpose afford an adequate explanation. (b) Some
differences there are in the theology. The Epistle
gives a prominence to Christ's atoning death and His
forgiving and cleansing grace which is not found in
the Gospel, although as will be shown in the discussion
of vi. 51c and vv. 52-57, this theme is not altogether
absent. Apart from certain clauses which may be
regarded as editorial additions, the Gospel does not
lay stress on the Second Coming (the apocalyptic
teaching), but rather on the relation of Jesus to His
disciples in His Spirit (the mystical teaching), whereas
the Epistle has the common apostolic hope of a speedy
outward appearance of the Lord. The Epistle, how-

ever, departs from the common apocalyptic standpoint
in identifying Antichrist with false teaching, and in
insisting on Christ's spiritual presence with believers
and eternal life as a present possession. A striking
difference, that this Gospel speaks of abiding in Christ,
and the Epistle of abiding in God, is easily explained
by the change of standpoint. 'The special theme,'
says Dr. Ramsay,[1] ' of the Gospel is the Word who
imparts life ; the special theme of the Epistle is the
life which the Word imparts. It is with the historic
presentment that the one has to do ; the other is
concerned with God as He is revealed in Christ.' It
would be beyond the scope of the purpose of this
volume to deal more fully with this subject, as there
is no intention to deny the identity of the evangelist
and the author of the Epistles.

(9) While the writer believes that the Christian
Church in forming its doctrine of the Person of Christ
need not confine itself to the Synoptics as the sole
reliable historical testimony, but may use the Fourth
Gospel in so far as Jesus' self-witness renders explicit
what is implicit in the Synoptics, yet it must not be
forgotten that in the Fourth Gospel doctrine does
blend with history, and even, as has just been shown,
doctrine of a somewhat aggressive type. There is a
Johannine interpretation of the person of Christ just
as there is a Pauline ; only that as regards the one the
doctrine is presented in the guise of history as it is
not in the other, but criticism can separate the two
blended elements, if not with certainty, yet with a

---

[1] *The Revelation and the Johannine Epistles,* by Alex. Ramsay
(*Westminster New Testament,* 1910), pp. 29-34. See also *The Epistles
of St. John,* by B. F. Westcott (Macmillan & Co., 1886), pp. xliii-
xlvi ; *The Epistles of John,* by David Smith (*The Expositor's Greek
Testament,* v. 1890, pp. 152-154) ; *The General Epistles,* by W. H.
Bennett (*The Century Bible,* 1901), pp. 71-73.

high degree of probability. When we have thus separated the doctrine from the history, we do not need to set it aside as valueless, just as we do not set aside the Pauline interpretation, and for the same reason. In the Johannine interpretation there is not only a historical basis, it rests, as does the Pauline, also on a personal experience (that of the witness transmitted to the evangelist) : for we can detect in the Fourth Gospel not only the impressions which the historical reality of Jesus left on the receptive and responsive soul of the witness, but also the influence in his inner life of the spiritual presence of Christ, and some of his reflexions on his own reminiscences may be described as *experimental* rather than *theological*.

(10) Regarding the presentation throughout the Fourth Gospel of the glory of the only-begotten of the Father, it may at this stage of the discussion be said that it is not so great a distortion of history by doctrine that we cannot go back from faith to fact. For (*a*) in the Synoptics Jesus is represented as the Son of God, and in one passage (Matt. xi. 25-27—Luke x. 22) Jesus is reported as making a claim for Himself beyond which the Fourth Gospel does not in the substance of its teaching go. (*b*) As subsequent discussion will show, the context of the passages in which a more supernatural endowment seems to be assigned to the person of Jesus than in the Synoptics allows us to correct the representation so as to get back to the facts. (*c*) While the Fourth Gospel does not expressly teach that the becoming *flesh* of the Word was a *Kenosis* or self-emptying, yet the Sonship is presented as an ethical and spiritual relation, such a dependence on, and submission to, as well as knowledge of and fellowship with the Father

as excludes the metaphysical attributes of absolute deity from the earthly life. (*d*) A historical exegesis yields a different impression of the teaching of the Gospel than a commentary such as Bishop Westcott's which reads into the Gospel the Christological dogma of a later age.

III

THE APPENDIX

(JOHN XXI.)

THE writer finds it quite impossible to regard the
Appendix as the work of the evangelist. It is true that
there is no textual evidence as in regard to Mark xvi.
9-20 to show that it is a later addition. It is true also
that the style closely resembles that of the rest of the
Gospel. But the author of such an addition would
make it his business to copy the style as nearly as
possible, and we cannot affirm that before our present
texts were produced, such an addition may not have
been made. ' Even within the brief space of the
Appendix, idiosyncrasies of language and style appear
which are practically sufficient to indicate another
hand.' [1] Neither of the considerations mentioned
above bars the way to the conclusion that the contents
of the chapter force upon us. The immediate purpose
of this addition was both to prove Peter's restoration
to apostolic authority (*vv.* 15-17), and to remove a
current misconception of a traditional saying about
the beloved disciple (*v.* 23), which his death or the
death of the person identified with him in common
opinion (probably recent) had made a stumbling-block
to faith. The occasion is also used to add a joint
attestation from the circle in which the writer of the
Appendix moved, of the trustworthiness of the evan-

---

[1] Moffatt's *Introduction*, p. 572, which may be consulted for
further details.

gelist, and so the worth of the Gospel (v. 24). It is
hard to believe that the evangelist could have borne
such self-witness. If, as is maintained, in this volume
the evangelist must be distinguished from the witness,
then the identification in this attestation of the
witness (ὁ μαρτυρῶν) and the writer (ὁ γράψας) contains an error. Further, the writer of the Appendix
desires to convey the impression that the beloved
disciple, the author of the Gospel, was John the son
of Zebedee.

(1) The first part of the Appendix (vv. 1-14) presents
a parallel to the account given by Luke (v. 1-11) of
the call given to Peter. While there are differences
in details it is difficult to resist the conclusion that
both passages contain variant traditions of the same
incident. The writer has elsewhere expressed the
opinion [1] that Peter's confession in Luke v. 8, 'Depart
from me; for I am a sinful man, O Lord,' found a more
appropriate context in the record of restoration to
discipleship after his denial, as given in the Fourth
Gospel, than in the record of the first call as found in
Luke. Further study has, however, modified this judgment. As will afterwards be shown, the Galilaeans
in the small company of disciples, whose attachment
to Jesus is recorded in John i. 35-51, followed Him
only for a time; and had to be recalled when the
Galilaean ministry began (Matt. iv. 18-22, Mark i. 16-
20). Had they wavered for a time in their allegiance
and gone back to their old calling, and was what the
Synoptics represent as a first call not only a recall but
a restoration? This would explain not only Luke
v. 8, but also John xxi. 15-17, if this passage belongs
to the same context, but for reasons given below this
is not likely. We must consider other possibilities.

[1] *Studies in the Inner Life of Jesus,* pp. 236, 443.

The story about the miracle may be due to a late tradition in which the figurative saying about the disciples becoming fishers of men was misunderstood, and was turned into an actual miracle of an abundant, unexpected draught. It is very difficult to understand how, if this account relates to the beginning of the Galilaean ministry, Mark, dependent as he was on Peter for his knowledge, has no trace of it. We cannot even conjecture whether, if we had Mark's Gospel complete, this story would have been found in the same context as in the Fourth Gospel. Whatever the original tradition may have been, it is clear that the writer of this Appendix has adapted it for his own purpose. This is obvious in regard to *vv.* 1 and 14. As regards the mention of the two sons of Zebedee (*v.* 2) it is to be observed that nowhere else in the Fourth Gospel is there any reference to them. The writer of the Appendix evidently intends to identify ' the disciple whom Jesus loved ' (*vv.* 7 and 20) with one of the brothers ; and yet there seems to be some doubt in his mind, and he leaves himself a door of escape from mistake by adding ' two other of His disciples ' without mentioning their names. Some questions may be suggested. Is not the statement in *v.* 3 abrupt ? Is not an explanation needed for the presence of these disciples in Galilee, and for their return to the calling which at the bidding of Jesus they had forsaken ? Is not also the restoration of Peter to his apostleship unduly delayed ? Would he after his denial have resumed his place in the apostolic company without such restoration ?

(2) We seem compelled to find in *vv.* 1-14 a tradition which we have no means of authenticating, or putting, if authentic, into its proper context, unless we accept Luke's setting as at least possible, which the writer

of the Appendix has with honest intention, if mistaken judgment, adopted as the occasion for the tender and touching talk of Jesus with Peter in *vv.* 15-19, linking the two separate stories together by the explanation in *v.* 15*a*, ' So when they had broken their fast.' For this conversation a context at once suggests itself. On their return the two disciples who had seen the Lord were told that He had appeared to Simon (Luke xxiv. 34) ; and Paul mentions an appearance to Cephas (1 Cor. xv. 5). What more probable than that Jesus among His very earliest appearances should show Himself to the penitent disciple to comfort and restore him ? The place of the appearance would be Jerusalem, and the time the day of Resurrection. The statement in *v.* 18 need not be treated as a prophecy after the event, as xiii. 36 indicates that Jesus anticipated that Peter would thereafter be faithful unto death, an anticipation which must be considered, as must all prophecy, as conditional. Such a prediction is surely not beyond the range of the foresight we may ascribe to the earthly Jesus even, not to say the heavenly Christ. Mr. Thompson denies that the saying in *v.* 18 has any reference to martyrdom. It is a description of an old man's helplessness in needing to be dressed and carried about. It is to be figuratively interpreted of ' the life of penitent and obedient discipleship which had not been possible for him at an earlier period in his spiritual development, when he preferred to be his own master and to go his own way.' Verse 23 must, in accordance with the contrast between Peter and the beloved disciple, receive a similar figurative interpretation. ' Jesus' promise is not that one of His disciples shall live to extreme old age, and witness the coming of the Messiah, but that spiritual insight and faith, the marks of true discipleship, as personified in the beloved disciple, shall never die out of the Church, and shall never lose their reward in the experience of the living presence of Christ.[1] This exposition is, however, too subtle to be at all convincing, and does not accord with the general character of this Appendix.

(3) If the whole Appendix is treated as a tendency writing with little, if any, contact with tradition, and with a skilful working up of materials suggested by the Fourth Gospel itself, as Dr. Strachan seeks to show in an elaborate argument which does not, however, command assent,[2] there is no difficulty in connecting vv. 20-23 with vv. 15-19. But it is here at least suggested that vv. 15-19 contain a tradition of Jesus' appearance to Peter on two grounds : (a) that it is probable that Jesus did restore Peter to apostle-ship after his denial before he resumed the prominent position he holds according to the record in Acts ; (b) that it is preferable to ascribe to the writer an adaptation of a tradition rather than free invention, if that charge can be at all avoided. If vv. 20-22 also rest on a tradition, they must have belonged originally to another context, as it is not likely that if the witness had been present when Christ appeared to Peter, as testified by Luke and Paul, the Gospel would have contained no account of the appearance. If the saying of v. 22 was current, it is not improbable that the writer of the Appendix in his own mind connected it with this occasion, even if there was no tradition to that effect. Jesus' saying in Mark ix. 1, ' There be some here of them that stand by which shall in no wise taste of death, till they see the Kingdom of God come with power,' was probably the ground for the

---

[1] *The Expositor*, 8th series, vol. xiv. pp. 226-229.
[2] *Op. cit.* vol. vii. pp. 255 ff.

expectation that one of the original disciples would
survive to the Parousia. What more inevitable than
that the expectation should attach itself to the only
survivor known in the circles where it was current.
The death (probably recent) of the beloved disciple
seemed to give the lie to the promise of Jesus, and the
writer of the Appendix seeks to save the veracity of
Jesus. But Jesus' saying in *v.* 22 may be interpreted
in two ways. Either the emphasis is to be laid on
if I will (ἐὰν θέλω) or on *tarry* or *abide* (μένειν).
In the first case Jesus is represented as simply affirming
that it lay in His power to preserve the disciple till
the Second Advent without any pledge that the power
would be used. In the second case μένειν must be
interpreted in accord with the use of the word μοναί
in xiv. 2. 'In his interpretation of μένειν,' says
Strachan, ' he seeks to save the veracity of our Lord
by implying that Jesus actually contemplated the
death of John when He so spoke, and meant that the
disciple would *abide* in the intermediate state until
the Parousia, when, with the other saints who inhabited
the μοναί of the Father's house (xiv. 2) he would be
received into glory.' The first explanation seems
adequate, and the second rather far-fetched. The
recent death is presupposed, and, as Strachan argues,
' the passage presents extreme difficulty to those who
hold the theory of the early martyrdom of John.' [1]
The way in which Dr. Moffatt seeks to remove the
difficulty [2] need not now detain us, as it does not exist
for those who do not identify the beloved disciple
with John the son of Zebedee.[3] If the writer of the
Appendix had heard this tradition of the early martyrdom, and because of his identification of the beloved

---

[1] *Op. cit.* pp. 269-271.　　　　[2] *Introduction*, pp. 575-576.
[3] To this point we shall afterwards return.

disciple with John disbelieved it, he was confronted
with a difficulty in the saying of Jesus to James and
John which appeared to be a prophecy of their martyrdom, ' The cup that I drink ye shall drink ; and with
the baptism that I am baptized withal shall ye be
baptized ' (Mark x. 39). He seems to meet it in *v.* 24.
There was recognized a ' white ' as well as a ' red '
martyrdom, a witness in continued life as well as in
life surrendered to death. The Gospel was ' the
martyrdom ' of the beloved disciple.

(4) Dr. Stanton's conclusion regarding the authorship
of the Appendix is this : ' Although, therefore, ch. xxi.
was by a different hand from chs. i.-xx., there appears
to be no good ground for interposing a long interval
between the composition of the one and the other.' [1]
He opposes Bacon's view that the Appendix was
added to the Gospel and that it was re-edited with
insertions from the Synoptic tradition in the middle
of the second century on the ground that some traces
of the earlier form of the Gospel would have remained. [2]
He argues that if, as Bacon contends, the purpose of
the Appendix and the other changes introduced into
the Gospel was to ' commend it to Roman Christians,
whose views as to the Gospel narrative and as to a
Petrine supremacy had been moulded by Mark,' he
should have done his work in so tentative a way.
' How could such extremely slight adjustments to the
Synoptic story have satisfied those who were wedded
to it ? How could such obscure indications of the
personality of the evangelist have served to establish
the Johannine authorship.' [3] It may be that Dr.
Bacon ascribes to the redactor of the Gospel, as he
calls him, too ambitious a design. For whatever

[1] *The Gospels as Historical Documents,* part iii. p. 27.
[2] *Op. cit.* p. 23,   [3] *Op. cit.* p. 27.

reason the passages which he assigns to the redactor were inserted, they do break the continuity of the evangelist's record, and may be regarded, mostly, if not all, as later additions. The Appendix does afford a starting-point for an investigation of what may be called the Synoptic elements in the Gospel, and we are justified in inquiring what are the passages which may be assigned to the writer of the Appendix.

IV

THE REDACTOR'S INSERTIONS

ONE of the problems of the Fourth Gospel, difficult to
solve, is its relations to the Synoptics. With the
general problem we are now not concerned, but only
with those passages which have Synoptic parallels,
or appear as Synoptic echoes. Stanton expresses the
opinion that ' the parallels with St. Mark certainly
seem to afford evidence of an amount and kind sufficient to prove that the fourth evangelist knew that
Gospel fairly well.' [1] Parallels, unless so close as to
prove literary dependence, may be explained by access
to a common tradition. Differences disprove literary
dependence, unless good reason can be shown for the
changes introduced. The writer is convinced that
the parallels are not close enough to prove, and that
the differences are great enough to disprove, literary
dependence. But the main objection against assuming
that either the witness or the evangelist knew St. Mark
is that such knowledge would have modified the
contents of the Gospel to a greater extent ; and that
the handling of St. Mark in the Gospel must on such
an assumption appear altogether arbitrary, putting
a strain on the scholar's ingenuity in finding reasons
for omissions, additions, or modifications. If it can
be shown, as the writer believes that it can, that the
Synoptic elements are due to a redactor, and bear the
marks of insertions interrupting the context, a diffi-

---

[1] *The Gospels as Historical Documents*, part iii. p. 220.

culty is removed ; and we need not ascribe either
to the evangelist or to the witness an unintelligible
treatment of one of the Synoptic Gospels. As it is
from the Synoptic tradition, if not one of the Synoptic
Gospels, that the redactor's interest in John the son of
Zebedee is derived, we may include under the present
heading the first of the insertions to which attention
may be called.

(1) Eager as is the redactor to establish the trustworthiness of the witness, and to identify him with
John the son of Zebedee, we need not hesitate in assigning to him the attestation, and even protestation, of
xix. 35, ' And he that saw it bare record, and his
record is true ; and he knoweth that he saith true,
that ye might believe.' There is ground for the
assumption that the redactor in inserting *the last clause*
had the statement of the purpose of the Gospel in xx.
31 before his mind, and wrote from the same motive
as in xxi. 24. The significance the evangelist finds in
the incident (*v.* 34) is indicated in *v.* 36. But the
redactor may have been thinking of 1 John v. 6, 8,
although that passage does not necessarily refer to
this statement, but more probably to the Baptism
and the Passion. The conclusion that this is ' an
early marginal gloss of *editorial* character ' [1] is
supported by the textual evidence dealt with by
Blass.

(2) The interest shown in the Appendix in Peter's
restoration to apostleship leads us to raise the question
whether other references to Peter may not be from the
hands of the redactor.

(i) Would he not be likely to insert the story of the
denial ? When we turn to the record in chapter xviii.
we find general agreement that there has been a dis-

[1] See Bacon, *The Fourth Gospel*, pp. 461-462.

location. Why is the story of Peter told in two parts, *vv.* 15-18 and *vv.* 25-27 ? Is the high priest referred to in *v.* 19 Annas or Caiaphas ? Verses 13 and 24 would indicate Caiaphas ; but if Caiaphas examined Jesus in the house of Annas, why did Annas send Jesus bound to Caiaphas (*v.* 24) to undergo presumably another examination. Even if the high priest was Annas, since he bears that title in Acts iv. 6, and shares it with Caiaphas in Luke iii. 2, why after the examination was Jesus sent to Caiaphas ? Dr. Moffatt [1] inserts *vv.* 19-24 between 14 and 15, and so makes *vv.* 15-18 continuous with *vv.* 25-27, while omitting 25*a* as a repetition of 18*c*, thus restoring the unity of the story of Peter's denial. But as this arrangement still requires us to assume that the high priest in *v.* 19 is Caiaphas the difficulty about *v.* 24 remains, and can only be removed if *v.* 24 be placed before *v.* 19. Such dislocation is surely an indication that the original text has been interfered with by an unskilful redactor. For such a conclusion other reasons may be offered. If *vv.* 15, 16 come from the redactor it is one of those indications of his desire to identify the author of the Gospel, but as these verses have no Synoptic parallel, it is more probable that they belong to the evangelist's record, and go back to the witness's indications of his own identity. If the other disciple was within while Peter was without the court he would not be an eye-witness of the denial ; and since, as will afterwards be shown, the witness probably confined himself to what he had seen and heard, the story is not likely to have come from him, but from another source. The redactor may have got it either directly or indirectly from one of the Synoptic Gospels. As will be shown in the course of the argument, what may be called Synoptic echoes are

[1] *The New Testament*, p. 139.

less likely to be due to the witness or the evangelist
than to the redactor.

(ii) If the story of the denial is from the redactor's
hand, can Peter's boast and Jesus' warning in xiii. 36-
38 be explained in the same way ? Here too scholars
find dislocations. Dr. Moffatt[1] places chaps. xv.
and xvi. after the middle of xiii. 31, and xiii. 31*b*-38
after xvi. 33 and before xiv. 1. But the exultation of
Spirit expressed in *vv.* 31-32 would seem more probable
immediately after the departure of the betrayer ; and
it is at least as probable that chaps. xv. and xvi. should
follow *vv.* 35.[2] Verses 36-38 (which now alone concern
us, although the probability of so large a dislocation
confirms the argument to be offered) would more
appropriately follow Jesus' statement in *v.* 33, and
how fittingly would xv. 1-8 follow *v.* 35. Again this
seems to be a Synoptic parallel which the redactor
has put in the wrong place. It is possible that it took
Peter some time to realize the import of Jesus' words,
and that he interrupted at a point unsuitable for his
question ; but on the whole the continuity of Jesus'
speech is but maintained by placing *vv.* 36-38 after 33.

(iii) Guided by the threefold clue, interest in Peter,
dislocation, Synoptic parallel or echo, we are brought
next to vi. 66-71. That the whole chapter should be
placed before chapter v. and that vii. 15-24 should be
joined to chapter v. will be argued in the subsequent
discussion ; meanwhile this passage may be assumed
to be part of a larger dislocation. As the whole chapter
is intended as a summary of the course of the ministry
in Galilee, this passage may be regarded as the counterpart of the Confession at Caesarea Philippi (Matt. xvi.
13-20). The redactor is more remote from the Synoptic

---

[1] *The New Testament*, pp. 134-138.
[2] See Wendt, *op. cit.* p. 104.

tradition here than in some Synoptic parallels ; and
we may rather call it an echo ; the voice is, as it
were, more confused. Peter is here also in the middle
of the stage as the Confessor. The differences from the
Synoptic records deserve notice. *Firstly*, as the Gospel
had already recorded (i. 41, 45, 49) franker and fuller
confessions of the Messiahship of Jesus at the beginning
of the ministry than any which the Synoptists record,
it is not a confession of the Messiahship that is reported.
The conception of the situation is that there is danger
of relapse from the faith already attained (*v.* 67).
Secondly, as the interest of the Gospel is in the truth
taught by Jesus, the confession runs : ' Thou hast the
words of eternal life ' (*v.* 68) ; words which, so far as
Peter is revealed to us by the Synoptists, are not likely
to have fallen from his lips. The next phrase, ' the
Holy One of God ' (*v.* 69), is nearer the Synoptic language. *Thirdly*, the anticipation of Judas' betrayal
is antedated, as in the Synoptic tradition a reference
to betrayal occurs only in the Second Announcement of
the Passion (Mark ix. 31), although it is possible that
the First Announcement of the Passion (viii. 31) produced a revulsion of feeling in Judas, which Jesus at
once detected. It is not at all probable, however,
that if Jesus at once uttered a word of warning, it
would be put in the terms of *v.* 70. Can this verse
possibly be an echo of the rebuke of Peter, ' Get thee
behind me, Satan ' (Mark viii. 33) ? Did tradition
confuse the rebuke of Peter with the exposure of
Judas ?

(iv) The preceding passage (vi. 60-65) has also some
Synoptic affinities. Verse 65 recalls to us the saying
of Jesus to Peter : ' Flesh and blood hath not revealed
it unto thee, but my Father which is in heaven '
(Matt. xvi. 17). The contrast in *v.* 63 between the

return to Galilee (vii. 1), but visited Jerusalem again at the Feast of Tabernacles (*v.* 10). A confirmation of this order of events is suggested by the indefinite reference in v. 1 to ' a feast of the Jews ' or ' as many ancient authorities read, the *feast* ' (R.V. *marg.*). If in the original Pentecost was mentioned, and chapters v. and vi. were transposed, the Passover would be mentioned between Pentecost and the Feast of Tabernacles, and the indefinite reference might be an attempt to get out of a chronological difficulty. The witness was too familiar himself with Jewish affairs not to be able to name this feast.

(*c*) Additional reasons for the redactor's insertion of this account of the Galilaean ministry may be suggested. He may have desired to contrast the enthusiasm of Galilee, however mistaken, with the hostility of Judaea, and to heighten the impression of Peter's fidelity by contrasting it with the desertions which followed even that enthusiasm in Galilee.

(*d*) Before going any further in our analyses of this chapter we may compare the narrative in *vv.* 1-21 with the Synoptic record. The story in Mark vi. 30-44 offers an altogether more probable explanation of the occasion of the miracle. Jesus, absorbed in His teaching, moved thereto by His compassion, needs to be reminded by His disciples that the people have been all day without food, and that it will be desirable to dismiss them before nightfall. The record in John bears far less the marks of historical probability, and shows clearly the pragmatism of the Gospel. Is it probable that as soon as Jesus saw the multitude coming to Him, He began to be concerned about how they should be fed (*v.* 5) ? Is not this situation more artificial and less natural than that presented in Mark ?

Again, *v.* 6 is written from the standpoint of a later Christology, and accords with other passages in emphasizing the supernaturalness of Jesus' knowledge beyond what seem the necessary limitations of a real incarnation. That after the disciples had brought the perilous position before Jesus He put such a question to Philip is not improbable, nor that Andrew offered the information about the five barley loaves and two fishes. This statement is given, however, in a doctrinal rather than a historical setting.

(*e*) It is not improbable that the multitude did follow Jesus to the other side of the lake, and that a conversation bearing on the miracle did take place, although it is strange that the Synoptists, Mark and Matthew, have no record of it. Luke does not come into consideration here, for he passes at once from the feeding of the five thousand to the Confession at Caesarea Philippi (ix. 17-18). Does not the summary of the ministry in Gennesaret (Mark vi. 53-56) in its lack of precise details suggest the possibility that either some of the disciples, in their disappointment, for a time withdrew from their Master, or were sent away by Him in order to allay the popular excitement, and were not with Him at the time referred to here? It is difficult to suppose, however, that Jesus on this occasion delivered the discourse as it is recorded. The language and the thought are distinctive of the Fourth Gospel, and not of the Synoptic reports of the teaching of Jesus. The conversation at the seashore and the controversy in the synagogue are combined, and it is too easy a solution of the last difficulty to suppose that the conversation ends with *v.* 40, and the controversy begins at *v.* 41. ' The unexpected ἐν συναγωγῇ of vi. 59 coming after vi. 25 and vi. 30 after

vi. 14 suggest a conflation of two traditions.' [1]
' Chastand,' [2] says Moffatt, ' distinguishes a speech
in the synagogue (vi. 28-30, 36-40, 43-46) from one by
the seaside (vi. 26-27, 31-35, 41-42, 47-58).' Before
considering this analysis, however, another solution
of the problem may be suggested.

(f) Two audiences are distinguished, a great multitude
(v. 2), the people (v. 14), the multitude (v. 22), and the
Jews (vv. 41 and 52). The multitude was addressed
on the seashore (v. 24) and the controversy with the
Jews took place in the synagogue at Capernaum
(v. 59). Assuming that this is correct, who were the
Jews ? The answer is offered by Mark vii. 1, ' And
there gathered together unto Him the Pharisees, and
certain of the scribes, which had come from Jerusalem.' If these opponents were not Galilaeans but
Judaeans, the nature of the controversy with them
can be more easily understood, for Jesus was then
dealing with the same kind of opponents as He dealt
with in Jerusalem. These enemies would thus in
some measure be responsible for Jesus' loss of popularity even in Galilee. If we can thus regard the two
references in John vi. 41, 52, and the one reference in
Mark vii. 3, as not to Galilaeans, but to Judaeans, then
we are warranted in affirming that the term Jews is
not applied to Galilaeans anywhere in the Gospels,
but is always used either of Judaeans in contrast with
Galilaeans, or of the Jewish nation as a whole. The
writer does not profess an adequate knowledge of the
contemporary Jewish literature to affirm whether
this is in accord with the more general practice, or
may be regarded as a peculiarity of the Gospels. The

---

[1] Moffatt's *Introduction to the Literature of the New Testament,*
p. 554.
[2] *L'apôtre Jean et le quatrième évangile,* pp. 241 ff.

problem of the contrast between the subjects and
manner of controversy between Jesus and His opponents as recorded in the Synoptics and the Fourth
Gospel may not be solved ; but its difficulty is somewhat mitigated if in John vi. Jesus is confronting in
Galilee His Judaean opponents. Otherwise we cannot
appeal to the difference of place, Galilee in the one
case, Judaea in the other, for an explanation of the
contrast between the Synoptics and the Fourth
Gospel.

(g) But another solution of the problem has been
suggested to the mind of the writer as at least more
probable. There may have been a conversation at
the seashore with the multitude, and a controversy
in the synagogue with the Jews, who may have been
those referred to in Mark vii. 1, but it does not follow
that what is before us is an exact report of what was
spoken on each of these occasions. For, having got
his historical framework, the redactor may have fitted
into it a discourse that he found in the Gospel without
any definite historical setting. In that case we
might assume that the conversation extended to the
end of v. 29. The request for a sign in v. 30 would
come very strangely from the multitude which had
just witnessed the miracle (vv. 1-14). To the controversy vv. 41-45 may refer, although the reason given
for the controversy in v. 41 is doubtful, if Jesus had
not called Himself on this occasion, ' the bread which
came down out of heaven.' Verse 42 would certainly
be more likely to be spoken in Galilee than in Jerusalem, and seems an echo of Matt. xiii. 55. As it is
held by many scholars that vii. 15-24 should follow
v. 47, is it not possible that a discourse on the Bread
of Life may belong to that place, between vv. 14 and
25, a discourse which the redactor has distributed

between the seashore and the synagogue as an appropriate sequel to the miracle. This he did unskilfully, as an analysis will show. As the Feast of Tabernacles was associated with the Wanderings in the Wilderness, such a demand as vi. 30-31 contains would be much more probable in Jerusalem on that occasion than in its present context. Thus would be explained the disorder in the report of the conversation and the controversy and also the peculiar character of the teaching, unlikely to have been given in Galilee.

(h) As this is offered only as a conjecture, we may look more closely at the passage to examine the possibility of such teaching having been given on this occasion. Chastand refers vv. 28-30 to the controversy in the synagogue, but it has already been suggested that vv. 28 and 29 would not be inappropriate as addressed to the multitude at the seashore. For an alternative explanation of vv. 30-31 we might recall Mark viii. 11, where a similar demand is recorded after the feeding of the Four Thousand. If that passage (viii. 1-10) is a variant tradition of vi. 30-44, then possibly the redactor with his second-hand knowledge of the Galilaean ministry may have introduced this incident at what seemed by association of ideas the proper place. Verse 33 is evidently a theological reflexion, but vv. 32, 34, 35 might be the substance of a conversation with the people. Verses 36-40 seem to contain teaching far too advanced for the multitude, and may belong to the controversy with the Jewish opponents. Unlikely even in that setting is the phrase in v. 38, ' down from heaven,' as also so plain a reference to His power in raising from the dead at the last day (vv. 39-40 ; cf. v. 19-29), which appears to go beyond the claim which from His other teaching we conclude He ever made for Himself, at least in the

present context, although at a later date He may
have challenged Jewish unbelief by such an assertion.
Chastand ascribes *vv.* 41 and 42 to the multitude, but
this is unlikely for three reasons.   *Firstly*, a distinction
seems to be intended between the multitude and the
Jews.   The Judaean opponents would make any
claim Jesus made to the multitude a ground of controversy on the first convenient occasion.   *Secondly*,
would the multitude, after having been fed, murmur
at such a claim ?   *Lastly*, *v.* 42 recalls Mark vi. 3, and
comes from another context.   Verses 43-46 may belong
to the controversy in the synagogue, and what has been
said above in reference to *vv.* 36-40 applies here also.
In *vv.* 47-50 possibly we return to the seashore, as the
thought is continuous with *v.* 35 ; but *v.* 50 looks like
a later reflexion, and the last clause of *v.* 51 makes us
pause.   Would Jesus at this time refer to *His giving
His flesh for the life of the world* ?   Is it likely that He
would make even an obscure allusion to His death
when dealing with the multitude before He had made
any announcement of His coming Passion to his own
disciples ?   The allusion to the flesh is developed in
vv. 52-57 ; but the thought of *vv.* 32-35 is resumed in
v. 58.   Chastand assigns *vv.* 47-58 to the conversations
at the seashore, but this seems impossible.   The last
clause of *v.* 51 and *vv.* 52-57 belong to another context.
Possibly Jesus may in the Upper Room to some of
His disciples, if not all, have expanded the thought
implied in the words of institution of the Supper, but
more probably there is here the reflexion of a later
time, possibly due to controversy regarding the
Eucharist.[1]   We may now in the light of this analysis

---

[1] For a treatment of the question from this standpoint see *The
Fourth Gospel and the Sacraments*, by John Naish.   (*The Expositor*,
8th series, vol. xxiii. pp. 53-68.)

reconsider our conjecture. It is more probable that the redactor had not an independent tradition before him ; but that as this teaching has so close affinities with the other discourses in the Fourth Gospel, that was the source ; he used his material unskilfully.

(i) It does not seem necessary, however, to abandon the historical character of the narrative, and to subordinate it so completely to the doctrinal interest as is done in the following statement by Dr. Strachan.[1] 'The mysterious appearance of Jesus is thus made prominent, and it is for this reason in particular that the evangelist uses this story, along with the previous one, as a prelude to the eucharistic narrative. Note also the rather elaborate and involved statement, vv. 22-25, intended to point out that Jesus could not have arrived by a boat, and culminating in the wondering question of the crowd at His sudden appearance (v. 25). What is the connexion of all this with the Eucharist ? The evangelist seeks to teach that Jesus is able to transcend the laws of space, and that His presence is to be looked for elsewhere than only in the eucharistic meal. The storm-tossed ship symbolizes the Church, and Jesus communicates Himself to its needs in a fashion that transcends limitations of sense. In our interpretation, the chapter refers to exaggerated ideas, current when the Gospel was written, as to the exclusive presence of Jesus in the Eucharist. Not only in the Eucharist, but amid the storms of life does Jesus appear. He is a real spiritual presence everywhere.' The writer must confess that all this is too ingenious and arbitrary to be convincing.

(j) Although the conjecture has been adopted that in this chapter in the parts indicated in the analysis we have a discourse of Jesus included by the evangelist,

[1] *The Fourth Gospel*, p. 119.

but re-edited by the redactor, the occasion of which
was possibly the Feast of Tabernacles ; yet in order to
avoid a return in a subsequent chapter a few words
on the theological significance may be added. Jesus
demands faith of the multitude on the ground that He
alone can offer men the absolute satisfaction of their
needs, because He comes from God, and brings God's
resources to men. This one thought is repeated again
and again, and this repetition may be due to the
witness's reflexions rather than his reminiscences. He
turned over in his mind a pregnant saying of Jesus.
The subtle distinctions which Bishop Westcott observes [1]
seem to show only a misplaced subtlety ; for an
effective popular teacher, as Jesus was, does not make
them. In His reply to His opponents Jesus affirms
the impossibility of His being understood and believed
except by those who have experienced an inward
change (vv. 44-45). It is the same demand as He made
of Nicodemus (iii. 3, 5), and the same assurance as He
gave Peter (Matt. xvi. 17). Next He affirms that He
knows God as no other has known Him (v. 46).
The same claim is made in Matt. xi. 27. He reproaches
His hearers with having failed to exercise the faith in
Him which their knowledge of Him warranted (v. 36),
and explains their failure, not as due to any unfaithful-
ness on His part to His calling, but as proving that they
have not experienced this inward change (vv. 37-40).
We may here note a contrast between Jesus' standpoint
and ours. We lay stress on the subjective process in
man of unbelief or faith, He lays stress on the objective
purpose of God (as in Matt. xi. 27). For Him the
inward change is a divine gift (vv. 37, 39). But we
should misrepresent His mind if we considered that
there was anything arbitrary in the exercise of the

[1] *The Gospel of St. John*, pp. 99 ff.

divine will or any disregard of the exercise of the
human will, for *v.* 40 makes this plain. God gives to
Christ all who choose to know Him and trust in Him.
On an intelligent interpretation there is in this teaching
no moral dualism or fatalism, as though God doomed
any man to inevitable unbelief, and so to consequent
condemnation. In the address to the disciples, or a
few of them (51c, 52-57), the figurative language here
ascribed to Jesus would be startling had He not in
the institution of the Supper compared His body to
the bread, and His blood to the wine which He called
on His disciples to partake. These sayings, if not the
reflexions of a later age, can be understood only as an
expansion of the words of institution. We need not
follow Westcott in his far too subtle exposition, as
when he writes : ' " Flesh " describes human nature in
its totality regarded from its earthly side. . . . The
thought of death lies already in the word, but that
thought is not as yet brought out, as afterwards, by
the addition of *blood*.' [1] What the passage teaches can
be put quite simply. The soul's sustenance and satisfaction is found only in Christ by faith in Him, and in
Him not only as living, teaching, working, but as dying,
as offering Himself in sacrifice for the world's salvation.
If the words are in some sense Christ's, to read later
eucharistic ideas into them is to indulge in dogmatic,
and not historical, exegesis. If they are the reflexions
of a later age, such interpretation could claim justification. Interpreted in the setting of the Last Supper,
the passage would not be inharmonious with Jesus'
other teaching about His sacrifice. Without affirming
that all the perplexities of chapter vi. have by this
treatment been resolved, the writer is convinced that
only on such lines can the problem be solved at all.

[1] *Op. cit.* p. 106.

(4) It is quite uncertain whether the account of the second visit to Cana in Galilee (iv. 43-54) is to be ascribed to the redactor or to the witness. (*a*) If the incident belongs to the public ministry in Galilee, and should be directly attached to chapter vi., it is not likely, for reasons elsewhere given, that the witness was present.   If, however, it preceded the formation of the Galilaean company of disciples, of whom he was not one, he may have been.   Even if he were not present, his reason for recording it at second-hand may have been his interest in the place itself, awakened by the previous visit (ii. 1-11).   As Mary the mother of Jesus had a connexion with Cana (ii. 1), she, who afterwards made her home with him (xix. 27), may have been his informant.   If the story is to be ascribed to the redactor, it is possible to regard it as a variant of the Synoptic story of the healing of the centurion's servant (Matt. viii. 5-13) with an exaggeration of the super-natural character of the cure as wrought at a distance. This, however, is by no means necessary.   For the difference between the distance from Cana to Caper-naum and the distance from the spot where Jesus was where He spoke the word of assurance to the centurion's house in Capernaum cannot really be supposed to in-crease the supernaturalness of the act of healing.   If Jesus' miracles were answers to His prayers, as xi. 41 suggests, distance would make no difference to the omnipresent God.   Only if we regard the miracles as due to *moral therapeutics* can we consider the personal presence of Jesus as essential.   It is from the modern scholar's standpoint, and not from the witness's or the redactor's, that the one kind of cure would appear more miraculous than the other.   On account of the character of the miracle we need not assign the record to the redactor rather than the witness.   On the whole

the writer himself inclines to ascribe the story to the witness.

(b) A difficulty emerges in v. 44. Does it mean that Jesus Himself quoted the proverb, 'A prophet hath no honour in his own country,' as He did on another occasion (Matt. xiii. 57) in reference to Nazareth 'His own country' (v. 54) as a reason for leaving Judaea and going into Galilee, or did Jesus' action in the judgment of the witness in so doing confirm the truth of the proverb ? In other words, are we to interpret the words from the standpoint of Jesus or of the witness. If from the former, the conclusion would be inevitable that Jesus meant by His own country Galilee, but that would be a reason for leaving Galilee, and not for returning to it. On the lips of Jesus at the beginning of His ministry, when He had not yet tested the feeling of Galilee, the words would be inappropriate as they are not on the other occasion. If from the latter standpoint, then the words reveal the witness's conviction which he may have transferred to Jesus that Jesus as Jewish Messiah, wherever His early home may have been, properly belonged to Judaea, and this intensified the tragedy of His having to turn from Judaea to Galilee. 'It looks,' says Dr. Strachan, 'as though the Evangelist regarded Judaea, and not Galilee, as "the country" of Jesus, which of course is wrong.' [1] In view of the explanation offered is it 'of course wrong' ? A parallel thought is in i. 11 : 'He came unto His own place (τὰ ἴδια) and His own people (οἱ ἴδιοι) received Him not.' For in this respect probably the evangelist would share the witness's standpoint. Does not such a touch indicate a Judaean and not a Galilaean ? [2]

---

[1] *The Fourth Gospel*, p. 110.

[2] Bacon's suggestion that the words ἀλλ' οὐκ εἰσῆλθεν εἰς Ναζαρέτ have fallen out between *vv.* 43 and 44 would supply a good explanation. (*The Expositor*, 8th series, vol. xxiii. p. 42.)

(*c*) The answer of Jesus to the request (*v.* 48) suggests that He was unwilling to repeat in Galilee the kind of ministry which had proved so fruitless in Judaea, the working of miracles which evoked an untrustworthy belief (ii. 23-25). If we now turn to Mark i. 14 for the continuation of the story after *v.* 54, we may infer that Jesus' plan was to avoid the working of miracles as far as possible, and to undertake with a few chosen companions a preaching tour in the synagogues of Galilee (*v.* 38). For this work the two pairs of brothers were first called (*vv.* 16-20) and then Matthew (ii. 14) ; and the witness as a Judaean returned to Jerusalem to rejoin Jesus on His subsequent visits.

(5) One other passage falls to be considered as a probable insertion by the redactor. It is the interview with the Greeks and the discourse of Jesus on that occasion (xii. 20-36). (*a*) The request of the Greeks is reported, and the response of Jesus ; but there is no record of the interview if it did take place. Dr. Strachan comments on this : ' Our interest is fixed not on the historical fact, but on its significance. These Greeks are symbolic of the world-wide significance of the death of Jesus. This meaning is brought out in the discourse that follows.' [1] But may not the historical fact have suggested to the mind of Jesus Himself the subsequent train of thought ? In view of the Synoptic echoes in what follows we may ask whether such an interview would not be more likely on the borders of Galilee as at Caesarea Philippi than in Jerusalem. If it was the redactor who placed a tradition of such an interview where it now is, *v.* 20 would be his explanation of the assumed presence of these Greeks in Jerusalem. Philip and Andrew again come into prominence as in chap. vi.

[1] *Op. cit.* p. 159,

(*b*) We must now examine each verse. Verse 23 is characteristically Johannine in form, but may be genuine, if not in this context. (Cf. xiii. 31.) Verse 24 sounds an authentic utterance of Jesus, suitable to such an occasion. The possibility of a wider ministry to the Gentiles suggested by the request of the Greeks is set aside in view of the necessity of His death. He must die as Jewish Messiah before He can become the world's Saviour. Dr. Strachan [1] here again comments : ' Note that the analogy of the death of the corn of wheat is peculiarly suitable to Greek thought.' Was it not just as probable for the mind of Jesus Himself, who spoke the parable of the Sower ? Paul was more familiar with streets than with fields, and he uses the same analogy (1 Cor. xv. 36). Do not *vv.* 25 and 26 recall Mark viii. 34-38 modified by the channel of transmission ? We cannot but think of Gethsemane, of the agony in which the Fourth Gospel has no record, as we read *vv.* 27 and 28. The voice from heaven recalls the experiences of the Baptism and the Transfiguration, although the possibility of some unusual manifestation during Passion week cannot be excluded. But *v.* 30 must make us hesitate. It was not the method of Jesus to give signs from heaven ; and does not the voice as recorded in *v.* 28 give the response to the prayer. There is a contradiction here (compare for a similar misrepresentation, xi. 42). If we compare these verses with the Synoptic record of Gethsemane when Jesus left all but three chosen disciples behind, and even withdrew a little from them (Mark xiv. 32-35) when He prayed, it will seem incredible that He should have laid bare His soul before the multitude. Surely the sacred intimacies of Father and Son were not for profane ears to hear. An apologist's ardour here over-

[1] *Idem*, p. 160,

comes love's insight. Verse 31 would most fitly follow
v. 23, but it might also follow *v.* 24, as the Sacrifice of
Jesus was the world's judgment and Satan's overthrow.
In *v.* 32, which quite properly follows *v.* 31, Jesus Himself probably intended a wider reference than is found
in it in *v.* 33 ; and iii. 14, 15 would find a better setting
here than in the conversation with Nicodemus. The
question in *v.* 34, 'Who is this Son of man ? ' assumes
that that title has just been mentioned—an additional
reason for placing iii. 14, 15 here. The saying in vi. 62,
which is out of place in its present context, could more
suitably be placed here after *v.* 34, as it is just the kind
of answer Jesus would give to such a question. Chapter
iii. 13, 11, 12 would also fit in here, and such an arrangement would give us a connected series of sayings.
Verses 35-36 would offer quite an appropriate sequel
to such teaching on whatever occasion it may have been
given, concealing the truth from the indifferent and
hostile, and yet revealing it to those who were able and
willing to receive it.[1]

(*c*) As *vv.* 37-40 clearly should follow and not come

[1] These sayings on the death and resurrection may be placed in
succession : xii. 24, ' Verily, verily, I say unto you, Except a grain
of wheat fall into the earth and die, it abideth by itself alone ; but,
if it die, it beareth much fruit.' Verses 31-32, 'Now is the judgment
of this world ; now shall the prince of this world be cast out. And I,
if I be lifted up from the earth, will draw all men unto myself.'
iii. 14, 15, ' As Moses lifted up the serpent in the wilderness, even so
must the Son of man be lifted up : that whosoever believeth may in
Him have eternal life.' xii. 34, ' The multitude therefore answered
him, We have heard out of the law that the Christ abideth for ever ;
and how sayest thou, The Son of man must be lifted up ? Who is
this Son of man ? ' vi. 62, ' What then if ye should behold the Son
of man ascending where he was before ? ' iii. 13, ' And no man
hath ascended into heaven, but he that descended out of heaven,
even the Son of man which is in heaven.' Verses 11-12, 'Verily, verily,
I say unto thee, We speak that we do know, and bear witness of that
we have seen ; and ye receive not our witness. If I told you earthly
things, and ye believe not, how shall ye believe if I tell you heavenly
things ? ' We need not assume that nothing else was said and that
all was said at the same time.

before *vv.* 42-50, which would suitably follow *v.* 19,
this dislocation points here as elsewhere to the activities
of the redactor. We cannot, however, assign the whole
of this passage (*vv.* 20-36) as echoes of Synoptic tradition, as we must recognize Johannine elements in *v.* 23
and *vv.* 35-36. He may here, as in chapter vi., be confirming what he found in the Gospel with what he derived
from some other source. Here his combination is
unskilful. The reason for such a series of sayings about
the necessity of Jesus' death appears more probable
at the close of His Galilaean ministry in the circle of
His disciples than before the multitude, as *v.* 34, which
betrays the redactor's standpoint, indicates. So scanty
and bare are the indications about the Passion in the
Synoptics that these sayings would form a welcome
supplement to them, and the words about the lifting
up would cover both the Crucifixion and subsequent
Resurrection as there foretold.

(6) The writer, while fully recognising a deep debt
of gratitude to Dr. Bacon for the clue to these insertions,
cannot regard as such some of the insertions he ascribes
to the redactor.

(i) ' Conspicuously is this the case with the interview
with Nicodemus which Tatian's order, Synoptic affinity,
and the intrinsic consistency of the Fourth Gospel
alike require should stand after 7 : 30. This scene is
linked by the editorial comment 2 : 23-25 to the incident of the Purging of the Temple 2 : 13-22, a passage
which over and over again we have found evincing
its alien origin. There was indeed nothing in the content of 3 : 1-21 to connect it with Passover : but it
dealt with the doctrine of baptism, and this, it would
seem, was enough for an editor in search of material
for the additional Passover he had interjected into the

section on Jesus and the Baptist.' [1]   The subsequent discussion will endeavour to prove that the historical framework of the Gospel can be accepted ; that there was a ministry in Judaea at the Passover, two years before the Passover of the Passion (the intervening Passover being referred to in vi. 4) ; that both the cleansing of the Temple and the conversation with Nicodemus belong to that period, and that if the repetition of the act of cleansing should appear incredible, the Johannine position is more probable than the Synoptic.   Hence the writer cannot accept Bacon's confident conclusion, as it seems to him to rest on an insecure foundation.

(ii) In a note he adds : ' We must also attribute to R the supplement to the Baptist's discourse in 3 : 31-36. This paragraph, of similar composition and style to 12 : 44-50, reiterates the thoughts and expressions of Jesus' discourse to Nicodemus, placing them now in the mouth of the Baptist ! '

The writer does not see a good reason for regarding xii. 44-50 other than as a report (reminiscence possibly mingled with reflexion) of what the witness said that Jesus had said.   With iii. 31-36 he has already dealt as a reflexion or comment of either the evangelist or the witness, not on *vv.* 22-30, which have probably been displaced, but on iii. 1-21.   Into any further consideration of Bacon's views it is not necessary for the purpose of this volume to enter.   Having with the help his discussion has offered sought to discover in the Gospel the contribution of the evangelist on the one hand and the redactor on the other, we come now to the most important part of the task, to ascertain and appraise what has come to us from the witness, ' the beloved disciple.'

[1] *Op. cit.* pp. 523-524.

V

THE REMINISCENCES AND REFLEXIONS OF THE WITNESS : INTRODUCTORY

(1) Having separated from the main contents of the Gospel the contributions of the evangelist and the redactor, we have now to examine the contribution of the witness. How far his report may have been affected by the evangelist in recording it we cannot accurately determine, neither can we rigidly fix the frontier between his own reminiscences and his reflexions, although sometimes the transition from the one to the other may be indicated with some degree of probability. In examining his contribution we may discover some of his characteristics, and thus gain some clues to his identity ; but the consideration of the authorship will be reserved for the close of the volume.

(2) Before entering on this examination, it seems desirable that the course of the ministry of Jesus as presented in the Fourth Gospel by the witness should be sketched as the background of the self-revelation of the Son of God which is its distinctive content.

(i) The Baptist's testimony (i. 19-34) was followed by the call of the first disciples (35-51), and the confirmation of their faith in the first miracle at Cana (ii. 1-11). After a brief stay in Capernaum (v. 12), Jesus and His disciples came into the land of Judaea ; and there He exercised a ministry similar to John's. The jealousy of the Baptist's disciples evoked from him an emphatic testimony to the superiority of the Messiah's work (iii. 22-30). The ministry in Jerusalem itself was begun at the feast of the Passover by the Cleansing of the Temple, an act which aroused the antagonism of the priestly party (ii. 13-22). Although only a superficial impression was made on the common people (23-25), the Pharisaic party sent Nicodemus to discover whether this new movement should be encouraged or not ; but Jesus' demand of a thorough-going change as a condition of discipleship was contemptuously rejected (iii. 1-10). The brief visit to Jerusalem had proved that the distinctive Messianic ministry could not yet be begun owing to the unpreparedness of the nation. To avoid any further dispute with John's disciples, Jesus withdrew even from Judaea itself to Galilee through Samaria, where He met with a promise of success, which, probably that He might not prejudice the chance of acceptance in Judaea or Galilee, He left to be fulfilled at a later time (iv. 1-23, 25-42).

(ii) While it is not certain that the witness accompanied Jesus into Galilee (iv. 43-45), it is not improbable that he did visit Cana a second time, and so was present at the interview with the nobleman of Capernaum (46-54). But when the public ministry in Galilee began, and the Galilaean circle of disciples was formed, he returned to his home in Jerusalem. After a period in Galilee (the report of which is contained in vi. 1-65) a second visit was paid to Jerusalem at a feast (v.). This feast was probably not the Passover (vi. 4) but Pentecost, fifty days later, as the excitement in Galilee (vi. 15) would have been fanned into a dangerous flame had Jesus gone up with the Galilaean pilgrims at once. The visit was a private one ; no disciples were with Him ; and the man cured

did not know his benefactor (v. 13).   His defence of
the act of healing on the Sabbath day (v. 30-47 continued in vii. 15-24), referred not only to the immediate
charge but to the relation to God which He claimed
for Himself.   It was probably when the Galilaean
ministry was again resumed that the confession at
Caesarea Philippi of the Synoptic record, of which
vi. 66-71 is an echo, took place.

(iii) A third visit, 'not publicly, but as it were in
secret,' was made at the Feast of Tabernacles (vii.
1-14) ; but publicity could not long be avoided, and
in accordance with the ceremonial of the feast Jesus
offered Himself to the multitude, many of whom were
now favourably inclined, as the Living Water (25-39).
The divided state of public sentiment prevented the
carrying out of the hostile designs of the priestly
party (40-52).   Jesus resumed His appeal to the
people, and again in accord with the festival ritual
offered Himself as the Light of the World.   He was
driven in controversy with His opponents to make
ever bolder claims for Himself, until by asserting His
pre-existence He excited such fury that an attempt
was made to stone Him (viii. 12-59).

(iv) Probably a retirement to Galilee at once took
place ; but Jerusalem was again visited at the Feast
of Dedication (x. 22).   On this occasion the blind man
received his sight (ix.), and Jesus had again to defend
Himself against the charge of Sabbath-breaking, and,
as always, to assert the claims regarding His relation
to God (x. 19-29).   The faith of the blind man contrasted with the unbelief of the Jewish rulers suggested
the theme of the public discourse on the Door of the
Fold and the Good Shepherd (x. 1-18) ; and the mention
of the Shepherd's sacrifice on behalf of the sheep in
obedience to the Father led again to a declaration of

His oneness with God, which provoked another out-burst of fury against Him (30-39), necessitating a retirement beyond Jordan. From this retirement Jesus was summoned by the tidings of Lazarus' death (xi. 1-16, a second-hand report). The visit to Bethany and the raising of Lazarus there caused so great enthusiasm among the people (17-46) that in secret counsel it was resolved that He should be put to death (47-53), and this resolve once more drove Him into retirement (54-57).

(v) Probably on the Friday evening preceding the Passion Jesus came to Bethany, and at a feast given in His honour was anointed by Mary (xii. 1-8). The popular enthusiasm found vent in the triumphal entry on the Sunday morning (9-19) ; and it was this public movement which probably excited the interest of the Greeks, an interview with whom led Jesus to a definite declaration of the necessity of His death for the universality of His influence (20-24, 32, and iii. 13-15, probably also vi. 62).[1] The perplexity of the multitude because of these sayings was met by a final appeal for faith (34-36*a*, 44-50), which a prophetic quotation showed for the majority of the nation to have been vain (36*b*-43). The witness makes no mention of the controversies during Passion week, nor of the eschatological teaching to the disciples, recorded by the Synoptists. Possibly he was not himself present. He writes as an eye-witness, however, of the Last Supper, although he does not record the institution of the Memorial Feast (xiii. 1-30). In the long discourse which he records there has been con-siderable displacement. If chapters xv. and xvi. do not report teaching given in the two or three days

[1] The difficulties of this passage have been dealt with in the pre-ceding chapter.

spent in retirement prior to the Supper, they are to be placed either between xiii. 31a and 31b, or after 35. The farewell discourse would thus be reported in xiii. 31b or xiv. 1-31, and this would be followed by the prayer (xvii.) while Jesus and His disciples stood around the table, before starting for Gethsemane. The arrest in Gethsemane (xviii. 1-11) was followed first by a preliminary inquiry before Annas (12-14, 24) and then by a formal trial before Caiaphas (19-23), during which Peter's denials probably took place (15-18, 25, 27).[1] The Fourth Gospel passes over the public trial before the Sanhedrin reported by the Synoptics, but gives an account of the trial before Pilate (xviii. 28-xix. 16). The account of the Crucifixion and Burial, though different, is not inconsistent with the Synoptic (xix. 17-42). The record of the Resurrection has points of contact with that in Luke's Gospel (xx. 1-29). The Gospel ends with a frank declaration of its purpose to awaken faith in Christ (30-31).

(3) The course of the ministry so presented makes clear the plan of the record, which can be given in three words, *testimony, judgment, glory*.

(i) The testimony is contained in the first four chapters, and is borne by John the Baptist, the first disciples, and the first sign. To the priesthood, the multitude, and the Pharisees, the three classes of Judaean society, the testimony is offered in vain. In Samaria there is a promise of faith, the fulfilment of which is, however, deferred. The sixth chapter, though a later addition, as has been already argued, falls into the same plan, a confirmation of the view that it should precede the fifth. In Galilee there is the testimony

---

[1] See preceding chapter for a discussion of this passage as of xiii. 36-38.

of the popular enthusiasm, real or mistaken, but there already the transition to the judgment or crisis begins. The Judaean opposition invades Galilee, and turns the tide of popularity; and the multitude who forsake are separated from the disciples who cleave to Jesus.

(ii) It is in Judaea, however, that the crisis of reception or rejection is mainly placed (chaps. v., vii.-xi.). It is connected with the three miracles of the cure at the Pool of Bethesda, the giving sight to the man born blind, and the raising of Lazarus from the dead, and with the three feasts of Pentecost (or Passover), Tabernacles, and Dedication. Unless we connect the second miracle with the second feast instead of with the third, and the third miracle with the third feast as Dr. Bacon does [1] instead of putting it after that feast, for which there are no adequate grounds, we are not entitled to charge the witness with such indifference to historical fact as would be the case if he had arbitrarily attached a miracle to each feast.

(iii) Just as in the first section there is a transition to the second, as has already been indicated, so the story of Lazarus, which closes the judgment section, serves as the transition to the account of the Passion and Resurrection, in which the Glory is revealed. But the idea of testimony as well as of judgment is taken up into this last section. It is surely testimony which is borne in chapter xii. by the anointing in Bethany, by the triumphal entry, by the request of the Greeks, by the perplexity of the multitude, and by the prophetic oracle. While the glory of Jesus is being revealed in the circle of His disciples (xiii.-xvii.) and before the Jewish people (xviii.-xix.), there is also judgment, resulting in faith in the one, and unbelief in

---

[1] *The Fourth Gospel*, p. 409.

the other. The work is crowned by the glory of the Resurrection (xx.).

(iv) This careful arrangement shows that the interest of the witness is not primarily historical but doctrinal and practical ; yet it would be rash to conclude on that account that he does not merely select, but that he also invents. He has not a historical interest in the mere record of facts apart from their significance and value ; but he is interested in history because the doctrine he desires to commend is not a speculative opinion, but the interpretation of a historical person-ality, and the practice he desires to evoke is the exer-cise of faith, not in an idea or an ideal, but in a personal object. The purpose demanded fact, and not fiction, although it allowed a freer handling of fact than the modern historian admits as legitimate.

(4) One of the most formidable objections to the historicity of the Gospel must here be dealt with. It records a number of visits to Jerusalem at the time of the feasts, whereas the Synoptics record only the last visit, and confine the ministry to Galilee and the surrounding regions. Does this difference justify our dismissing the Fourth Gospel as unhistorical ? Some reasons in arrest of such hasty judgment may be given.

(a) The completeness of the Synoptic record is an assumption which the results of modern scholarship are more and more disproving. According to the Two-Document hypothesis, the main sources of the Synoptics are two : Mark's reports of Peter's reminis-cences and the collection of sayings of Jesus. In his book on *Gospel Origins*, Prof. Holdsworth gives this hypothesis a form which at least challenges close scrutiny and respectful consideration. He maintains that Mark himself prepared three editions of his own

work, so accounting for some of the differences of
Matthew and Luke from Mark, and from one another ;
and that it was Matthew who first arranged a mere
collection of detached sayings of Jesus in a series of
discourses, which he fitted in a Markan framework.
' We have only to suppose,' he says, ' what bears
every mark of probability, that St. Mark wrote down
what he remembered of St. Peter's preaching both while
he superintended the Church in Alexandria and later
on when he was again associated with St. Peter in
Rome, to see that the apparent contradiction between
the Fathers may be resolved.   Chrysostom and Jerome
are right in ascribing the Gospel to Egypt, and Clement
is equally right in declaring Rome to be its birthplace.
We shall show presently that the Markan narrative
in the first Gospel bears unmistakable marks of an
Alexandrian origin, while canonical Mark as distinctly
points to Rome.   But if these marks appear in these
two Gospels, the Lukan Mark has many traits which
indicate a Palestinian origin, and there is no reason
why St. Mark should not have written an even earlier
edition of his Gospel which was left at Caesarea, where
it would pass into the hands of St. Luke when he visited
that town.' [1]   This hypothesis is stated to throw into
bolder relief the fact that the other Synoptists are so
dependent on Mark, that they cannot be regarded as
giving an exhaustive account of the ministry of Jesus.
While Luke had access to another source dealing with
a ministry in Peraea on the way to Jerusalem for the
last visit, and may have gleaned a few additional facts
on his visit with Paul to Jerusalem (Acts xxi. 15),
yet for the record of events Peter is the only eye-witness.
His interest as a Galilaean was in the ministry in Galilee.
His silence about his first meeting with Jesus, as recorded

[1] *Op. cit.* p. 117.

in John i. 41-42, is certainly difficult to explain.   One
would have thought that the story would often be
upon his lips ; but is not a possible explanation this,
that after a short period of intercourse Peter and
Andrew returned to their homes and their calling, until
Jesus transferred His ministry, for reasons to be immediately noted, from Judaea to Galilee ; and that he
regarded his discipleship as beginning with the call to
constant companionship in the Galilaean ministry, and
so made no mention of the previous less intimate and
constant relation ?   It is extraordinary that there is
no mention of Peter's presence with Jesus in Jerusalem
at any of the feasts except the last, although, in the
sixth chapter, when the scene of the ministry is shifted
to Galilee, he is mentioned.   We have no evidence
that all the twelve (or any) went with Jesus on all these
visits to Jesusalem.   The organisation was probably
less formal and fixed than later ecclesiastical associations lead us to regard it as being.   And it may have
existed primarily for the work in Galilee, as all the
twelve, except Judas, were Galilaeans.[1]   Peter, therefore, may have said nothing about the visits to Jerusalem, as he had nothing to report as an eye-witness.   For
it is certain that in his discourses nothing was further
from his mind than to furnish a complete biography
of Jesus.   The writer may throw out a suggestion
which has occurred to him, but which would require
further testing before it could be urged with any confidence.   May not Mark have first heard Peter give an
account of the Galilaean ministry for the instruction
of the primitive community in Jerusalem, for whom
any report of visits in Jerusalem would be unnecessary,
even if he had been able to speak with special knowledge ?   This local circumstance may have given its

[1] See Chap. x. for a full discussion of this subject.

form to the Petrine tradition of the life and work of
Jesus. The account of the last visit would be added
when Peter went on his missionary travels ; and Mark
as a Jerusalemite would not be dependent here on
Peter. The present form of the Gospel according to
Mark would be determined by the needs of the readers
to whom it was addressed. Is it not highly probable
that Peter's teaching in Jerusalem would mainly consist of the account of the Galilaean ministry ? We must
always remind ourselves of how great is our ignorance
of the life and work of Jesus ; and there is room for
conjecture which accords and does not conflict with
the evidence we have.

(b) If the Synoptic records are incomplete, we may
welcome an additional source of information, if its
authenticity can be maintained on historical grounds.
(i) Is it not only probable, but even certain, that
Jesus as the Messiah of the Jewish nation could not
be content to offer Himself for its acceptance or
rejection in the comparatively insignificant province
of Galilee, but must have felt constrained to press
His claims upon it at the very centre of its national
religious life at the seasons when Jews from all parts
of the world had come together to worship? More
than London is to the British Empire was Jerusalem
to the Jewish nation ; it had a sanctity such as Rome
has for the Roman Catholic, if not even greater.
Could the full responsibility of refusing His claims
be cast on the nation, if the full opportunity of considering these claims had not been given ? (ii) But
the Synoptic record of the last visit to Jerusalem
presupposes a previous ministry there. The mere
reports of His sayings and doings in Galilee would
not have affected the priests and scribes and the
populace in Jerusalem, as the story shows. Surely

the lament over Jerusalem (Matt. xxiii. 37-39) would become unreal rhetoric if Jesus had not made a more persistent and passionate endeavour to overcome unbelief and hate than the Synoptists record. How could He have said ' How often ' if He only at the end of His ministry made such an attempt ? (iii) Other evidence may be mentioned. Luke records the visit of Jesus to the home of Martha and Mary (x. 38-42), and there is no ground for suspecting John's statement that it was Bethany. Had this been a first visit to former strangers, would such a conversation be credible ? Jesus had adherents near or in Jerusalem before the last visit. The same fact is proved by the arrangements Jesus made for the use both of the ass for the entry and of the upper room for the supper (Matt. xxi. 2, 3 ; Mark xiv. 13-14). In neither case need we suppose supernatural knowledge, but a preconcerted sign with a devoted disciple, ready to put his possessions at the Master's disposal. It is even not improbable that the witness himself was that disciple. There was a Judaean as well as a Galilaean circle of disciples, and these, and not the Twelve, may be referred to in some passages in the Fourth Gospel.

(c) This consideration exposes the weakness of one of the links in the chain of argument by which Bishop Westcott tried to prove that the beloved disciple, the author of the Fourth Gospel, can have been no other than John the son of Zebedee. (i) If one so appreciative of and devoted to Jesus as Mary of Bethany was not one of the women following and ministering to Him, but remained in her home in Bethany ; if a disciple in Jerusalem not only was ready to offer a room for the Master's use, but seems even to have been unknown to the disciples who were sent on the errand, is it impossible that ' the beloved disciple,' who could receive and retain the deeper teaching of the Master, after a short period of following Jesus, even in Galilee, returned to his home in Jerusalem, and was afterwards with Him only when He renewed His ' forlorn hope ' to win the city from its doom to Himself ?   (ii) We have evidence in the Synoptics that Jesus after the confession at Caesarea Philippi failed to find in His constant companions the responsive sympathy with His teaching about His death that He sought.   Their quarrels about precedence in the Kingdom show how far their minds were from His.   It was John the son of Zebedee who joined in the request for the nearest places to the throne in the Kingdom of God (Matt. xx. 20-28).   It was he too who forbade the disciple who was casting out demons in the name of Jesus, although he was not following Him, and wanted to call down fire on the inhospitable Samaritan village (Luke ix. 49-54).   It will not do to say that it was the grace of God which afterwards changed one of the sons of thunder (Boanerges, Mark iii. 17) into the apostle of love in the later years, for the capacity to receive and retain this deeper teaching must seem credible in this disciple as he was at the time of the ministry, and not as he might afterwards become.   (iii) We may, at least provisionally, conclude that the beloved disciple was with Jesus in Jerusalem, but did not usually follow Him in Galilee.   That he was not John the son of Zebedee would offer an adequate explanation of his silence about the ministry in Galilee, the references to which have already been assigned to the redactor. That he was a Jerusalemite would explain his familiarity with the ministry in Judaea and Jerusalem. Thus would two difficulties in regard to the historical trustworthiness of the Fourth Gospel be removed.   It

is historically probable that in Galilee a public movement was possible which would have been at once
suppressed in Jerusalem ; and so probably the Judaean
disciples were doing secretly a work for the Master,
which showed their devotion, and tested their courage
not less, but even more, than the open following of
Jesus in His Galilaean ministry. The reason why
Jesus went up only at the feasts was probably that
the presence of the Galilaean pilgrims in the city and
its environs did offer Him a measure of protection
which at other times would have been denied Him.[1]
Judaean disciples would apprehend the danger as the
Galilaeans could not, and hence would be readier to
give ear to Jesus' warnings regarding the death
awaiting Him in Jerusalem. (iv) A confirmatory
consideration may be mentioned. While ' disciples '
are mentioned in chapters ii., iii., and iv., no names
at all are given, and it is only in chapter vi. when
we are again in Galilee that the familiar names, Philip,
Andrew, Simon Peter, of chapter i. occur. If that
fact does not warrant us in confidently asserting that
these ' disciples ' did not include any of the Twelve,
it forbids our confidently assuming, as is usually done,
that they must have been some of the Twelve. It is
possible that these were Judaean disciples, who afterwards fell from their faith, or at least shrank back
from continued companionship, and that the one who
afterwards proved ' faithful among the faithless ' in
loving kindness and tender mercy made no mention
of their names. Let these suggestions not be dismissed as rash conjectures ; for the call of Peter and
Andrew, James and John, as recorded in the Synoptics
(Mark i. 16-20), is unintelligible if it was addressed

---

[1] See Mark xiv. 2, ' Not during the feast, lest haply there shall
be a tumult of the people.'

to men who had for months been close companions
of Jesus. The truth is that we have formed our
conception of the disciple company from the Synoptic
records, and when we come to the Fourth Gospel we
assume without warrant in the narrative itself, and
contrary to the plain meaning of the Synoptic story
of the call, that the disciples there mentioned must
be some of the Twelve.

(d) Accordingly, to maintain the historical accuracy
of both the Johannine and the Synoptic records, it
seems to the writer necessary to venture on the following historical reconstruction. The ministry of the
Baptist had attracted the Galilaeans mentioned in
chapter i. By their contact with Jesus they had been
won to a measure of faith in Him sufficient to detach
them from the Baptist, and to attach them to Him.
Other disciples may have been brought in the same
way, but these are mentioned by name because they
were afterwards included in the chosen company of
the Twelve. The first call was to a less constant companionship than the call recorded in the Synoptics,
when Jesus had definitely decided on a public ministry
in Galilee. The unnamed disciple was probably the
witness. After the marriage at Cana (ii. 3) it is
possible that the Galilaeans went back to their homes,
as while ' His disciples ' are said to have gone down
with Jesus to Capernaum (v. 12) where we meet the
pairs of brothers in the Synoptic record, Jesus only is
mentioned as going up to Jerusalem for the Passover
(v. 13). During the interval between the first visit
to Capernaum (John ii. 12) and the second (Mark i. 21)
the witness and other Judaean disciples alone may have
been Jesus' companions, and may have left Him only
when He decided on Galilee as the scene of His ministry.

(5) A brief statement seems relevant at this point

regarding the way in which the growth of the Gospel
may be conceived.   (a) The evangelist was the scholar,
and the witness the teacher.   Either in a small band
of disciples, or in the public assembly of the Christian
community, he dealt with the life and teaching of Jesus.
He began with an account of events or report of discourses, just as the modern preacher starts with his
text ; and then he went on to comment on what he
had reported.   We cannot throughout the Gospel
analyse this preaching or teaching into its components
as will be done in regard to iii. 1-21, but we may assume
a similar process of composition even where the
analysis cannot be made so distinctly and confidently.
It is probable that neither the hearer nor even the
speaker was aware of the passage from reminiscence
to reflexion.   The scholar reporting his teacher would
feel no need for indicating the points of transition ;
and his conscience would not trouble him for thus
blending (or, as the modern critic, conscious of his own
integrity, would possibly say, confusing) history and
doctrine.   So much in extenuation of the reporter's
offence, if offence it be ; what of the witness himself ?

(b) We may conceive the process in his mind as
follows.   He had not merely a retentive memory, but
also an active intelligence ; he meditated on what he
remembered, and so gradually, inevitably, and insensibly reflexions attached themselves to, or even
modified, reminiscences.   A non-thinking person is
more likely to retain the *ipsissima verba* of a remembered conversation than a thoughtful one ; the more
active the intelligence, the stronger the influence of
meditation on recollection.   It is quite credible that
when preaching or teaching the witness could not
always have distinguished the original germ of reminiscence from the subsequent development of reflexion.

(c) Would he have made the attempt, or felt any obligation to make it ?   He was not a modern scholar, aiming at historical accuracy, but an ancient teacher, conscious of the guidance into all the truth of the Spirit of God, promised by the Master.   His reflexions would be to him as much part of the given revelation as his reminiscences.   He would confidently claim with Paul that he had the mind of Christ.   And great as for us is the significance of the earthly life of Jesus, can we confine the divine revelation through Him to His spoken words alone ?   We must include the experience of His truth and grace through the Spirit, which has been given to seers and saints.   The value of the revelation of Christ in the witness is fully tested by the influence the Fourth Gospel has exercised on Christians of all lands and ages.   If we may make a comparison, we may confidently affirm that it has probably been more of a spiritual treasure than any of the others. We can recover, if not with absolute certainty, yet with adequate probability, the history, and we can retain the theology as a valid interpretation of the history of the Word who became flesh.

(d) The mode of composition would account for some of the displacements in the Gospel—a subject which has already been dealt with in so far as these displacements are related to the insertion in the Gospel of Synoptic material [1] and may be due to the unskilful hand of an editor.   For this feature two other explanations may be suggested, not necessarily alternative, but more probably even complementary.   (i) There may have been ' accidental disarrangements of whole leaves in some parent MS. of the present text.'   This hypothesis Mr. Thompson works out in detail by showing that the transposed parts correspond to one or

[1] See Chap. IV.

more pages of the MS.[1] (ii) There may have been imperfect recollections on the part of the witness, or of the evangelist. A correspondent has suggested this explanation to the writer. His words may be quoted. ' If one tries to recall an address delivered long ago, and endeavours to write down what one recalls, probably one would remember *sections*. One would recall, say, a passage of a few lines' length, then similar passages. If one then tried to rebuild the whole discourse the unity of utterance would be obscured, and the whole present a result very much like what we have in the Fourth, and indeed in the other Gospels. This might account not only for the disconnected nature of the discourse, but also for the repetition that in some measure occurs.' A teacher of the writer in his old age used to reproduce in public utterance isolated passages, remembered with extraordinary accuracy, from sermons and lectures, but without any logical continuity of thought or historical continuity of fact.

[1] *The Expositor*, 8th series, vol. ix. pp. 421 ff.

VI

THE TESTIMONY

(JOHN I.-IV.)

(1) THE FIRST TESTIMONY OF THE BAPTIST (i. 19-34)

(a) IN vv. 19-28 the writer at least does not find anything that need be regarded as in substance unhistorical.
If the witness was a disciple of John the Baptist it is
probable that he was more fully informed regarding the
testimony borne to Jesus than was Peter, the probable
source through Mark of the Synoptic account. This
testimony contains nothing theologically distinctive,
and is in substantial agreement with the Synoptic
representation, except in the affirmation of the presence
of the one greater than himself in v. 26. If there was
current in Ephesus a tradition that John was greater
than Jesus, as the Prologue also indicates, there would
be an additional reason for the present record.

(b) In vv. 29-34 statements emerge which demand
explanation. Verse 30 has already been dealt with
as a variant of v. 15 in the Prologue, and as a probable
gloss. In v. 29 the description of Jesus, as ' the Lamb
of God which taketh away the sin of the world,' is
in so marked contrast to the description of the function
of the Messiah in the Synoptic account of the Baptist's
teaching that it has often been dismissed as unauthentic.
In his book, *Studies in the Inner Life of Jesus*,[1] the
writer has tried to show that Jesus thought of His

[1] Pp. 125-126.

vocation as presented in the picture of the suffering servant (Isaiah lii. 13–liii. 12), and has suggested that Jesus had had some conversation with John, and had raised him for a time at least to the height of His own ideal, and that John in this declaration was echoing the words of Jesus. No more satisfactory explanation has since presented itself to his mind. Dr. Strachan admits this possibility, although he places the communication at a later date. ' It is by no means so improbable historically as it seems, that the Baptist should have known the mind of Jesus. They were related by birth, and must have had opportunity of conversation on the work of the Messiah.' [1] In *v.* 34 the Baptist claims that he recognized the Messiah [2] by the descent of the Spirit (*v.* 32). In Mark's account (i. 10) the opened heavens and the descending dove are seen, and the voice of approval is heard by Jesus alone. The account of the heavenly utterance in Matthew (iii. 17) suggests rather that the voice was heard by, and was addressed to others, and not to Jesus alone. Luke appears to substitute an event for a vision (iii. 21-22). It is not intrinsically improbable that the vision was granted to the Baptist to instruct him as well as to Jesus to confirm His sense of His calling. The statement need not in itself cast doubt on the trustworthiness of the witness's record of the Baptist's teaching. While the Baptist's recognition of Jesus as the Messiah is not impossible (*vv.* 31-34), yet if he testified even to his disciples Jesus' Messiahship, the representation in Mark's Gospel of the gradual process which resulted in the confession of Caesarea Philippi is inexplicable ; and

---

[1] *The Fourth Gospel,* p. 80.
[2] If the Baptist used the phrase ' Son of God ' on his lips it must have meant that.

it does seem more probable that the witness is ante-
dating the belief of a later time. This consideration
applies also to the disciples' confession (*vv.* 41, 45, 49).

(2) THE CALL OF THE FIRST DISCIPLES (i. 35-51)

It is not improbable that the repetition of the
declaration (*vv.* 29, 36) was the occasion of two of
the Baptist's disciples following Jesus.

(*a*) In this narrative two questions present themselves for answer. First it is usually assumed that
John the son of Zebedee was one of the two disciples ;
and that as Andrew found first (πρῶτον, *v.* 41) his own
brother Simon, so John next found his brother James,
and thus the two pairs of brothers were the earliest
disciples of Jesus. It is true that John the son of
Zebedee is closely associated with Peter in the records
of the ministry ; but it does not necessarily follow
that he was one of the two who first came to Jesus,
and it is also mere conjecture that James as well was
brought to discipleship at this time. If the unnamed
disciple was the son of Zebedee, the fact would be one
reason for assigning to him the authorship of the
Gospel. If this identification is challenged, however,
the question remains : Was the witness the unnamed
disciple ? The grounds on which the question may
be answered affirmatively are *first*, the tokens of an
eye-witness which the narrative offers in its minute
and vivid details ; and *second*, the probability that
the witness for the most part, if not altogether,
confined his record to first-hand reports of what he
himself had passed through.

(*b*) While the narrative bears the signs of an eye-
witness, it must be admitted that reminiscences are
coloured by reflexions in two respects. *First*, the

witness assigns to these disciples a much more definite
confession of Jesus' Messiahship (*vv.* 41-45, 49) than
in view of the Synoptic representation is at all probable.
If Jesus welcomed Peter's confession at Caesarea
Philippi as a revelation, not of flesh and blood, but of
the Father (Matt. xvi. 17), is it at all likely that the
confession would be made by any of the disciples at
the very beginning of their contact with Jesus ? Even
if in His intercourse Jesus was less reserved than He
found it needful to be afterwards it is not at all likely
that so definite a conception was given to the first
disciples. In recollecting the past, it is almost impossible to exclude the influence of later experiences,
or of our reflexions upon them ; and we must admit
that the witness here represents Jesus as already being
to His disciples what He became to them only at a
much later stage. We must also raise the question
whether the words to Peter in *v.* 42 are not ante-dated,
and must be assigned to a time when Jesus had gained
a more intimate knowledge of the character of His
disciples (Mark iii. 16 ; Luke vi. 14). *Secondly,* this
verse and *v.* 48 also illustrate the tendency of the
witness as well as the evangelist to exaggerate the
supernatural character of Jesus' knowledge, unless
the evangelist has transformed the report the witness
gave. That Jesus had an exceptional foresight based
on insight regarding those with whom He came into
contact, the Synoptists also testify ; but it is evident
that *v.* 48 is intended to record something altogether
miraculous. That Jesus may actually have seen
Nathanael with the bodily eye as he was engaged in
his devotions, need not be questioned. How did He
in that moment gain the knowledge of Nathanael's
life that the commendation of him implies ? One
cannot exclude the possibility of a supernatural in-

F

tuition given to Jesus in the case of Peter as well as
Nathanael. But we must also admit the probability
that here history has been influenced by theology.
Some indications of insight of an exceptional kind
must have been given, which excited wonder and
stimulated faith ; for that seems implied in *v.* 51,
which may be accepted as a genuine saying of Jesus.
Jesus based His insight into man, as all His other
gifts, on His relation to God ; and what He promised
His disciples was that in His companionship they
should witness a constant and intimate communion
of God and man.

(3) The Marriage at Cana of Galilee (ii. 1-12)

In this story three matters call for notice. (*a*) As
we find that in the rest of the Gospel the witness
confines himself almost entirely to Jesus' work in
Judaea and Jerusalem, and that the simplest explanation of the fact is that he was a Judaean disciple who
did not, at least usually, accompany Jesus in Galilee,
we may raise the question whether he himself was
present at the marriage feast ? If he were not here
an eye-witness, we might conjecture that he had got
an inaccurate report of the actual occurrence, and
that would relieve the difficulty about the nature of
the miracle, to which we must return ; it might be
conjectured to be a natural provision misunderstood.
As the mother of Jesus was entrusted to the care of
the beloved disciple (xix. 26, 27), she might be supposed
to be his informant, especially as the incident had a
pregnant personal interest for her (*v.* 4). It is more
probable, however, that the witness did on this journey
accompany Jesus, as he would not be inclined so soon
after the first interview to depart from Him.

(*b*) We must accordingly face the difficulty of the nature of the miracle. The writer is a firm believer in the supernatural endowment in knowledge and power of Jesus, and His miraculous activity, but he must admit that this miracle as well as that of the feeding of the five thousand (of which the story of the feeding of the four thousand is probably only a variant tradition) presents a greater difficulty than the healing works, or even the stilling of the storm and the walking on the sea ; one cannot conceive the process by which loaves and fishes were multiplied, or water was transformed into wine. The explanation of accelerated natural process, poetically expressed in the hymn,

> ' 'Twas springtide when He blest the bread
> And harvest when He brake,'

does not afford adequate relief to the mind. Probably we must be content to say that the unimaginable to us need not be impossible. As we are here concerned primarily with the Fourth Gospel, it may be added that the difficulty here is of the same kind, not more and perhaps even less than in the miracle of the feeding of the five thousand, which the Synoptics record, so that in this respect the Fourth Gospel does not fall any more under suspicion as regards its trustworthiness than the other Gospels.

(*c*) The miracle is sometimes treated as symbolic of the transformation of human life by the influence of Christ. ' He came,' says Dr. Strachan,[1] ' to turn the water of the Jewish ceremonial religion into the wine of the Christian Gospel.' Its reality even is denied on the ground that it is a misunderstood allegory. There is, however, no hint in the story that the witness him-

[1] *Op. cit.* p. 87.

self so regarded it. If he had, would he not, as he has
not hesitated to do in other cases, have added reflexions
to reminiscences to fulfil this intention ? Surely we
need not go beyond *v.* 11 for his interest in the event,
the confirmation of his own faith. Was the glory
manifested only in the supernatural power exercised,
or in the independence of human direction, the dependence on divine prompting, and the compassion for
human need ? The witness represents Jesus as dis-
trustful of the belief which rested on beholding His
miracles (ii. 23-24) and as rebuking the desire for
miracles to evoke faith (iv. 48) ; and the contradiction
can be removed only if we suppose that he saw a
revelation evoking the true and proper faith in the
manner of the deed apart from the power exercised.
The sign would then be of divine character and not
merely divine power. We need not turn aside from
our main purpose to defend the character of Jesus
against the charge suggested by the jest of the
ruler of the feast (*v.* 10).

(4) THE SECOND TESTIMONY OF THE BAPTIST (iii. 22-30)

(*a*) The Rev. J. M. Thompson, in an article on the
Accidental Disarrangement in the Fourth Gospel,[1]
maintains that this passage should be placed between
ii. 12 and ii. 13. ' The sequence of thought in iii. 1-15
(the interview with Nicodemus), 16-21 (the first commentary on it), and 31-36 (a second commentary) is
broken by 22-30, a narrative passage describing the
relations between Jesus and the Baptist. At the same
time a paragraph seems to have slipped out of the text
between ii. 12 and 13, where the sudden transition from
Capernaum to Jerusalem without the usual mention

---

[1] *The Expositor*, 8th series, vol. ix. pp. 421-437.

of Judaea is as awkward as the subsequent journey
from Jerusalem to Judaea in iii. 22. If, however, we
suppose that iii. 22-30 originally stood between ii. 12
and 13 both passages are remedied. The continuity
of iii. 1-21 and 31-36 is restored, the journey (from
Capernaum) to Judaea precedes the arrival in Jerusalem,
and other improvements which need not be specified
are effected.' [1] This view commends itself as almost
certain to the writer.

(b) It is probable that Jesus did at first continue the
work of His forerunner, although the actual baptizing
may have been done by the disciples. It is also probable that the success of Jesus in attracting the multitudes would arouse the jealousy of those disciples of
John who had not left him for Jesus. Whether this
second testimony is given *verbatim*, or has been a little
coloured by the channel of its transmission, the mind
of the witness, there is nothing in the words inconsistent
with what we know of the Baptist from the other
sources. The Baptist asserted the superiority to
himself of Jesus as the Messiah, and consequently his
willingness to rejoice in His greater popularity. The
trustworthiness of this declaration depends on whether
we assume that the Baptist did recognize Jesus as
Messiah. For a former disciple of John this renewed
testimony would be of special interest, and may have
come to the witness from one of his former companions.

(5) THE FIRST VISIT TO JERUSALEM (ii. 13-25)

In the preceding chapter the writer has already dealt
with one of the most formidable objections to the
historicity of the Gospel, which at once confronts us
in this narrative, as it affects not only this passage,

[1] *Op. cit.* p. 422.

but the whole representation of the course of the ministry of Jesus in the Fourth Gospel. This passage, however, has a difficulty of its own, which may here be dealt with.

(*a*) A similar action is recorded in the Synoptics at the end of the ministry. We need not, with Dr. Strachan, assume that the key to its position at this part of the Gospel is found in the fact that the evangelist uses it merely to illustrate the third stage in the faith of the disciples, [1] if the present position can be historically justified. (i) The quotation in *v.* 17 suggests that it was in the mood of prophetic inspiration, in ' holy enthusiasm,' under the influence of the Spirit manifested at His Baptism, which in Mark's vivid phrase ' driveth Him into the wilderness ' (i. 12), and sustained Him through His long fast, that He performed this act. It was not an open claim of Messiahship, but such a challenge to the corrupt priesthood as any zealous reformer might have offered. The second cleansing, taken in conjunction with the triumphal entry, was an assertion of His Messianic authority, not less but more significant because of the repetition. The claims He had made with growing frankness and boldness on successive visits He confirmed by this act ; the first cleansing was an appeal for reform ; the second was a condemnation of resistance to that appeal. Notice the greater severity of the rebuke on the second than on the first occasion. ' Make not my Father's house a house of merchandise ' (*v.* 16) becomes ' Ye have made it a den of robbers' (Mark xi. 17). What makes this difference the more significant is that the tone of the Fourth Gospel towards the Jews is usually more severe than that of the Synoptists. Imprudent the act was not, as it was necessary for Jesus to test

[1] *Op. cit.* pp. 87-88.

the feelings of the Jewish rulers towards a reform movement, so that He might adapt the method of His ministry to the actual situation. There was zeal, but it was according to knowledge.

(ii) To the writer this explanation seems sufficient; but an alternative may be considered. If the cleansing of the Temple took place once only, it may be argued that the position the Fourth Gospel gives to the incident is the more probable. *Firstly*, we may ask: Would Jesus, knowing the hostility which was felt towards Him, have added fuel to the flame, if the act was not related, as has just been indicated, to a previous similar act investing it with a significance which as solitary it would not have had? *Secondly*, is it at least not possible that the Synoptists brought together in the record of the last visit incidents which belonged to earlier visits as well as those of the last visit, for they do not follow a strictly chronological order? If, as has been suggested in the previous chapter, Mark's Gospel consists of the report of Peter's account of the Galilaean ministry for the Jerusalem Church, and of the account Mark could give of events in Jerusalem, of which he himself was an eye-witness, the possibility becomes at least a probability. The writer does not need to resort to this assumption.

(b) Attention may be called to what may be regarded as comments of the evangelist, if not of the witness, the reference to prophecy in *v.* 17, the probable misunderstanding of a saying of Jesus in *v.* 21, and the emphasis on the supernaturalness of Jesus' knowledge in *vv.* 24-25. A minor difficulty is the mention in *v.* 23 of ' the signs which Jesus did.' The Gospel has not recorded any miracles in Jerusalem at this point. If they had occurred, had the witness passed them over, as he could not attach any symbolic significance to

them, nor find any other personal interest in them ?
Or is it unlikely that at so early a stage in the ministry
Jesus would freely work miracles ? The reference in
iii. 2 excludes the second assumption. It is possible
that *vv.* 23-25 are not an immediate sequel to *vv.* 13-22,
and that we must allow a considerable interval of time
for a continuous ministry in Jerusalem between the
cleansing of the Temple and the widespread movement
of untrustworthy belief to which these verses refer. It
is not improbable that in the first inspiration which
followed His baptism Jesus did use His supernatural
power more freely than He did afterwards, when the
evident peril of His being treated as merely a wonder-
worker inspired a restraint, which only urgent need
and confident faith could overcome. Had the witness
been possessed by the desire of miracle-mongering
he would assuredly not have been content with noting
only the failure of the signs to produce the kind of
faith which Jesus desired, and to which He could trust
His person and His cause.

(6) The Interview with Nicodemus (iii. 1-21)

In this narrative there are two issues quite subordinate to the present purpose, and one of primary
importance.

(*a*) Nicodemus has often been regarded as an individual anxious inquirer ; but Jesus does not treat him
with the gentleness which in such a case we might
expect, and He addresses him as representing a class
while Nicodemus himself passes from condescension
to incredulity. It is probable that Nicodemus was
sent by a section of the Pharisaic party, who, as religious
leaders of the people, felt their influence imperilled by
the growing popularity of the new Teacher, and thought

it might be for their advantage to come, if practicable, to some sort of understanding and alliance with Him. Jesus sternly rejects the professed patronage, and severely demands an entire change of attitude as the first condition of understanding or taking part in His movement. As He had tested the Sadducees by the cleansing of the Temple, so He tested the Pharisees by the demand for the new birth, or the birth of water and the Spirit ; and both parties failed to stand the test, even as the people failed to offer the belief which He desired.

(b) If our exegesis is to be at all historical, we cannot find in Jesus' words about the new birth, or the birth of water and the Spirit, any allusion to the ecclesiastical dogma of regeneration, to the Christian ordinance of baptism, or to the Christian experience of the descent of the Spirit at Pentecost. For Jesus was not speaking to Nicodemus in riddles. His reference was to the baptism of repentance which John administered and the gift of the Spirit which John announced as the Messiah's prerogative, and which Jesus Himself had experienced when baptized by John. Let the Pharisees come to Him in penitence, and in expectation of blessing, and they would both see and enter into the Kingdom. When such an explanation which preserves the historical character of the interview is not only possible, but probable, it seems gratuitous to offer another such as Dr. Strachan offers in his reference to Christian baptism.[1] The teaching here is in no way at variance with, although in terms it may be different from the Synoptic ; and in this interview with Nicodemus one feels oneself on the solid ground of reminiscence. A few words on the import of the conversation may be added. Even the leaders of religion and morals

---

[1] *Op. cit.* p. 93.

of His people needed the inward change of repentance and inward renewal by the Spirit before they could either understand or submit themselves to His new order of grace. God's Spirit in His teaching, example, and influence was as incomprehensible to them as the movement of the wind, and even their religion and morals belonged to the natural earthly order, and not to His supernatural heavenly order. His confidence in Himself as the witness to and agent of the new order was as decisive as His judgment of the unfitness of Sadducees, Pharisees, and Jewish multitude for any share or place in it. He knew Himself so far above His own people and age.

(c) It is generally acknowledged that reminiscence passes soon into reflexion, although there is difference of opinion as regards the exact point of transition. (i) The Revised Version begins a new paragraph at v. 16, and the writer welcomes the opportunity of quoting so conservative a scholar as Bishop Westcott in support of this view. 'This section,' he says, 'is a commentary on the nature of the mission of the Son, which has been indicated in Christ's words (vv. 13, 14), and unfolds its design (vv. 16, 17), its historic completion (vv. 18, 19), the course of its apparent failure (vv. 20, 21). It adds no new thoughts, but brings out the force of the revelation already given in outline (vv. 1-15) by the light of Christian experience. It is therefore likely, from its secondary character, apart from all other considerations, that it contains the reflexions of the evangelist, and is not a continuation of the words of the Lord. This conclusion appears to be firmly established from details of expression.' [1] The case need not be argued further.

(ii) The writer is convinced, however, that the

---

[1] *Gospel of St. John*, p. 54.

narrative of the interview with Nicodemus does not
extend to *v.* 15. Is it at all likely that Jesus would
have spoken to Nicodemus about His heavenly descent,
or His heavenward ascent by way of the Cross and the
Resurrection, when He even with His disciples exercised
such reserve of utterance ? There seems no doubt that
vv. 13-15 must be excluded from the story of the
meeting with Nicodemus. But are they to be at once
reckoned to the witness's reflexions ? To use Bishop
Westcott's phrase, ' details of expression ' bar this
hasty judgment. The Son of man is a term used of
Himself in the Gospels by Jesus only ; the witness
speaks of the Son as the Son of God (*vv.* 17, 18). If
Jesus did speak of pre-existence at all,[1] it is not improbable that He described His entrance into the world
as a descent from heaven, for did He not describe God
as ' Our Father which art in heaven ' ? ' Many ancient
authorities omit *which is in heaven* ' (R.V. *marg. v.*
13) ; and, whatever may be the balance of the textual
evidence, if we are to accept the saying at all as an
authentic utterance of Jesus, these words must manifestly be rejected as a gloss, as they are entirely inconsistent with Jesus' conception of His earthly life
as relatively a separation from His Father, and His
Death and Resurrection as a return to His Father (xiv.
12, 28 ; xv. 5-7, etc.). The descent is contrasted with
the ascent in the lifting up. And the whole thought
is quite congruous with the other teaching of Jesus.
It bears a resemblance to the saying in i. 51. We may
conclude that here we have a genuine logion, but
belonging to another context, at a later stage of the
ministry. Probably, as has already been shown,[2]
vv. 14-15 should follow xii. 31, 32, and *v.* 13, xii. 34
and vi. 62 in a series of sayings, now scattered through-

---

[1] See Chap. I. p. 11.   [2] See Chap. IV. p. 58.

out the Gospel, on the Death and Resurrection, spoken about the same time towards the close of the ministry, when the shadow of death was already falling. These verses may have been attracted to this place by association of ideas with the reference in the preceding verse to the earthly and heavenly things.

(iii) About these verses (11, 12) the same question may be raised : Can they belong to the story of the meeting with Nicodemus ? The question in *v.* 10 would form a deserved dismissal of Nicodemus. It is true that the plural is used in *v.* 7, so that Nicodemus is treated as the representative of a class ; but in *vv.* 3, 5, 7, in direct address, the singular is used. Accordingly *vv.* 11 and 12 in their whole tone, as well as mode of address, seem more appropriate to a public discourse than to an individual interview. If without any irreverence the illustration may be used, we may recall the story, now challenged, of Queen Victoria's complaint that Gladstone addressed her as if she were a public meeting. A similar incongruity seems to obtrude itself here. That the words are authentic utterances of Jesus need not be doubted, only by an association of ideas, not hard to discover (*v.* 6), they have been attracted here from some other context. Probably, as has been shown, they should with iii. 13 follow xii. 34. We may summarize the results of our inquiry thus : the interview with Nicodemus is reported in *vv.* 1-10 ; sayings of Jesus from another context have been attracted by an association of ideas in *vv.* 11-15 ; the witness offers his comments on his report in *vv.* 16-21.[1]

(*d*) The experimental rather than theological character of the passage in *vv.* 16-21 has led the writer to

---

[1] Verses 22-30 have already been dealt with as properly following ii. 1-12, and *vv.* 31-36 as the evangelist's comments.

the conclusion that it should be included in the reflexions of the witness rather than the comments of
the evangelist.   The starting-point of this meditation
is the logion of Jesus about the necessity of His death,
and all else which may be included in the word ὑψωθῆναι,
for man's salvation.   He is led to three thoughts :
the purpose of the Incarnation—salvation, and not
condemnation (*vv.* 16, 17), the contrast between the
divine intention and the human result, the salvation
of the few and the condemnation of the many (*vv.* 18,
19), and the explanation of this contrast in the opposing
tendencies of human nature towards light or darkness,
good or evil (*vv.* 20-21).   As the Synoptics present the
Christian good as *the Kingdom of God*, and Romans as
the *righteousness of God*, so the Fourth Gospel presents
it as *eternal life*.   But the witness is at one with all
Christian teachers in making faith in Christ the condition of the possession of this good.   The conception
of the Kingdom of God is not unknown to the Fourth
Gospel (iii. 3, 5), nor the conception of eternal life to
the Synoptics.   The rich young ruler is concerned
about the means of inheriting eternal life (Matt. xix.
16 ; Mark x. 17 ; Luke xviii. 18), and so is the lawyer
who asks the question about the greatest commandment (Luke x. 25).   But ' eternal life ' is as characteristic of the Johannine as the ' Kingdom of God '
of the Synoptic teaching.   It is a qualitative and not
merely a quantitative conception ; it refers to the
character, and not only the duration of life ; it is
moral and spiritual and not merely eschatological.
It is life in the truth, holiness, love, and blessedness
of God in Christ.   The witness conceives this good as
a universal possibility.   No trace is there here of the
doctrine of election of only some thereto, while others
are predestined to perdition.   But he recognizes

human freedom, and the actuality this involves of
the rejection as well as the acceptance of the gift.
Thus the human result does contradict the divine
intention of the Incarnation. In the explanation of
this result he does not fall back on any natural inevitable dualism in human nature. He does affirm
what every candid inquirer into human life must
admit, that human choice is not absolutely uncondi-
tioned, but that the previous character will affect the
present decision ; for good or evil conduct reacts on
the disposition. Continuance in evil does produce
aversion to God, and continuance in goodness has as
its reward greater attraction to it. The acceptance
or rejection of Christ justly and fitly decides the soul's
destiny, as it makes manifest the permanent tendency
of the life. This is a valuable thought, as it proves
that the crucial importance assigned to faith in Christ
is no arbitrary condition, but true and just. We
must not assume that the witness would have denied
the possibility of a moral and religious change ; if he
had, he would have been in conflict with the teaching of
Jesus about the new birth (iii. 3-8). The persistent,
violent, and irreconcilable opposition to Jesus which
he records, leads him naturally to emphasize the one
aspect of the truth to the neglect, but not denial, of
the other. Faith or unbelief towards Christ results
in life or death, because each reveals the soul's essential
attitude to goodness and God ; since He is related as
Son to God as Father.

(7) THE JOURNEY THROUGH SAMARIA (iv. 1-42)

(*a*) The narrative of the journey through Samaria,
if it is not a record of fact, is a masterpiece of literary
realism. The conversation moves from point to

point naturally. The great truth about the spiritual worship of God (*vv.* 21-23) arises in the mind and falls from the lips of Jesus almost inevitably in the reaction of His spirit against the religious exclusiveness of the woman (and it may be of His own disciples, who may have expressed some hesitation about taking this route to Galilee, to which, though shorter, some very strict Jews took exception). The declaration in *v.* 22 is not an instance of Jewish exclusiveness, but an appeal to the woman to recognize the inferiority of her own religious standpoint, of which she was too confident, so that she might be prepared to receive the instruction which Jesus, whom she had repelled as a Jew, desired to impart to her. Since the woman, with her countrymen, thought of the Messiah as the ' Converter ' or the ' Guide,' and did not, at the time at least, seem to cherish the political expectations of the Jews, Jesus could reveal Himself to her as the Messiah without fear of the political complications that such an avowal would have involved in Judaea and Galilee. Josephus [1] does tell us of a subsequent Messianic insurrection on Mount Gerizim, but that fact does not prove that the conditions were the same at the earlier and the later date. The way in which the narrative passes from one circumstance to another as determining Jesus' spirit and action shows that a ministry in Samaria was as remote from His purpose as a mission to the Gentiles, not, as the words here (confirmed elsewhere) show, because of His own Jewish exclusiveness, but because He was dominated by His consciousness of His vocation as the Jewish Messiah, through the fulfilment of which alone He could reach forth to the wider function of the Saviour of the world. Accordingly He does not embrace the oppor-

[1] *Ant.* xviii. 4, 1.

tunity which Samaria now offered, but leaves it to
His disciples to enter afterwards into the harvest
of which His ministry now was the seed-sowing.
(See Acts viii.) Jesus had the insight to perceive
that, ready as had been the response of the Samaritans,
the soil was not so well prepared for the seed of the
Word as in Judaea or Galilee among those who were
waiting for the consolation of Israel. The historical
probability lends support to the trustworthiness of
the record before us. While it may be admitted that
the language may have been coloured by the subsequent experience of the Christian Church, it is surely
applying the critical method with needless rigour
to set aside the reference to the immediate occasion
altogether, and to recognize only a reference to the
witness's own surroundings, as for instance, Dr.
Strachan does. ' This is a typical Johannine passage.
The immediate historical situation is forgotten, and we
feel that Jesus is speaking to the Church as it was in
the evangelist's day. As we read *v.* 38, for example,
we recognize that those addressed can only be the
earliest preachers of the Gospel, already engaged in
their mission.' [1]

(*b*) There are, however, a few points demanding
explanation.

(i) As Jesus was alone with the woman, the record
of the conversation may have come to the witness
either from Jesus, or from the woman ; or it may
be that he included parts of the story the woman
was so eagerly telling in the instruction Jesus Himself
repeated to His disciples as the explanation of His
unusual action, and its still more surprising results.
In *v.* 18 there is a statement which raises a difficulty.
Moral and spiritual insight, however exceptional, does

[1] *Op. cit.* p. 109.

not include the knowledge of a fact such as that the woman had had five husbands. Jesus was doubtless aware as He spoke to her of her moral degradation, and the discomfort that on account of it she may in His presence have been feeling, since her frank confession, ' I have no husband,' shows that her conscience had been stirred ; but the ability to know how often she had been divorced does not seem to fall within the scope of His supernatural endowment. Possibly the witness, having afterwards learned the fact from the woman herself, may have, quite unconsciously, reported this later information as part of Jesus' own speech to her. Or, more probably, the woman herself in her excitement may have failed to distinguish what Jesus said and what her own conscience spoke in His presence. Her words in *v.* 29 show that she thought Jesus had laid bare all the secrets of her life. Another possibility has been mentioned in a preceding chapter, that the statement is due to the evangelist under the influence of his tendency to emphasize the supernaturalness of Jesus' knowledge. This is one of the cases where we cannot with certainty distinguish what the witness may have said and what the evangelist may have written.

(ii) While *vv.* 21-23 arise spontaneously from the context, the more abstract statement in *v.* 24 may be a reflexion of the witness or a comment of the evangelist. Further, the title *the Saviour of the World* (*v.* 42) goes beyond anything that the previous record has prepared us for, and may well reflect the faith of a later age, and not of this historical occasion.

(*c*) The content of the conversation may be briefly sketched. The same confidence is shown in this conversation as in that with Nicodemus. Only here the symbol of water was put to another use, not the

cleansing from sin which repentance brings, but the
satisfaction of the soul's deepest need and keenest
desire (vv. 10-15). But that the need might be felt,
and the desire awakened, conscience must be roused
(vv. 16-18). The attempt to escape this appeal by
an inquiry on ritual questions was at once met by a
demand for sincerity and inwardness of worship ; and
an assurance that the localized worship of Samaritan
and Jew alike would be superseded by such worship
(vv. 22-23). The challenge to the priesthood (ii. 19),
and the demand on the Pharisees (iii. 7) are both
in close correspondence with this assurance, and
all three utterances indicate the exaltation of spirit
in which Jesus entered on His ministry (ii. 17 ; cf.
Mark i. 12, 27). The challenge of His authority in
the postponement of the question to the decision of
the Messiah compelled His avowal of the Messiahship
(vv. 25-26). So absorbed was He by the new order
He had come to establish that He was indifferent to
bodily needs (v. 34), and so confident was He of His
success that He saw harvest where others could see
only the seed-sowing (vv. 35-38), but gratefully He
recognized all in the previous history of Samaria
which had prepared for that success, in which His
disciples were called to share. But if in His judgment
success in Samaria was so assured, why was the visit
so brief (v. 43) ? Probably recognition as Messiah
in Samaria would have been no help but a hindrance
to His acceptance as Messiah in Judaea, owing to the
prejudice of Jew against Samaritan ; and the Gospel
makes clear that His main purpose was to offer Himself
as Messiah to the Jews, to whom He was divinely
promised.

(d) Looking backward on this section of the Gospel
—the Testimony—as a whole, the conviction of its

historical accuracy is confirmed. It is probable that Jesus began His ministry in Judaea, that He attached that ministry to the work of His forerunner, that at first His disciples were not His constant companions, and that the company of Twelve was formed only for the Galilaean ministry, that He began His ministry with the enthusiasm of the Spirit-filled, certain of His message, confident of His mission, that accordingly He challenged the priesthood, the scribes and the Pharisees, and the multitude as a reformer, if not avowedly as Messiah, and that He was compelled to turn from Judaea to Galilee to seek the faith He claimed.

VII

THE JUDGMENT

(JOHN V., VII.-XI.)

(1) THE CONTROVERSY AT THE FEAST OF PENTECOST
(v., and vii. 15-24)

(a) IN Chapter IV. reasons have been given for placing
chapter v. after chapter vi., and for regarding chapter
vi. as an insertion by the redactor. It is uncertain
whether the account of the visit to Cana (iv. 43-54)
is also to be regarded as due to the redactor ; but this
is much less probable. The activity of the redactor
must be regarded as responsible for the displacement
of vii. 15-24, which is the sequel of v. If the Feeding
of the Five Thousand took place about the time of
the Passover (vi. 4), then it is probable, as has already
been suggested, that the unnamed feast of v. 1 was
Pentecost. As no disciples are mentioned, and the
man cured does not know his benefactor, it is likely
that this visit too, like the next at the Feast of Tabernacles, was made ' not publicly, but as it were in secret '
(vii. 10). Another transposition still is suggested by
Mr. Thompson : [1] ' The discourse attached to the
healing of the impotent man in v. has really nothing
to do with this particular miracle, and would be
more appropriate (v. especially the emphasis on
$\zeta\omega o\pi o\iota\epsilon\hat{\iota}\nu$ in v. 21, 25, 28) to the raising of Lazarus,

---

[1] *The Expositor*, 8th series, vol. ix. p. 423.

which, as it stands, has no accompanying discourse.
It is therefore possible that v. 19-47 is a case of disarrangement.' This displacement is not, however,
so probable as is the other. The first reason given—
its irrelevance to the occasion—will be deprived of
its force if the view is correct that most of this passage
is either reflexion, and not reminiscence, of the
witness, or more probably even comment of the
evangelist, as has already been shown.[1] The second
reason is also not convincing, unless on the assumption
of an altogether artificial arrangement of the Gospel.
The circumstances of the raising of Lazarus did not
give occasion for a discourse.

(b) We may now look more closely at the passage
itself. The explanation of the troubling of the
waters in v. 4, which might be used to charge the
witness with too ready a credulity, is absent from
the best MSS. How Jesus knew that ' he had been
now a long time in that case ' we are not told. We
might suppose that here again the witness assumed
supernatural knowledge, but γνοὺς is the verb used.
The warning in v. 14 indicates that Jesus had knowledge of the man's past, but neither are we told how
that was gained. Jesus had disciples in Jerusalem,
and the man would be well known. Some previous
knowledge, and not only the sight of the moment,
may have stirred in Jesus the compassion which moved
Him to offer spontaneously the cure in awakening
the desire for it (v. 6). That the act of cure on the
Sabbath provoked hostility is entirely in accord
with the Synoptic record (v. 16), although the hostility
in Judaea was more violent than in Galilee. Jesus'
justification in v. 17 carries us into another circle
of ideas than the defences of Sabbath cures offered

[1] See Chap. II. p. 21.

in the Synoptic records ; but in vii. 22-23 the defence
is of the same kind as was usual in Galilee. That
Jesus claimed His Father's example, the constant
beneficent activity of God in nature (Matt. vi. 26-32)
as a justification of His own act is, however, not
itself unlikely, especially in view of the probability
that in Jerusalem, in face of more violent embittered
opposition, He asserted His claims more openly and
persistently than He did in Galilee, where these
claims, being misunderstood, might lead to an un-
desired Messianic movement. It was His purpose
to bring the Jewish people at the centre of its faith
and worship to a decision for or against His claims,
and not His desire to excite a merely local disturbance.
Whether the witness accepted the interpretation of
the words which Jesus' opponents put on them we
cannot tell, as *vv.* 20-29 (excepting *v.* 24) have been
shown to be due to the evangelist. The theology of
this passage is the theology of the Prologue, and not
of the witness's reflexions or his reminiscences. The
context itself justifies this assumption, for throughout
the discussion which follows it is the Son's dependence
on and submission to the Father which is insisted
on. If we find the ὁμοούσιον here our exegesis is
dogmatic, and not historical. That the saying aroused
so fierce an outburst of hate shows that there must
have been previous controversy, and that there had
been gathered fuel of hate, ready to kindle at the
feeblest spark. Without assuming that *vv.* 30-47
are a *verbatim* report, it seems to the writer that we
can accept them as a substantially accurate account
of the controversy of Jesus with His opponents. The
same assumption seems justified as regards the sequel
of the controversy in vii. 15-24, as the connexion of
thought is obvious. The reference of Jesus to the

writings of Moses leads to the question about His knowing letters.

(c) The course of the controversy can be sketched in a few sentences. Whatever objection the opponents had made to Jesus' direct appeal to God as warranting His action, He justified that appeal by His claim of His perfect knowledge of His Father's will due to His entire dependence on and obedience to God (v. 30; cf. Matt. xi. 25-30). Discarding self-witness He appeals to the witness of John, held in so high favour by the people (vv. 32-35) and to the greater witness of His works as proving His divine mission (v. 36). Reproaching His hearers with their unbelief, He sends them to the witness of the Scriptures, although He expects this appeal also to be vain (vv. 37-40, which v. 24 as an explanation and confirmation of v. 40 might follow). Next, the reason for and the results of the rejection of His manifold witness are stated. Themselves selfish, because lacking the love of God, His unselfishness as revealing God provokes their refusal, a refusal on which falls the condemnation of the law which bare Him witness (vv. 41-47). Jesus' appeal to the Scriptures calls forth the taunt : ' How can this uneducated fellow manage to read ? ' [1] The taunt is met by the declaration that the source of His teaching is not in Himself, but in God, as any one willing to obey God may discover for himself ; and that the selflessness of His aim guarantees His own sincerity (vii. 15-18). The taunt is also flung back upon them. Their enmity to Him because of His supposed breach of the law is proof of their ignorance of the law (vv. 19-21). Then follows the kind of argument in defence of Sabbath cures, such as we have in the Synoptics ; if the rite of circumcision may be performed on the Sabbath,

[1] Moffatt's *New Testament*, p. 120.

why not an entire cure ?   The controversy ends with a pregnant saying as to false and true judgment (*vv.* 22-24).

(*d*) As we follow the course of this controversy and subsequent discussions, the impression is fixed upon us that we have here sayings direct from the lips of Jesus, such as *v.* 24, which should probably follow *v.* 40, *v.* 35, *v.* 39, vii. 17, and *v.* 24 ; but that for the most part reminiscence has been affected by reflexion in the sharpness of the controversial tone, the vehemence both of the self-assertion and of the condemnation of others. While pregnant sayings might be remembered *verbatim*, a discussion like this is not likely to have been, although its general import may, with these pregnant sayings as points of attachment ; and its temper may have been insensibly altered.   We are tempted to ask here and elsewhere, Could these words fall from the lips of *the meek and lowly in heart* ?   The possibility must be admitted that the witness in his passionate devotion to his Master, and his no less vehement indignation against his Master's enemies, may have unconsciously exaggerated the polemic character of both the spirit and the content of Jesus' teaching.   Dr. Strachan may be right in saying : ' We cannot conceive Jesus thus exasperating His opponents.   The tones of contemporary controversy are heard here, and right through this passage.' [1]   On the contrary side, however, it must also be remembered that Jesus combined severity with gentleness, and even of His earthly ministry we might use the paradoxical phrase ' the wrath of the Lamb.'   We must not forget His woes on Chorazin, Bethsaida, and Capernaum (Matt. xi. 20-24), and His terrible denunciation of the scribes and Pharisees at the close of His ministry (xxiii. 1-36) : also His solemn

[1] *The Fourth Gospel*, p. 136.

warning about the unpardonable sin against the Holy
Ghost (xii. 31-32). The hostility in Jerusalem was
more persistent, vehement, and ruthless than any
experienced in Galilee. As it came from the rulers, the
teachers, and the leaders of the nation, it was more
fatal to the acceptance of Jesus as Messiah by the
Jewish people. These enemies were responsible for
the rejection of Jesus, and the doom that would fall
on the nation. The lament over Jerusalem (Matt.
xxiii. 37-39) follows the denunciation of the scribes
and Pharisees ; it was Jesus' compassion for the people
which intensified His indignation against *the blind
leaders of the blind*. We abstain from judging, because
we know that we ourselves deserve to be judged.
Surely the sinless and perfect had a right to condemn
as no other man has. His insight enabled Him to know
the unreality both of the piety and the patriotism under
which pride, greed, conceit, censoriousness, self-indul-
gence and self-interest hid themselves. The Synoptic
records leave unexplained the hatred which pursued
Jesus to death ; but the record of the controversies in
Jerusalem offers an intelligible explanation. Are we
not, in finding a difficulty in the severity of Jesus, con-
demning our own moral and religious standpoint ?
Was not His burning indignation against falsehood,
wrong, and hate the reverse of the moral perfection
of which passionate devotion to God, truth, and goodness was the obverse ? Because He as Son was so
certain of God as Father could He be so confident in
His judgment of those who not only rejected that
Fatherhood in Him, but stood in the way of others
accepting its blessings.

(2) THE CONTROVERSY AT THE FEAST OF TABER-
NACLES (vii. 1-14, 25-52, viii. 12-59)

(a) It has already been maintained that vii. 1 is
the sequel to vii. 24, and that vii. 15-24 continues the
story of v. 1-47.   It was the attempt made on His life
at the Feast of Pentecost (vii. 19) which led Jesus, not
only to withdraw to Galilee (vii. 1), but also to abandon
what seems to have been His usual practice of going
up to the feast with the Galilaean pilgrims (v. 10) ; and
the precaution was wisely taken, as His opponents were
on the outlook for Him (v. 11).   The attitude of His
brethren here described (vv. 3-8) is also attested by
Mark iii. 21, 31-35 ; and His refusal to be guided by
their advice is exactly paralleled by His reply to His
mother at the marriage in Cana (ii. 4), in which also
His sole and entire dependence on God is asserted.   An
intimation of the Divine will that He should go to the
festival, accompanied doubtless by an assurance of the
Divine protection if He went, is probably the explanation of the change of plan (cf. xi. 6-10).   We cannot
be sure what change of conditions made it safer for
Him to appear publicly at the middle of the Feast
than at the beginning.   But possibly the presence of
large numbers of friendly pilgrims may have offered
some security ; and His non-appearance at the com-
mencement may have for a time thrown His enemies
off their guard, so that He gained His brief opportunity
of appealing to the people before steps were taken to
seize Him (vv. 43-46).

(b) We seem in this record to be in the region of
historical probability, and only a few matters claim
closer scrutiny.   We may note how carefully the witness distinguishes the different currents of opinion.   In
vii. 12 the phrase, ' among the multitudes ' (R.V. ἐν τοῖς

ὄχλοις) is used to describe ' the different groups of
strangers who had come up to the festival, and such as
consorted with them ' ; [1] and a conflict of opinion is
here recorded. The Jews (*vv.* 11 and 13) are the openly
and bitterly hostile party, described in *v.* 26 as the
rulers, and composed, according to *v.* 32, of the *chief
priests and the Pharisees.* ' The combination occurs
also in St. Matthew (xxi. 45, xxvii. 62). The phrase
probably describes the Sanhedrin under the form of its
constituent classes.' [2] The Pharisees were the demo-
cratic party in close contact with the people, and so
kept well informed of the popular opinions (vii. 32,
viii. 13), and through them the aristocratic party of
the priesthood was moved to action. In vii. 25 another
group is mentioned, distinguished on the one hand
from the multitudes, the pilgrims, and on the other
from the members of the Sanhedrin, and described in
the phrase τινὲς ἐκ τῶν Ἱεροσολυμειτῶν, citizens of
Jerusalem, ' who were acquainted with the designs of
the hierarchy, and yet not committed to them.' [3]
Probably the witness himself was in close contact with
this group, and may even have been seeking to influence it to a favourable judgment. The opinions
ascribed here would not be spoken openly ; and how
could one of the Galilaean disciples become aware of
what was being thus privately discussed ? While the
term Jews is usually applied to the hostile party of
priests and Pharisees, in viii. 31 it is used of another
group, whose hostility, if it had existed, had been so far
overcome that they *had believed Him* (τοὺς πεπισ-
τευκότας αὐτῷ Ἰουδαίους). But their belief is distinguished from the faith of the numbers who
' believed in Him ' (*v.* 30, πολλοὶ ἐπίστευσαν εἰς αὐτόν),

---

[1] Westcott's *St. John,* p. 117.   [2] *Idem,* p. 121.
[3] *Idem,* p. 120.

if we may assume that 'the change in the construction of the verb' has some significance. According to Westcott this group 'acknowledged His claims to Messiahship as true, were convinced by what He said, but still interpreted His promises and words by their own prepossessions.'[1] In the warning Jesus recognizes the imperfection of their faith ; and their quick resentment of His speech shows the superficiality of the impression made on them (v. 33). To the writer it seems incredible that one who was not an eye-witness, and had no concern for historical reality, should so carefully have distinguished the varied and the varying attitudes assumed towards Jesus, and have presented them with so striking verisimilitude.

(c) A second indication of trustworthiness is surely to be found in the figures in which Jesus made His appeal to the multitude.[2] In vii. 37 He offers Himself as *the living water* ; and in viii. 12 as *the light of the world*. The appropriateness of the first may be indicated in the words of Dods : ' On each of the seven feast days water was drawn in a golden pitcher from the pool of Siloam, and carried in procession to the Temple, in commemoration of the water from the rock with which their fathers in the desert had been provided. On the eighth day, which commemorated their entrance into a " land of springs of water " this ceremony was discontinued. But the deeper spirits must have viewed with some misgiving all this ritual, feeling still in themselves a thirst which none of these symbolic forms quenched, and wondering when the vision of Ezekiel would be realized, and a

[1] Westcott's *St. John*, p. 133.
[2] In this connection may be recalled what has been said about the teaching regarding the manna, which the redactor has placed in chapter vi.

river broad and deep would issue from the Lord's
house.' [1] As regards the fitness of the second figure,
the same writer's words may also be quoted : ' Not-
withstanding Meyer and Holtzmann, it seems not
unlikely that this utterance was prompted by the
symbolism of the feast. According to the Talmud,
on every night of the feast the Court of the Women
was brilliantly illuminated. This brilliant lighting
was perhaps a memorial of the Pillar of Fire which
led the Israelites while dwelling in tents.' [2] The
witness was assuredly one who was thoroughly familiar
with Jewish customs, and also with the mode of the
teaching of Jesus, whose language was always appropriate to the occasion and to the environment, as
the Synoptic reports show. The comment in vii. 39,
however, is probably a misunderstanding of the
meaning of Jesus due to the witness, or the evangelist
as Mr. Thompson contends.[3]

(d) The appropriateness of the imagery in viii. 12
seems to be a reason against accepting Mr. Thompson's
suggestion that viii. 12-20 is also a displacement.
' The removal from the Gospel of the undoubted
interpolation vii. 53–viii. 11 (the *pericope adulterae*)
leaves viii. 12-20 in an awkward position after vii. ;
for the end of vii. is a climax, yet in viii. 12 we are
back in the middle of an argument. If this paragraph
has been displaced, its original position was probably
at the beginning of vii. immediately after vii. 15-24.' [4]
What is not adequately taken into account in this
statement is that we are not following the plot of a
cunningly made drama, which moves right on to its
completion ; but the ebb and flow of a tide of human

---

[1] *Expositor's Greek Testament*, i. p. 767.   [2] *Idem*, p. 773.
[3] *The Expositor*, 8th series, vol. xiv. pp. 220-222.
[4] *Idem*, vol. ix. p. 423.

passion and purpose ; and so we must not expect
absolute continuity. There were several crises before
the final one was reached. The possibility must,
however, be admitted that viii. 12-20 should be placed
between vii. 36 and 37 (cf. vii. 34 and viii. 14).

(i) Mr. G. N. C. Macgregor favours the suggestion
that viii. 12-20 should follow vii. 15-24, and precede
vii. 1-14, vii. 25 ff. on the following ground : ' Chapter
vii. 24 standing by itself would form a very abrupt
conclusion, the transition thence to vii. 1 being sudden
and harsh. Insert viii. 12-20 at this point, and we find
that *v.* 20 forms an admirable conclusion to the incidents in Jerusalem during Pentecost narrated in
chapters v. and vii. 15-24.' [1] The same objection
here also applies, the appropriateness of the imagery
to the later Feast of Tabernacles. What seems a
more attractive suggestion is set aside by Macgregor :
' Burton would place it outside the chapters under
discussion after x. 21 (x. 19-21 being transposed to
follow immediately after ix. 41). This setting appears
good, Jesus' proclamation of Himself as the Light of
the World following most appropriately after the
healing of the man born blind, the Pharisees' question,
" Are we blind also ? " (ix. 40), and the question of
" others," " Can a devil open the eyes of the blind "
(x. 21).' [2] We can here only weigh the probabilities
and cannot affirm any certainty.

(ii) Mr. Macgregor [2] also proposes to place viii.
21-59 after vii. 1-14 plus vii. 25-36, as he does not
regard the transition from vii. 52 to viii. 21 as satisfactory. Jesus cannot possibly be thought of as
present at the private inquiry of the chief priests and
Pharisees, including Nicodemus, into the failure of
' the officers ' to arrest Him. Yet at viii. 21, He is

---

[1] *The Expository Times*, xxxiii. p. 75. [2] *Idem*, p. 75.

suddenly introduced as renewing to this audience
a discourse exactly similar to that broken off at vii. 36,
and this in spite of the fact that *v.* 37, marking the
transition to a different occasion altogether, has
intervened.' [1] The need for this transposition depends
on the transposition just discussed having been
accepted, as *vv.* 20 and 21 form quite a satisfactory
sequence, and in the kind of controversy Jesus was
engaged in a resumption of a previous thought is not
improbable. If the possibility of viii. 12-20 being
transposed after vii. 36 be admitted, then viii. 21-59
could, but need not, go with it to this new position.
One transposition of viii. 12-59 is more probable than
two transpositions of viii. 12-20 after vii. 15-24 and
of viii. 21-59 after vii. 36, and on other grounds is
to be preferred, if the necessity of the transposition
is at all accepted.

(iii) Mr. Macgregor holds that ' one more transposition makes the sequence of the two chapters
under consideration perfect. Transpose vii. 45-52
before vii. 37-44 (as Burton suggests, so that *v.* 45
follows immediately on viii. 59). How perfectly
natural the train of events. . . . At vii. 32 the officers
are sent to arrest Jesus, at viii. 59 they allow Jesus
to escape, and in the very next verse, vii. 45, they
are called to account for their remissness ; moreover,
these events can now take place during the course
of a single day. We are now left with vii. 37-44 as
a climax to the whole section dealing with Jesus'
visit to Jerusalem at the Feast of Tabernacles. This,
as so often in this Gospel, concludes with a summing
up of the impression left by Jesus on the people.' [2]
This conjecture has much to commend it ; although
we must remember that the actual course of events

[1] *The Expository Times,* xxxiii. p. 75.   [2] *Idem,* p. 76.

need not closely correspond with the unfolding
of a historical drama, as it presents itself to our
imagination as most appropriate. To none of these
suggestions need serious exception be taken, except
the proposal to transpose viii. 12-20 after vii. 15-24,
and so transfer it from the record of the Feast of
Tabernacles to that of the Feast of Pentecost. We
need not follow further this writer in his discussion
of the possible explanation of these displacements,
i.e. ' Spitta's theory that the pages of a papyrus
roll had got out of order.' While he recognizes that
' the whole theory is a precarious one on which to
work,' yet he holds that ' when it is applied to chapters
vii.-viii. the results are certainly arresting,' and the
application of the theory ' serves to corroborate the
results previously arrived at from a study of the
internal evidence, and, in addition, suggests a possible
explanation for the insertion of the much debated
Pericope de adultera.' [1] It is not necessary for the
present purpose to discuss the passage vii. 53–viii. 11,
as the general conclusion of scholars is accepted.
But it may be pointed out that the intrusion of a
passage not authentic affords some justification for
the assumption that there have been displacements
in the text of the Gospel, and that we may without
rashness attempt to restore the order of the original
document.

(*e*) The result of the controversy at the previous
feast was a division of opinion among the people ;
but no open confession by even the favourably inclined
owing to the terrorism exercised by the influential
opponents of Jesus (vii. 12, 13).   (i) The freedom for
a time allowed Him at the Feast of Tabernacles,
to which He came only at the Divine prompting

[1] *The Expository Times*, xxxiii. p. 78.

(*vv.* 6-10) after rejecting the advice of His unbelieving brethren (*vv.* 3-5), led some of the multitude to believe that even the rulers might be restrained by the belief in the possibility of His Messiahship (*vv.* 25-26) ; and yet the surmise was set aside on the ground that, while Jesus' home and family were known (Nazareth, and not Bethlehem being thought of), the appearance of the Messiah, as commonly expected, would be sudden (*v.* 27). This objection Jesus at once met by reasserting His divine mission (*vv.* 28-29). A subsequent attempt at arrest evoked the declaration of His speedy return to God, and therewith the close of the opportunity of His hearers (*vv.* 30-34), some of whom were being moved to believe. This declaration suggested to some of His hearers the possibility of His undertaking a mission to the Dispersion (*vv.* 35-36).

(ii) On the last day of the Feast, Jesus made a direct, final appeal to the multitude. He promised the believer in Him not only full spiritual satisfaction, but also abounding spiritual power (*vv.* 37-38), a promise which had probably a more general reference than to the gifts of Pentecost. Such a declaration only increased the division of opinion among the people, and His arrest was deferred. Even in the Council Nicodemus pleaded for suspense of judgment. If viii. 12-20 and 21-59 are in the proper place, and should not be put between vii. 36 and 37, the controversy was soon after resumed. Having as the Water of Life offered satisfaction, Jesus next as the Light of the World offered illumination (possibly referring to the Shekinah, viii. 12). But this claim the Pharisees, jealous of their position as the authoritative teachers, at once challenged on the ground of the untrustworthiness of self-witness (*v.* 13). Jesus met the challenge by claiming truth for His

H

self-witness, because of His self-knowledge and knowledge of the Father whose companionship He is en-
joying as He is discharging His mission (*vv.* 14-16).
With an appeal to the requirements of the law, He adds
the Father's witness to His own (*vv.* 17, 18). Their
scornful question as to the identity of His Father He
rebuked by charging them with ignorance, both of
Himself as revealing and of the Father as revealed
in Him (*vv.* 19-20).

(iii) On another occasion, when Jesus repeated the
warning of the speedy close of the day of grace, a more
sinister suggestion than that of a mission to the
Dispersion (vii. 35) was made, even that He would
commit suicide ; and such a taunt called forth a declaration of the contrast in nature between Himself as
from above, and them as from beneath, and a warning
of judgment on their sin of unbelief (*vv.* 21-24). Their
plea of ignorance regarding Himself, and so His claim
to belief, probably intended to evoke a distinct assertion
of His Messiahship, which might have been charged
against Him before the Roman governor, was met
by a saying, of which there are different readings and
renderings. Nestle reads τὴν ἀρχὴν ὅ τι καὶ λαλῶ ὑμῖν ;
the A.V. has not got the point of interrogation, but
Westcott has, and ὅτι as one word. Taking it as
a question, Moffatt renders, ' Why should I talk to
you at all ? ' [1] If the words be taken as a statement,
Westcott translates, ' Altogether, essentially I am that
which I even speak to you,' but prefers the other
rendering himself.[2] In either case no direct answer
was given. Either further discussion was declined, or
the sufficiency of the information already given was
asserted (*v.* 25). Further teaching was needed, and,

[1] *The New Testament : a New Translation,* p. 125.
[2] *The Gospel of St. John,* p. 131.

as entrusted by His Father, would be delivered ; but
the unbelief of His hearers would make that teaching
judgment (*v.* 26 ; *v.* 27 is a comment probably of the
evangelist). As His hearers made no intelligent
response, a clearer warning was given that at His
exaltation even those who were now unbelieving would
recognize Him as Messiah, and His dependence on God,
message and mission from God, and possession of the
Presence of God because of His constant obedience
(*vv.* 27-29).

(iv) A faith, just beginning in a few, received the
assurance of spiritual liberation through the truth
on condition of continued discipleship ; but the assurance, instead of confirming the faith, provoked resentment that even the need of such liberation should
be suggested to descendants of Abraham (*vv.* 30-33).
The nature of the bondage, not as outward but as
inward to sin, was declared ; and a relationship to
God as sons through Him the Son was offered as a
condition of this freedom (*vv.* 34-36). A sudden
change either in the feelings of the crowd, or in the
persons composing it, can alone explain the swift
change of tone at *v.* 37. The murderous intentions
of those who boasted their descent from Abraham
were exposed, and another descent was with ruthless
severity assigned to them. As His words revealed
His divine, so theirs their diabolic descent, and contradicted their claim to relationship with Abraham
(*vv.* 37-40). It is not probable that in *v.* 41, ' We
were not born of fornication,' there is any reference
to the current slander about Jesus' birth, which was
of much later date ; but fornication is used as is
adultery in the Old Testament for any departure
from God through idolatry ; and in the words spiritual
descent from God as certain as the physical descent

from Abraham is claimed. This claim Jesus, however, will not allow ; their rejection of Himself, coming from, sent by, and in His teaching revealing God, proves their kinship with the devil, the source of the falsehood opposing the truth, and of the hate planning the murder of its bearer (*vv.* 42-45). The challenge to His opponents, ' Which of you convicteth me of sin ? ' may mean either that no moral offence showing His kinship with the devil could be proved against Him, or that He could not be shown in error regarding the account He had just given of the nature and origin of the sin of His opponents. The second would imply the first ; only moral perfection could claim moral infallibility. He was not in error ; their rejection of Him was a rejection of truth, and that was evidence that their spiritual descent was not from God (*vv.* 46-47). Stung to the quick by this charge, His opponents applied to Him the hateful name Samaritan, and even suggested that the words proved Him possessed (*v.* 48). Repelling the charge, He reaffirmed the disinterestedness of His motives and His regard only for God ; and from their judgment He confidently carried the appeal to God's unerring tribunal (*vv.* 49-50). At this point (*v.* 51) Jesus made a declaration which, while consistent with the teaching elsewhere, broke rather abruptly the continuity of the argument ; yet, as its subsequent course depends on it, the saying cannot be regarded as interjected from another context. Yet the saying may be explained in this way. Weary of the profitless wrangle, Jesus turned again from His opponents, to whom at *v.* 37 He had begun to address Himself in tones of so great severity, to the less hostile persons whom He had been addressing in *vv.* 31-32. It was like Him to do this, for judgment was His strange work, and in mercy was His delight.

He now added to the promise of liberation the promise
of deliverance from the power of death as a reward
of discipleship. The promise was suitable to the
occasion, for what His opponents were bringing on
themselves was their own doom. His opponents
would not, however, desist, but at once replied that
such a claim proved possession beyond doubt or question, since even Abraham and the prophets had died,
as it asserted superiority to the greatest men of the
nation. What megalomania was this on His part
(*vv.* 52-53) ! Disclaiming all vain ambition, He
represented the dignity He claimed as a trust from
God, which it would be falsehood in Him to deny
(*vv.* 54-55). Opposition instead of depressing elevated
His spirit. He declared His mission to be a good,
the prospect of which brought joy to the breast of
Abraham, so conscious was He that in Him all God's
promises which had comforted His people had at
last found their fulfilment. It is a saying which
cannot be taken with prosaic literalness as it was
taken by His opponents. Against their taunt that
His age forbade any such knowledge of Abraham, He
declared His pre-existence, a declaration which has
already been dealt with in connection with the Prologue. This provoked an attempt at stoning.

(*f*) In estimating the historical value of the record,
the considerations advanced in regard to the previous
controversy must be recalled. Here the final issue
of His acceptance or rejection as Messiah was involved ; and He laid aside reserve and restraint, and
used the whole of the resources of argument, appeal,
and authority. It is not improbable too that the
more His claim of sonship was contradicted and challenged, the more distinct, confident, and dominant
would His self-consciousness become. To the writer

it does not seem improbable that the intuition of
pre-existence (viii. 58), the certainty that His relation to God as Son to Father was not temporal but
eternal, antecedent to the very beginnings of God's
revelations to the chosen people, flashed upon Him
as a gleam from heaven, when the shadows of unbelief
and hate were gathering thick and close around Him.
The teaching of those chapters does not seem to go
beyond what was possible, and even necessary, for
the occasion.

(3) THE CONTROVERSY AT THE FEAST OF DEDICATION
(ix. and x.)

(a) The incident recorded in the ninth chapter
leaves a vivid impression of historical reality; the
development of the faith of the man born blind,
to whom sight was given, is shown in a most convincing way.   As the incident closely connects itself
with the teaching given in x. and the note of time
there (v. 22) fixes the date of that teaching, we may
regard both chapters as an account of a visit to Jerusalem at the Feast of Dedication.   The disciples mentioned in ix. 1 need not be the Twelve, but may be
Judaean disciples, including probably the witness,
whose account here seems to be given at first hand.
Would the Galilaean disciples be interested in the
question of v. 2 ?   Is there convincing proof for
Dr. Strachan's statement that the suggestion that
the man himself had sinned is ' a Hellenistic and not
a strictly Jewish idea ' ?   Must we find in the process
of healing ' two points of rather subtle symbolism ' ?
In regard to the statement in v. 34, ' they cast him
out ' (ἐξέβαλον αὐτὸν ἔξω ; cf. v. 22, ἀποσυνάγωγος
γένηται), may we not find the reference to the imme-

diate historical occasion, or must we ignore it altogether, as does Dr. Strachan ? 'We must realize again,'
he writes, ' that the synagogue of which the Evangelist
is really thinking would be in Asia Minor, and not
in Palestine. The chapter is founded on an actual
incident, but we know that excommunication in
the time of Jesus could not be pronounced by the
authorities of a synagogue. The Sanhedrin alone
could do this. Among the Jews of the Dispersion,
on the other hand, the synagogue became more and
more a central authority ; for the Jewish colonists
were separated by long distance from the ecclesiastical
authorities at Jerusalem. There may have been
some minor form of excommunication that could be
exercised by a local synagogue in our Lord's day,
but there can be no doubt that the strong words
used in *v.* 34 imply the severest sentence possible.' [1]
Even if in respect of this word we may admit a slip
of memory on the part of the witness, we need not
sacrifice the trustworthiness of the narrative as a
whole.

(*b*) Dr. Moffatt in his *New Translation* makes a
transposition which seems justified. He connects
x. 19-29 directly with ix. 41. An appropriate comment on Jesus' action and speech in chapter ix. is
offered in x. 19-21 ; and *vv.* 22-29 follow quite naturally
on *vv.* 19-21, *vv.* 26 and 29 continue the thought of
vv. 24, 25, and very appropriately lead up to the
teaching in x. 1-18. Also it seems more probable
that such a declaration as ' I and my Father are one '
(*v.* 30) would follow on the frank declaration of His
intention to lay down and take up His life again
(*vv.* 17, 18), than on the assurance of God's power
over all (*v.* 29). Altogether there is a decided gain

[1] *The Fourth Gospel*, pp. 140-141, 142.

in the continuity of the teaching by this rearrangement. Mr. Thompson also connects x. 19-21 as
the appropriate climax with ix. 41 ; and maintains
that x. 1-18 has been displaced on the ground that
a new episode obviously begins with x. 22. He places
this passage, however, not, as Moffatt does, after
x. 29, but between *vv*. 28 and 29 ; and even suggests
another position. 'Perhaps it is more seriously
astray, and belongs to the gap between xvi. 24-25,
where a παροιμία (x. 6, xvi. 25) with an eschatological
reference (the true Shepherd contrasted with the
false prophets, x. 8—there are also points of contact
with xvii.) would be in place.' [1] This suggestion is
less probable than the other, which assigns to the
passage an altogether appropriate context.

(c) Points of theological interest in the narrative
of the miracle are the following : Jesus' denial of
the necessary connexion between suffering and sin,
and His declaration that man's necessity is God's
opportunity (ix. 3) ; His claim for faith as the Son
of Man (reading ἀνθρώπου instead of θεοῦ as do Nestle
and Westcott) ; and His assertion of a present judgment of men in their attitude to Himself (*vv*. 36-41).
His charge of wilful blindness so irritated His enemies
that madness was ascribed to Him ; but the wonder
of the miracle so impressed some that the suggestion
was rejected (x. 19-21). Pressed vehemently to
assert His Messiahship, Jesus replied that both in
word and deed He had offered sufficient ground
for faith, and that unbelief could be due only to
alienation of spirit from Him : 'Ye are not of my
sheep' (*vv*. 22-26). Thinking doubtless of the blind
man's growth from darkness to light, Jesus at this
point turned from His enemies to describe His disciples

---

[1] *The Expositor*, 8th series, ix. pp. 423-424.

as His sheep, obedient to Him, and kept securely
by Him because given to Him, and held for Him
by the Father's almighty power (*vv.* 27-29).

(*d*) The passage in chapter x. 1-16 is interesting
as an example of the allegory into which, according
to the Fourth Gospel, Jesus expanded His metaphors.
(i) In this Gospel there are no parables exactly similar
in structure to those in the Synoptics, and we may
raise the question, whether and why Jesus avoided
in Judaea a mode of teaching so attractive and effective.
Is it not more probable that the witness, transforming
reminiscence by reflexion, has changed parables into
allegories ?   This at least is Wendt's opinion in regard
to this passage, for he finds here companion parables.
' The first of those parables (*vv.* 1-5) describes how the
sheep obey and follow only the shepherd who enters
by the door into the sheepfold, while the one who
breaks in by another way is a stranger and a robber,
from whom the sheep flee.   Its application, according
to the explanation in *vv.* 7-9, is that Jesus is the
one essential Mediator of salvation for men :   " I am
the door : by me if any man enter in he shall be saved,
and shall go in and out, and find pasture " (*v.* 9).   But
since this comparison of Jesus to the door of the sheepfold, which in a merely passive sense gives entrance
to the flock, makes no account of the devoted care
with which Jesus ministers salvation to His people,
therefore this additional idea is brought out by a
second parable (from *v.* 10) in which the same figure
of a sheepfold is employed in another relation.   As
the good shepherd, in contrast to the robber who will
only injure the flock, and in contrast to the careless
hireling who leaves it in the lurch in time of danger,
devotes his life to the welfare of the sheep, so Jesus
exhibits Himself as the true Saviour, in lovingly

devoting His life for them.' [1]   This solution does
not seem to the writer satisfactory, and he would
suggest another.   In *v.* 7 Moffatt seems right in
substituting ὁ ποιμήν for ἡ θύρα.   Verse 9, which
Moffatt brackets, appears a genuine logion, but from
another context ; for would Jesus not have confused
His hearers if, just after calling Himself the Shepherd,
He had called Himself the door also ?   Verse 8, if it
is genuine, although its tone of unqualified condemnation of all previous teachers makes it doubtful, is a
comment on *v.* 1.   In *vv.* 1-5 we have a parable of the
relation of the sheep to the shepherd.   In *vv.* 7-8, 10-16
it is the relation of the shepherd to the sheep that
is made prominent.   Wendt does not point out clearly
enough how the witness has altered the parabolic
form : probably in the original parable the first personal
pronoun was not used, as it is used in *vv.* 10, 11, 14-16,
although not found in *vv.* 1-5, but a description of
the Good Shepherd's ways was given in the third
person ; and the evangelist has blended explanation
(his reflexions) with parable (his reminiscences).
So restored, the companion parables would fall into
the first of the two classes which Wendt distinguishes,
i.e. that which gives ' a rule in frequently recurring
cases.' [2]

(ii) The teaching in these parables may be briefly
summarised.   His relation to His disciples is presented
as that of the shepherd who in contrast with the thief
and robber (His rivals and opponents) has unhindered
entrance into the sheepfold, and whom the sheep
willingly follow, as they know Him (x. 1-5).   The
evil intention of the thief is contrasted with that of
the Good Shepherd (*v.* 10).   This forms the transition

---

[1] *The Teaching of Jesus*, Eng. tr., i. pp. 128-129.
[2] *Op. cit.* p. 117.

from the one to the other parable. The desertion of
the sheep by the hireling in time of danger is next
contrasted with the Good Shepherd's devotion to their
interests even to death (*vv.* 12-15). In *v.* 16 Jesus
looks beyond the immediate present, the circle of His
Jewish disciples, to the wider range after His death of
His future ministry to the Gentiles. This suggestion
of a universal purpose need not be suspected. In
v. 9, which probably belongs elsewhere, Jesus asserted
that faith in Him, such as the blind man had exercised, was the condition of even beginning the life of
discipleship.

(*e*) The intimation of the voluntary sacrifice (x. 17,
18) follows easily and simply on the teaching about
the Good Shepherd, who is ready to lay down His
life for the sheep. It is appropriate to the occasion,
for Jesus knew that His enemies were purposing and
intriguing for His death. He admitted that they
would accomplish their end. What He was concerned
to make plain to them was that the death they were
seeking to inflict would nevertheless be a voluntary
sacrifice on His part in loving obedience to God and
loving solicitude for man, and would be approved
of God as evidence of the identity of His purpose
with God's (*vv.* 17-18 and 30). The declaration in
v. 30 is not improbable, if we do not impose on it the
meaning of later dogmas, but understand it as the
context indicates. The words are not to be interpreted
metaphysically, whatever metaphysical inferences may
or may not legitimately follow. The neuter ἕν does
not signify unity of substance, and the plural ἐσμέν
difference of person. It is unity of purpose which
is primarily intended, and the words must be interpreted morally and religiously. It is the Son's
obedience to the Father's commandment which makes

Him one with the Father. His opponents were not
sound Christian theologians, because He did not make
Himself God in the sense they meant (*v.* 33). The
attempt to stone Him (*v.* 31) for His supposed blasphemy in claiming deity evoked a self-defence which
confirms this view. It is based on the use of the
word *gods* in the Psalms for God's messengers. While
He does not place Himself merely on an equality
with *the persons to whom the word of God came,* it is as
sanctified and sent into the world that He claims to be
the Son of God (*vv.* 31-36). He then offered as the
test of His claim to faith the conformity of His actions
to God's will. The mutual immanence of Father
and Son is proved by moral resemblance (*vv.* 37-38).
This mutual immanence is not unity of substance.
It is not the correctness or otherwise of the orthodox
formula that is here in question, but the historical
exegesis of the passage. Another attempt at arrest
followed, and compelled withdrawal from Jerusalem ;
but many disciples had been won (*vv.* 39-42).

(4) THE RAISING OF LAZARUS AND ITS RESULTS (xi.)

(*a*) The raising of Lazarus from the dead raises the
problem of miracle in a very acute form. For the
naturalistic explanation of the acts of healing as
moral therapeutics it must appear as an absolute
impossibility, and so the record must be rejected
as entirely unhistorical. Whether a rationalistic
explanation as restoration from a prolonged trance [1]

---

[1] Mr. Edward Grubb has resort to this explanation. He prepares
for it by calling attention to ' the agitation of Jesus continuing until
he reached the tomb,' and accounts for that agitation by the assumption that ' Jesus was seeking with the most intense earnestness to
know His Father's will, which had not yet been fully revealed to
Him.' When ' He saw clearly what He was to do, He called Lazarus
from the tomb, and Lazarus came.' Then follows his explanation :

has any probability from the standpoint of modern medical science is a question which the writer claims no competence to decide.

(i) This is not the only instance in the Gospels of the raising of the dead by Jesus. The case of the daughter of Jairus is recorded by the three Synoptists (Matt. ix. 18-26 ; Mark v. 35-43 ; Luke viii. 49-56). The words of Jesus, ' she is not dead, but sleepeth,' are interpreted in two ways. ' Either Jesus, confident of His power to recall from death, speaks of death as a sleep from which He will awaken (cf. John xi. 11), or He declares that the girl is not dead, but in a trance. Wonderful insight, if the latter is the case, takes the place of wonderful power, if the former. The words are ambiguous, but the evangelists convey the impression that they are recording a restoration to life, not a recovery from a trance.' [1] The case of the widow's son of Nain is recorded by Luke alone (vii. 11-17) ; and in this record there is no ambiguity of language. Although the circumstances do not exclude the possibility of a trance, yet it would be

' I do not myself suppose that Martha's fears about the opening of the tomb were justified. I do not take it that Lazarus was so completely " dead " as to be beyond the possibility of resuscitation if the right methods could have been employed. There are death-like trances which may last for many days ; and I imagine the few cases in which Jesus is reported to have raised the dead to life were of this character. The patients were probably beyond the power of any medical skill or methods available in those days, and would, I suppose, soon have succumbed completely if Jesus had not intervened with a supernormal control of matter by spirit. These " miracles " I take to have been simply an extension to persons apparently dead of His ordinary works of healing, and to have been wrought in the same way. The fewness of the reported cases suggests that He never attempted to restore the dead indiscriminately, and only did so when He had an inward intimation that it was the Divine will for Him to act.' (The Expository Times, xxxiii. p. 407.) These cases were thus providential coincidences, in which Jesus enjoyed the unerring Divine guidance. The view is attractive, if not convincing.

[1] 'St Luke,' in Westminster New Testament, p. 169.

a marvellous coincidence that the revival should take
place at the moment when Jesus spoke the word of
recall. The record in no way suggests such an explanation.

(ii) Luke is charged with outbidding in this record
the common Synoptic account about Jairus' daughter
who had just died (Mark v. 35). One may ask whether
the difference in point of time would be as significant
for the evangelist as it may appear to the modern
scholar who is casting about for a naturalistic explanation. If the reality of death is conceded, is the
restoration any more marvellous after the lapse of
a number of hours than after the lapse of an hour ?
Do we know enough about the relation of soul and
body to be able to declare confidently at what moment
an irrevocable separation takes place ? We need
not speculate, as do Weiss and Beyschlag, regarding
this insoluble problem.[1] Many scholars charge the
Fourth Gospel with trying to outbid Luke's record
in marvellousness.

(iii) It is impossible to escape the impression that
the witness or the evangelist in *v.* 39 desires to magnify
the greatness of the miracle. If normally the process
of putrefaction must have set in in the interval, we
must suppose either an arrest or a reversal of the
process by the miraculous power of Jesus. ' Beyschlag,' according to Bruce, ' remarks that the ἤδη ὄζει
of Martha cannot have been intended by the writer
to exaggerate the miracle by making it consist in
restoring life to an already putrefying corpse. One
bent on magnifying the miracle would have represented the interval that had elapsed from death,
not as four days, but rather as four years or centuries,
and would not have put the ἤδη ὄζει in the form of a

---

[1] See Bruce, *The Miraculous Element in the Gospels*, p. 200.

mere inference, a mistaken one, as the author thinks.' [1]
'That may be so,' continues Bruce, ' but it is difficult
to think of a body out of which life has fled four days
as still having within it " echoes of life " as if the soul
had not quite left it.' [1] But are not Martha's words
quoted expressly to indicate the probability in the
known conditions that the process of dissolution had
begun. The witness has increased our difficulty by
his manner of telling his story.

(iv) Can the difficulty be relieved by assuming
that the story of the witness has been worked over
by a later hand ? Dr. Strachan traces the changes
in the story to the redactor of the Gospel : 'I believe
that the historical fact which lies behind the narrative
is a story of the same character as the raising of
Jairus' daughter. The suggestion is that R has
transformed, especially in *vv.* 38-44, the raising of
Lazarus from his death-bed into the more stupendous
miracle of reviving a putrefying body. The passages
assigned to R are *vv.* 2, 17, 19, 30, 31, 38-46. In
the case of *vv.* 38-44, R's work and the original
Johannine material are inextricably intermingled.
In the account, as we have it, the miracle is performed
before a crowd, and in public. Evidently R felt
that the story must be altered so as to take the place
in his chronological scheme of the Cleansing of the

---

[1] *The Miraculous Element in the Gospels,* p. 200, note. Westcott's
note *in loco* may here be added : ' The full significance of the words
appears from a passage (cf. " Bereshith R," p. 1143) quoted by
Lightfoot. " It is a tradition of Ben Kaphra's ; the very height of
mourning is not till the third day. For three days the spirit wanders
about the sepulchre, expecting if it may return into the body. But
when it sees that the form or aspect of the face is changed (on the
fourth day) then it hovers no more, but leaves the body to itself."
" After three days," it is said elsewhere, " the countenance is
changed " ' (*St. John,* p. 172). If the evangelist or redactor shared
this common belief, it was clearly his intention to show that death
had fully taken place without any hope of recovery.

Temple, which, in the Synoptics, provokes the hostile
attention of the authorities. Note the use of the
word " crowd " in chapter xii.' In a note he adds :
' Remember that there is no reason to doubt the
sincerity of the witness, and that we are moving
in an atmosphere of literary ethics entirely different
from our own.' [1] This explanation would need some
modification to bring it into accord with the view
of the Gospel here presented. It is not likely that
the redactor, the author of the Appendix and other
material connected with the Synoptic tradition, so
transformed the record of the evangelist, but the
evangelist himself may have worked over the report
of the witness, following his tendency to exaggerate
the supernaturalness of Jesus.

(v) Forbes,[2] as quoted by Dr. Moffatt, goes even
further than Dr. Strachan. ' The whole evidence,'
he says, ' points strongly to the conclusion that the
evangelist, using some tradition to us unknown, and
the Synoptic material mentioned, elaborated them
freely into a narrative designed to be at once : (a) an
astonishing manifestation of the Logos-Christ ; (b) a
pictorial setting forth of the spiritual truth of Christ
as Life ; (c) a prophetic prefiguration of the death
and resurrection of Jesus, as shown by the fact
that the names Jesus and Lazarus have the
same meaning, and that the narrative forms a
transition to the final struggle and to death.' [2] The
writer cannot, however, assign to the evangelist so
definite an intention or so deliberate an invention,
so free and bold a manufacture of history in the
interests of theology. He desires to guard his own
mind against credulity, and, therefore, would welcome

---

[1] *The Fourth Gospel*, p. 155.
[2] *Introduction*, p. 273, quoted *op. cit.* p. 539.

any explanation which would ascribe to a later hand
a heightening of the marvel of the story as it may
have been told by the witness. With some hesitation
he accepts the reality of a miracle of raising from the
dead on the grounds that on the one hand he cannot
bring his mind to believe that whoever was responsible
for the story was capable of sheer invention when
he seems most desirous of conveying the assurance
of truth, and that, on the other, he does not feel
competent to fix the limits of the possibility of the
miraculous action of the supernatural person of the
Conqueror of death as the Risen Lord.

(b) Apart from this wider problem of miracle, the
narrative in John xi. raises other difficulties. It
has been urged as an objection to the historicity of
this event, that *the silence of the other Gospels is inexplicable*. ' It is just conceivable,' says Dr. Moffatt,
' that the incident failed for some reason to be included
by the Synoptic Gospels : their silence would not by
itself be absolutely conclusive against the historicity.
The difficulty is to give any adequate psychological
reason why so stupendous and critical an episode
(witnessed *ex hypothesi* by all the disciples) should
have failed to win a place in the Synoptic tradition,
even when that tradition is admitted to be incomplete
at certain points, and this difficulty is heightened
by the obvious motives of the writer, who makes
this miracle the pivot of the final Jewish attack on
Jesus, instead of the purging of the temple, which
he transfers to the beginning of the ministry.' [1] In
spite of the concession at the beginning, this passage
sets forth clearly the difficulty which the silence of
the Synoptists involves, and so deserves close scrutiny.
(i) The incompleteness of the Synoptic tradition

[1] *Introduction*, p. 539.

I

needs to be asserted more unreservedly, as has already
been shown in a previous section, and can be explained
by the limitation of Peter's knowledge or interest.
He was concerned solely about the Galilaean ministry
apart from the final tragedy ; and an event, however
significant or crucial for the Judaean ministry, about
which the Fourth Gospel is concerned, might quite
probably be passed over by him.   If such limitation
of interest be held incredible, there remains the possibility of his limitation of knowledge.

(ii) The parenthesis in Dr. Moffatt's statement,
' witnessed *ex hypothesi* by all the disciples,' appears
a conclusion going beyond the data.   If, as has already
been argued, the Twelve, though the constant companions of Jesus in Galilee, did not accompany Him
on all His visits to Jerusalem, and if there was a circle
of disciples in Judaea regarding whom because of the
extreme hostility of the Jewish rulers secrecy had
to be maintained, when disciples are mentioned in
the Fourth Gospel we are not entitled at once to assume
that the Twelve are meant.   If the mission of the
Seventy in Luke x. 1-20 is an historical reality, a wider
circle of disciples accompanied Jesus in the wanderings
of the last stage of His ministry.   Even if the disciples
mentioned in *vv*. 7-8, 12, and 16 included some of the
Twelve, it is not at all improbable that Peter was not
one of the number.   Had the disciple who was always
ready to speak for and take the lead of the others
been present, would he have left it to Thomas to
propose that they should go, if necessary, even to death
(*v*. 16) ?   Verse 17 does not mention any disciples,
and as the word *secretly* in *v*. 28 indicates, public
observation was being avoided.   Is it not likely then
that, even if some of the disciples went part of the
way with Jesus, He came to Bethany alone ?   These

conjectures are offered as no more than conjectures ;
but as at least forbidding the confident assertion that
the Twelve must all have been present on this occasion.

(iii) Even if the episode appeared so critical to the
witness, with his dominant interest in the Judaean
ministry and the influence of that ministry on the
Jewish authorities, as bringing to a head the purpose
of the rulers to rid themselves of Jesus once for all,
the event need not have had the same significance
for Peter, even if he knew of it, or any of the other
witnesses to the Galilaean ministry, as probably they
were entirely ignorant of the course of hostile action
against Jesus by the scribes and Pharisees in Jerusalem. If they had known, it is strange that they
cherished their hopes to the very end, and were so
taken by surprise when the blow fell. Verses 47-53
appear to come from one who was somehow in touch
with the inner circles of Jewish politics, as none of
the Galilaean disciples were at all likely to be.

(iv) It has been suggested that, as the Synoptic
tradition comes from a much earlier date than the
Fourth Gospel, regard for the safety of the family
in Bethany at a time of violent Jewish hostility to
the followers of Jesus may have been the motive of
silence. But this seems an improbable reason. If
the Jewish rulers were influenced in their actions by
this event, as the Fourth Gospel itself asserts, the family
in Bethany would already be known to them, and a
record of the events would not at a later date in any
way have increased their peril. This suggestion
does get some support, however, from the fact that
in Luke's reference to Martha and Mary, Bethany
is not mentioned, but only ' a certain village ' (x. 38),
and that in Mark's (xiv. 3) and Matthew's (xxvi. 6)
account of the anointing at the supper, the house is

described as ' of Simon the leper,' and the name of
the woman is not given.   Is it likely that the company
of disciples would know nothing about the family
in Bethany ?   Some reason which we cannot now
conjecture there must have been for silence.   In the
preceding paragraphs, however, an adequate reason
for the absence of any record of this event from the
Synoptic Gospels has been given apart from this
possible reason.

(c) A closer scrutiny of the record in its details
adds other difficulties.   While it is on general grounds
probable that the witness himself was at Bethany,
having a special interest in the family there ;   yet,
as has been indicated, his report must have undergone a more considerable transformation at the hands
of the evangelist than most of the Gospel.   Just as
improbable, however, is it that he was a companion
of Jesus in His withdrawal beyond Jordan, and that
what is recorded in vv. 1-16 is his personal testimony.
Either the witness himself got it at second-hand from
one of the disciples there present, or the evangelist
to complete the story made such inquiry as was possible
to him.   As one of the Galilaean disciples, Thomas,
is mentioned, it is possible even that the redactor
inserted it, having derived it from the same sources
as his other insertions.

(i) Few statements have touched the human heart
as the simple words, ' Jesus wept ' (v. 35 ; cf. vv. 33
and 38), revealing the depth of His compassion and
the breadth of His sympathy for man in the presence
of death.   But it is not easy to reconcile with this
' touch of nature that makes the whole world kin '
the declaration in v. 4, in which Jesus' interest in the
glory which is to be won by the performance of the
miracle is made to obscure His regard for His friends

in their anxiety and need ; or the further explanation
in *v.* 15 that He is glad of His friend's death because
of the opportunity it gives of strengthening the
disciples' faith. If *v.* 6 is intended to convey the
impression that Jesus delayed His return to Bethany
in order that Lazarus might die, and so He might
have the greater glory of saving from the dead instead
of healing disease, it surely puts Him in a false light,
and is doctrine misrepresenting fact. There would
be both less tenderness for His friends, and more
desire to display His power, than we have any
reason to ascribe to Him. We may, however, understand *v.* 4 as expressing confidence regarding Lazarus'
recovery, and recovery in such a way as would bring
honour to Jesus. He waited, however, for Divine
guidance as to His next step, as *v.* 9 indicates. While
we might, thus interpreted, accept *v.* 4 as an authentic
utterance, it is not likely that Jesus described Himself
as ' Son of God.' Probably the evangelist understood
the utterance as showing the supernatural foresight
of Jesus into what He was about to do in raising
Lazarus from the dead. Probably also he assumed
a supernatural knowledge by Jesus of Lazarus' death.
But this is not at all a necessary assumption, although
we may grant the possibility that there came to
Jesus so distinct a conviction of Lazarus' death that
He saw in it at once the Divine guidance He needed,
and so delayed no longer. The utterance in *v.* 15
raises an intolerable difficulty, and one is forced to
believe that it cannot have been correctly understood
and reported. After learning that Lazarus was
dead, and realizing as He must have done by His
intense sympathy the desolation which the sisters
were experiencing, could He, however confident of
a happy issue out of this affliction by the Father's

answer to His prayer, have said that He was glad
He was not there ? Can the confirmation of the
faith of the disciples have been so ample a compensa-
tion for the sorrow of the sisters so dear to Him that
the tender, pitiful heart of Jesus can have rejoiced
in His friend's death ? Was not the price of suffering
paid by the sisters too high even for such an end ?
Would not restoration from sickness have served
the purpose ? The Gospel itself shows that Jesus
did not value highly the faith which rested on
miracles (iv. 48), and that He was very compassionate to sorrow (xi. 35). Acquiescence in
God's will there may have been, confidence too
that God's power would be manifested through
Him, and expectation that even this event would
be overruled for good; but joy there surely cannot
have been. The dogmatic interest here as elsewhere
presents the words and works of Jesus in a distorting
medium.

(ii) Wendt,[1] in accordance with his partition hypothesis, derives from the source *vv.* 23-26, and also
probably *v.* 27, and then, as introductory to this utterance, he assigns the greater part in *vv.* 1-22 to the same,
except *vv.* 1*b*, 2-4, 11-15, taking similar exception
to the representation there of Jesus' attitude. Dr.
Bruce seeks to weaken the strength of the objection
by the following considerations : ' The glory which
is represented as the aim of the miracles is not of the
vulgar, worldly kind. Glorification and humiliation
are close of kin, or virtually identical, in John's Gospel.'
After quoting *v.* 4 he asks, ' How does the sickness
contribute to Christ's glorification ? As the exit of
the traitor did (xiii. 31)—by causing His crucifixion.' [2]

[1] *St. John's Gospel*, pp. 153-158.
[2] *Miraculous Element in the Gospels*, pp. 151-152.

But this does not relieve the difficulty, and is itself
rather far-fetched.

(iii) Another explanation has been suggested to
the author by a correspondent. ' Jesus " abode two
days in the place where he was." On His arrival
on the scene Lazarus had been dead *four* days. Lazarus
would therefore have been dead by the time the
messengers reached Him, or must have died on that
same day. From the report it might well have been
concluded, without the exercise of supernatural
knowledge, that, if Jesus had started at once, He would
have been too late to save His friend from death.
Having work to finish in Peraea, and knowing that
it was now of no use to think of preventing the death
of Lazarus by His presence, and also for the further
glory of God, " He abode " where He was. This I
believe is George Matheson's view.' Against this
view there are two objections : (1) The message sent
by the sisters cannot have indicated the probability
of death before Jesus' response to the summons, as
Martha expresses her disappointment (*v.* 21) that
Jesus had not arrived in time to cure. We should
need to infer supernatural knowledge, as indeed the
record before us assumes. (2) Would not Jesus'
knowledge that Lazarus was dead be sufficient reason
for hastening to comfort the sisters, unless He was
waiting God's guidance. To His entire dependence
on God even His most tender affections were ever
made subordinate.

(iv) This explanation has, however, suggested to
the writer another conjecture, which is given only
as such. The word *dead* in *v.* 39 is printed in italics
to show that it is not in the original Greek. What
we read there is τεταρταῖος γάρ ἐστιν (Vulgate, *quadri-
duanus enim est*). τεταρταῖος is defined in Thayer's

Greek-English Lexicon as ' an ordinary numeral, used in answer to the question, on what day ? ' Souter in his Pocket Lexicon adds, ' Greek idiom often personalises such adjectives.' The word need not be restricted to death ; it might have a wider reference. Is it possible that Jesus may have been inquiring about the duration of Lazarus' illness, and that this word may be an answer to that question ? If misunderstood as referring to the time of death, it may have been the starting-point of a tradition that issued in Martha's words ἤδη ὄζει. The evangelist could thus be acquitted of the charge of sheer invention. The writer is fully conscious of how precarious a defence this is.

(v) In chapter ii. the words in *v.* 42 in which Jesus gives a reason for declaring His assurance of answers to His prayers has already been treated as a comment of the evangelist ; but the assurance itself and the thanksgiving which it follows may be regarded as authentic utterances ; and they afford a most significant indication that He exercised His supernatural power in dependence on God through constant prayer.

(d) The account in *vv.* 47-53 has the marks of historical probability. The connexion of the witness with the high priest will be afterwards discussed in the more appropriate context (xviii. 15). Whatever it was, it placed him in a position to know the plans of the enemies of Jesus. The phrase ' high priest that year ' (*v.* 51) cannot be regarded as a proof of his ignorance of Jewish affairs in view of all the other evidence the Gospel contains of intimate acquaintance with the national conditions. It is adequately explained by many scholars as referring not to the length of Caiaphas' tenure of office, but to the significance of the year of the crucifixion of Jesus in human history. Probably the counsel of expediency given by Caiaphas has without any deliberate intention been so modified as to make it appear more obviously a prophecy (*v.* 50). Verse 51 belongs to the witness's theology rather than to history. The uncertain Synoptic account of the last stage of the ministry affords no good reason for challenging the substantial accuracy of the witness's representation of the historical situation.

(*e*) At the close of this critical discussion, attention may be fixed on the theological import of the record. (i) Martha's sorrowful reproach Jesus met by an assurance of Lazarus' resurrection, not in the remote future, but in the immediate present through Himself as the Resurrection and the Life, faith in whom secures eternal life. The appeal for her faith was answered by her confession of His Messiahship (*vv.* 21-27), a confession which is not incredible. The sorrowful reproach of Mary (*v.* 32) called forth no answer in words to comfort her, for Jesus Himself ' chafed in spirit and was disquieted,' and either in sympathy with the sisters, or in compassion for the hopeless grief of men in the presence of death, ' Jesus burst into tears.' [1] Confident of His power, because assured of His answered prayer, He called Lazarus out of the opened grave (*vv.* 32-44). If God cannot and will not raise the dead, then Lazarus was not raised. But if God can and will it is credible that the prayer of Jesus was answered, and the power of God was revealed through Him, and thus His filial confidence in God was justified. If we believe that Christ was raised from the dead, need we disbelieve that God through Him raised Lazarus ? Here we must leave

[1] Moffatt's *A New Translation*, p. 130.

the problem, as no logical demonstration can solve
it ; for the solution is bound up with the faith in
Himself Christ inspires in us, and the experience
of the eternal life through that faith which becomes
ours.

(ii) The impression of this miracle is represented
as so great that the enemies of Jesus were forced to
the resolve at any cost to repress the Messianic
movement, which might bring down on Judaea the
heavy hand of Rome.　It was as a measure of political
expediency that Caiaphas advocated the execution
of Jesus, although the witness attached to this
utterance in view of his office a prophetic significance.
Our faith does find the same world-wide meaning and
worth in the death of Jesus, although our modern
modes of interpretation forbid our finding in Caiaphas'
words a prophetic oracle (*vv.* 45-53).

(*f*) In this resolve on a judicial murder ended the
Great Judgment, the course of which this chapter
has endeavoured to sketch.　No attempt has been
made, as in Westcott's *Commentary*, to read Christian
theology into almost every phrase and clause, but
the intention has been through a critical discussion
to reach the historical situation, as it developed
from stage to stage, and to show its theological import.
Regarding the result two remarks may be made.

(i) The writer is more than ever convinced that
the witness is not romancing ; if he is, he is one of
the most consummate realists in fiction, for so vivid
is the impression he makes of reality.

(ii) The writer cannot find in Jesus' self-disclosures
the advanced metaphysics of the ecclesiastical dogma
of the person of Christ, but a moral conscience and
a religious consciousness of intimacy with, dependence
on, confidence in, obedience to God as Father, which

demands a metaphysical explanation; but none of the utterances is metaphysical in intention. Opposition threw Jesus back more and more on God, and evoked in Him a fuller and firmer sense of the uniqueness and absoluteness of His relation as Son to God as Father. A gradual human development was the medium of a progressive divine incarnation.

VIII

THE GLORY

(JOHN XII.-XX.)

AFTER the *Testimony* to what Jesus was, the Christ
the Son of God, through whose name believers may
have life, came the *Judgment* of the Jewish people
in rejecting Him. Adverse as was the Judgment,
it issued in the *Glory* of His sacrifice for the salvation
of men. Of that glory there was a twofold revelation,
in word in the discourse in the Upper Room, and in
passion and action in the Crucifixion and the Resurrection.

(1) THE WEEK BEFORE THE PASSION (xii.)

(*a*) Mark (xiv. 3-9) places the anointing in Bethany
in immediate connexion with the treachery of Judas
(*vv.* 10 and 11) ; and if the note of time in *v.* 1, ' after
two days,' applies to this incident also, on Wednesday
evening. Matthew gives it a similar position (xxvi.
6-16). Both may have intended to throw into bold
relief the contrast between Mary's devotion and
Judas' treachery. And it is not at all improbable
that the chronology of the Fourth Gospel is to be
preferred, and that it was on the Sabbath evening
that the feast was given. There is no serious difficulty
about harmonizing the Johannine and the Synoptic
accounts. The murmuring that is ascribed by
Matthew (*v.* 8) to the disciples is by the Fourth Gospel

140

limited to Judas (*vv.* 4-5). The charge against Judas in *v.* 6 may be justified ; but it may also be due to the witness's detestation, elsewhere shown in the Gospel, for the traitor, of whom he would on very slight evidence be ready to believe the very worst. The explanation of Mary's action by Jesus, according to the Synoptists, is much more intelligible than the saying reported in the Fourth Gospel (*v.* 7), although the import is similar. While the Synoptists pass at once to record the treachery of Judas, the witness, with his intense interest in and intimate knowledge of every detail of the growing hatred of the Jewish rulers, which at last resulted in the condemnation of Jesus, turns aside to deal again with their machinations (*vv.* 9-11).

(*b*) The account of the triumphal entry (*vv.* 12-19) is told with less detail than by the Synoptists. How the young ass was found (*v.* 14) the witness does not tell us. Either he did not know, not being one of the Twelve, or he himself was the citizen of Jerusalem who rendered the Master this service. He quotes the same prophetic oracle as Matthew in a shorter form without the Hebrew parallelism, which leads that evangelist to the absurdity of representing Jesus as riding upon two asses at once (Matt. xxi. 2-7). Characteristic of him is the reference to the lack of understanding of the disciples till after the Resurrection (*v.* 16). But did not the Twelve and the multitude alike intend a Messianic demonstration, even although the prophecy may not have been in their mind ? It is not improbable even that Jesus Himself intended His action, for it was He who took the initiative, as an acted parable, not only a claim to the Messiahship, but also a proof of the only kind of Messiahship He claimed, and that He had the prophetic oracle in

mind.   There are instances in which the fulfilment
of prophecy is assigned to Him which we must hesitate
in accepting as too artificial, as in xix. 28 ; but here
the objection does not hold.   Characteristic of the
witness too is the connexion indicated between the
demonstration and the raising of Lazarus from the
dead (*vv*. 17-18).   If some of the crowd from Jerusalem
were so influenced, the multitude from Galilee was
moved to their enthusiasm by their knowledge of
the Galilaean ministry.   Here again is his one-sided
Judaean interest.   A familiar trait in the Gospel
meets us in the account of the effect of the demonstration on the Pharisees, concerned about their own
popularity (*v*. 19).   The cleansing of the Temple,
recorded by the Synoptists, is not mentioned here,
as the witness had already recorded a similar action
at the beginning of the ministry (ii. 13-17).   We
need not assume that he has transferred an event at
the close to the beginning of the ministry, and reason
has been already given why the act may have been
repeated.   Knowing as he did the grounds of the
hostility of the Jews to Jesus, he probably did not
assign to this single event the importance given to
it by the Synoptists.

(*c*) The next section (*vv*. 20-36) has already been
dealt with as a probable insertion.   The witness's
confirmation from prophecy of the necessity of the
people's unbelief (*vv*. 37-41) is entirely in accord with
the common interpretation of the Old Testament in
the early Church.   The following statement (*vv*. 41-42)
again indicates one who was in close contact with
the ruling classes in Jerusalem, and not a Galilaean
fisherman.   The next paragraph is manifestly displaced
(*vv*. 44-50), as this final appeal of Jesus to the Jewish
multitude must have come before the witness's summing-

up of the results of the ministry as regards the Jewish
people ; and Dr. Moffatt in his *New Translation* [1]
seems entirely justified in placing these verses between
the two sentences in *v.* 36. Although *vv.* 20-36 are a
composition of Synoptic and Johannine elements, the
distinctively Johannine elements, such as *vv.* 35-36,
may belong to this context. It is significant here
again that there has been a displacement, where on
other grounds we have been led to suspect an insertion. [2]
It is perplexing to find out at how few points the
Synoptic and the Johannine tradition of Passion-week
coincide. It is probable that the witness only records
what he himself saw and heard.

(*d*) The anointing in Bethany and the triumphal
entry do not yield us any distinctively Johannine
theological material. The theological significance of
vv. 20-36 has been elsewhere discussed. The course
of thought in the final appeal recalls previous teaching.
Faith in Christ is faith in the God whose messenger
He is, and so is knowledge of Him knowledge of God.
His aim is to enlighten men, and even unbelief He does
not judge, as what He seeks is to save : and yet such
is His teaching that rejection of it must bring condemnation since He does not make His message, but gets
it from God, and delivers it in obedience to God
because He knows that faith brings eternal life.
After this final appeal the witness adds his own judgment of the unbelief of his nation, and shows that
it is in accord with prophetic prediction. He exposes
the cowardice of those who, moved by faith, were

---

[1] Pp. 132-133.
[2] Mr. Thompson offers a suggestion so improbable that it needs
only to be mentioned. It is very tempting to suppose that the
original climax of xii. 37-43 was xx. 30-31, and that these two
passages together formed the original conclusion of the Gospel.
(*Op. cit.* ix. p. 424.)

restrained from confession by prudence. Some of
the contents of this chapter suggest that it should
be joined to the previous section, *The Judgment*, but
not only does *v.* 23 require its inclusion here, but it
would be a pity to separate this part from the rest
of the story of the Passion.

(2) The Upper Room (xiii.-xvii.)

In these chapters there emerge a number of questions.
Is the record of the washing of the disciples' feet
historical, and why does the Fourth Gospel alone
contain it ?   Why is this Gospel silent regarding the
institution of the Lord's Supper ; and at what point
in the narrative should it be inserted ?   Is the discourse
assigned to Jesus authentic, and is the present the
original order ?

(*a*) Not only is the action of Jesus in washing His
disciples' feet characteristic, but the details bear the
marks of the eye-witness. The introductory verses
(1-3) give the witness's interpretation of the consciousness of Jesus in performing this service, and have
his theological peculiarity ; but even here, allowing
for some over-emphasis, the discourse which follows
affords a justification for this interpretation. The
writer has elsewhere [1] suggested that the witness was
himself the householder, who provided the Upper
Room. (i) The absence of a slave to perform the
menial office assumed by Jesus was a failure in
hospitality (cf. Luke vii. 44) which Peter, though
prominent in the incident, did not report, as that
would have appeared ' as a censure of a fellow-disciple,
and one whom, owing to his position in Jerusalem
and influence with the priesthood, it was desirable

[1] *Studies in the Inner Life of Jesus*, pp. 351-355.

not to offend.' The host records it himself as a personal confession. For, even if there had been danger in introducing a slave into the room, he ought to have assumed the task himself.

(ii) The reference in *v.* 23 is also probably to the host : ' Would this not be the place for the host, even if he had surrendered his function to Jesus ? Might not his claim for that favoured position explain the jealousy of the other disciples,' [1] and so have aggravated their disinclination, due to conflicting ambitions, to render this humble service. It is a common assumption, due to transferring to the ministry of Jesus the ecclesiastical traditions of a later age, that only the Twelve can have been present with Jesus in the Upper Room, and that accordingly the reference must be to John, the son of Zebedee. ' Had this disciple been John, the son of Zebedee, known as one of the apostles, such an allusion would seem an affectation ; but if the disciple was known as such only after many years to the circle of his own disciples, whose reverence and affection conferred on him this distinctive title, it seems natural.' An alternative explanation would be that the disciple described himself thus in humble penitence.

(iii) In *v.* 28 the witness asserts that none of the disciples knew why Jesus gave Judas the sop, and sent him on his errand of treachery. Evidently he is himself an exception. ' The beloved disciple alone heard Jesus' words, and probably by sign Jesus had made him understand that the secret was to be kept especially from inquiring Peter, who, had he known, would probably never have allowed the traitor to escape alive.' [2] May we not add the name of John the son of Zebedee, who was ready to call down fire

---

[1] *Op. cit.* p. 351.   [2] *Op cit.* p. 359

on the inhospitable Samaritan village (Luke ix. 54) ?
The witness had learned from Jesus the truth of
the necessity of His death, and thus, in submission
to the Master's teaching, did not hinder the departure
of Judas. It is probable that he was not an eye-
witness of Gethsemane, because when he left the
Upper Room it was to go to the High Priest's house
to be better informed of the plans of the enemies of
Jesus, who had now got a tool in Judas. It is possible
to find an intelligible consistency in the allusions
made in the narrative to the witness.

(*b*) For the silence of the Gospel in regard to
the Lord's Supper, the following reasons may be
suggested.

(i) He wrote at a date long after the apostolate of
Paul, and in a community, and to communities, to
which Paul had ministered, and to which Paul's account of the Last Supper, as found not only in 1 Cor. xi.,
but as probably given to all the Churches to which
he had delivered his Gospel, was thoroughly familiar.
There was no need of repeating an account which
had become a part of the order of worship.

(ii) It may be even that superstitious ideas were
so attaching themselves to the ordinance, that the
witness was unwilling to give them any sanction.
May not his attitude in the matter be represented
by the logion of Jesus (vi. 63), whatever may have
been the occasion of its utterance ? If vi. 53-56
contains an authentic explanation of the significance
of the words of institution by Jesus Himself to the
beloved disciple, the redactor may have placed the
passage in its present context by association of ideas,
and because the account of the Supper was absent.
There was some reason for which he felt that he could
not make use of this incident for the purpose of his

Gospel; and this seems as likely a suggestion as any that can be offered.

(iii) Does *v.* 34 refer to the institution of the Last Supper? 'It has been conjectured,' says Bishop Westcott,' [1] that the "new commandment" is the ordinance of the Holy Communion which was instituted to the end that Christians "might love one another" by recalling in that the crowning act of Christ's love. If this be so, the words *that ye love one another*, give the purpose and not the substance of the commandment. It is, however, difficult to suppose that such an institution would be spoken of as a "commandment" ($\dot{\epsilon}\nu\tau o\lambda\acute{\eta}$, 1 John ii. 7; iii. 22).' This objection seems altogether insufficient, and the suggestion is most attractive. If we accept it, then the departure of Judas was prior to the institution of the Supper, and he took no part in it. Matthew and Mark both place the announcement of this treachery before, and Luke alone after, the Supper. If we may here appeal to psychological probability, it is more likely that the spirit of Jesus was oppressed by the presence of the traitor, that only when he had gone there came to Him the exaltation of spirit indicated in *vv.* 31 and 32, even although the words may have been spoken at a later stage of the discourse, and that it was in this mood that the new commandment was given. Do not these words imply the accomplished sacrifice and salvation of which the Supper is the memorial? Although it is but a conjecture, yet it is probable that the institution of the Supper is to be placed in this context.

(*c*) Many who have difficulty about accepting some of the teaching of Jesus presented in the Fourth Gospel hesitate about challenging the authenticity

[1] *St. John,* p. 198.

for fruit, the promise of a speedy reunion, and of the
coming of the other Paraclete, the assurance of the
advantage to Himself as well as to them of His return
to the Father—there is nothing that need be regarded
as beyond the circle of Jesus' interest and knowledge
in the Upper Room.   It is the familiar filial consciousness which finds expression.   The announcements
of the Passion in the Synoptics were always accompanied by the assurance of resurrection, and this
implied a renewed intercourse, if under other conditions, with His disciples (cf. Matt. xxviii. 20).   The
Baptist declared that the Messiah would baptize,
not with water only, but with the Holy Ghost, and with
fire (iii. 11).   And Jesus recognized the operation of
the Spirit in His own ministry (xii. 28), and promised
His disciples the Spirit, who would speak in them in
times of persecution for their defence (x. 20).   After
the Resurrection the disciples were expectant of the
power from on high, the descent of the Spirit (Luke
xxiv. 49 ; Acts ii. 45).   If the Spirit's operation in
the Apostolic Church presents a double aspect, the
abnormal spiritual gifts (including the prophetic
referred to in xvi. 13), and the inward enlightening
and renewing influence, it is not at all improbable
that the latter conception was present in the teaching
of Jesus as well as the former.   Wendt's objection
to the last clause of xvi. 13 is not conclusive, although
it may be an insertion from the later standpoint.
The prediction of Judas' betrayal, to which he also
takes exception, is paralleled in the Synoptics.   It
is not necessary to find in xiii. 21-30 the ' purpose
to lay an express emphasis on the fact that Jesus
was not deceived and outwitted by the traitor.' [1]

(iv) Recognizing that there are probably various

[1] *St. John's Gospel*, pp. 161-162.

strands in the discourse, we must admit that after
rearrangement of several of the passages there is a
continuity and consistency in the argument which
makes it impossible for the most part to offer any
detailed analysis ; but there are verses here and there
which do not fit into their context, or betray so distinctly another than Jesus' standpoint, that we may
with a certain measure of confidence affirm that they
did not belong to the original discourse. Is it likely
that Jesus explained to His disciples that He had
uttered the prediction, not because it was rooted in
and grew out of the occasion, but in order that in
the future the fulfilment might confirm their faith
(xiii. 19 ; xiv. 29) ? Possibly the witness's or evangelist's explanation was changed from the third to
the first person, and so made to appear a saying of
Jesus.[1] Wendt connects *v.* 20 in chapter xiii. with
v. 17, and gets rid of the intervening verses as an
interpolation, but the connexion he suggests is rather
far-fetched ; and if we regard *v.* 18 as authentic,
v. 21 should immediately follow it, and *v.* 20 must
appear the interpolation. Not only is it inappropriate to the context, but it is similar to the saying
Matt. x. 40, which is in what seems the proper setting.
Verses 34 and 35 might appear an intrusion also,
as Peter's question in *v.* 36 seems to follow on Jesus'
declaration in *v.* 33. A possible explanation is that
it took Peter some time to realize the import of Jesus'
words, and he interrupted at a point unsuitable for
his question. But if, as has already been argued,
the passage about Peter has been inserted by the
redactor, this explanation is unnecessary. In chapter
xiv. *v.* 21 takes up the thought of *v.* 15, and the inter-

[1] Such explanations are found throughout the Gospel, *e.g.* ii.
21-22, xii. 33.

vening verses seem, if not an interpolation, yet a
digression. Similarly *v.* 26 breaks the continuity
of *vv.* 25 and 27 ; so also xvi. 1 attaches itself naturally
to xv. 25, and *v.* 16 to *v.* 6. These four passages
about the Spirit (xiv. 16-20, 26 ; xv. 26-27 ; and
xvi. 7-15) may have belonged originally to another
context, and have been inserted here where there
were points of contact, as undoubtedly there are.
The question does obtrude itself, would Jesus give
the whole company of disciples teaching about the
Spirit so much in advance of what we find afterwards
current in the Apostolic Church ? Regarding the
expanded metaphor or allegory of xv. 1-8, we may
ask, as we have already done in regard to x. 1-16,
whether it may not have been originally in the parabolic form ? It is at least probable that the figure
and the interpretation were not so blended together
in Jesus' utterance as in the report.

(v) The high-priestly prayer of xvii. also presents
some difficulties. It is not impossible, or even improbable, that, when the company had risen from
the table, Jesus did pray aloud, and so seek to
strengthen the disciples for what was awaiting them.
The language of the prayer is more like that of a
soliloquy in God's presence, with no reference to the
presence of others than that of public devotion ; but
we cannot deny the possibility that, moved by His
deep feeling, Jesus did lay aside all reserve, and did
lay bare His heart before His disciples. We cannot
assume, however, that we have the *ipsissima verba,*
unaffected altogether by the channel of their transmission, the reflective mind of the witness. Yet
the prayer does resume the varied teaching which
has just been given ; and if we can accept that as
authentic, we need not hesitate about the genuineness

of this utterance in its general features. One verse
there is which must be regarded as a gloss of witness or
evangelist. The theological definition of *v.* 3 cannot
have fallen from the lips of Jesus. MacGillivray,[1]
after referring to his personal experience in inter-
jecting an idea suggested by a speaker into rough
notes of his speech, concludes : ' John, in recording
the prayer, must have enjoyed intense spiritual
elevation, and it may be this sentence, which ordinarily
would be placed in the margin as a pious ejaculation,
was from the very beginning a part of the text.'

(*d*) While, with these qualifications, we may accept
the report as a whole as authentic, there is very good
reason for maintaining that there have been considerable displacements, and that to restore continuity
to the teaching we must rearrange a number of the
passages. While Mr. Thompson recognizes the possibility of displacements he also holds that ' xv.-xvi.
and perhaps xvii. might be an expansion of the Last
Discourse added subsequently to xiv. without altera-
tion of xiv. 30-31.' [2] If we reject so radical a solution,
we are driven to admit displacements. In his *New
Translation of the New Testament,* Dr. Moffatt inserts
chapters xv. and xvi. in the middle of *v.* 31 of xiii. ;
chapter xiv. follows 31*b*-38, and is followed by xvii.[3]
He offers the explanation in his *Introduction to the
New Testament.*[4]

(i) The words in xiv. 31, ' Arise, let us go hence,'
were a summons to the disciples to rise from supper,
and to start for the garden of Gethsemane. While
it is probable that, as the whole company stood, Jesus
did offer the prayer contained in xvii., it is extremely
improbable that He would then deliver the discourse

---

[1] *Expository Times,* xxv. p. 333.   [2] *Op. cit.* ix. p. 424.
[3] Pp. 134-138.   [4] P. 556.

contained in xv. and xvi. The passage xiv. 25-31
sounds like the conclusion of the discourse. Is it
likely that Jesus would have uttered the reproach
in xvi. 5, ' None of you asketh me, Whither goest
thou ? ' after Peter had asked the question in xiii.
36, ' Lord, whither goest thou ? ' or Thomas had made
the inquiry in xiv. 5, ' Lord, we know not whither
thou goest ; how know we the way ? ' The perplexity
expressed by the disciples in xvi. 18 seems incongruous
after Jesus' declaration in xiii. 33 and xiv. 18, 19.
There is general agreement that xv. and xvi. should
precede xiv., but there is difference of opinion as to
the place in xiii. where they should be inserted.

(ii) There are three theories current. Wendt [1] would
place these chapters between vv. 35 and 36. This
suggestion ignores the incongruity of having xvi. 18
after xiii. 33, although this is not an insuperable
difficulty. The allegory of the Vine in xv. 1-8 follows
very appropriately on v. 35, and Jesus' mood of
exaltation can be very fitly explained as due to the
relief He experienced when the traitor departed, and
He was left with faithful disciples. A serious objection,
however, is that v. 36 links itself so closely to v. 33, as
has already been indicated ; this, however, falls to the
ground if vv. 36-38 have been inserted by the redactor.
Bacon, according to Moffatt, places the two chapters
between vv. 20 and 21 ; but also puts vv. 36-38 after
xvi. 31-33.[2] But unless with Wendt we treat vv. 21-30
as an interpolation not belonging to the source, it
properly follows v. 18.[3] It is also probable that the
departure of the traitor did take place before Jesus

[1] St. John's Gospel, p. 101 ff.
[2] Op. cit. pp. 556-557. But see Bacon's The Fourth Gospel,
pp. 500-524.
[3] The interruption of the sequence by v. 20 and the peculiar
character of v. 19 have already been explained.

began fully to unburden His soul to His disciples.
The severance of *vv.* 36-38 from *vv.* 31-35 is a further
objection.   Moffatt's arrangement—xv. and xvi. between 31*a* and 31*b* in xiii.—is the same as Spitta's.
One objection to this arrangement is that the mood
of exaltation which is uttered in *vv.* 31-32 seems
probable as an immediate reaction from the withdrawal
of the traitor, but it fits into the context given to it
in the rearrangement.   Another objection is that
vv. 34-35 would come very appropriately before
xv. 1.   In favour of it are offered the following considerations.   The incongruity of xvi. 18 after xiii. 33
and xiv. 18, and the introduction of xvi. 5 after
xiii. 36 or xiv. 5-6, are avoided ; the sequence of xiii.
21-30 and 18-19, and also 36-38 and 31-35, is maintained;
the declaration of xiii. 31-32 follows fitly on the
expression in xvi. 32-33 of confidence in the Father's
presence and victory over the world ; the prediction
of Peter's denial appears more probable in the closing
conversation than before the more formal discourse.

(iii) To the writer Moffatt's rearrangement commends itself as the most probable, if chapters xv.
and xvi. were indeed spoken in the Upper Room.
The possibility must be admitted that the contents
of both were spoken at an earlier hour on the same
day, or even on a previous day.   The figure of the
Vine may have been suggested to Jesus as He and
His disciples passed the Temple, on one of the gates
of which the Vine was an ornament.[1]   A slight modification of his arrangement may, however, be made :
verses 34 and 35 may be placed after 31*a* as the
beginning of the talk, just after the Supper, and on
this xv. 1-8 would follow, the figure being suggested
by the wine which had just been used as the symbol

[1] Westcott, *St. John*, p. 216.

of the blood of the covenant. Moffatt clinches his argument by a summary of the discourse as thus rearranged. 'After the withdrawal of Judas, Jesus, in view of the wine at table (Mark xiv. 25 ; Luke xxii. 18 ; Didaché ix. 2), utters the parable of the Vine (xv. 1 f.), beginning with a special and warning allusion to the recent apostasy of His friend (an unfruitful branch, xv. 2=xiii. 30-31 ; xv. 6=xiii. 27) ; and urging brotherly love as the bond of life (xv. 9 f. carrying on xiii. 14 f. ; cf. also xiii. 10-11 echoed in xv. 2-3 ; xiii. 17-18 in xv. 4-5 ; xiii. 18 in xv. 16 ; and xiii. 16 in xv. 20). The connexion of thought between xiii. 1-30 and xv. grows in fact more vivid as the two passages are set in juxtaposition ; thus the love of the disciples suggests to Jesus (xv. 18) the hatred shown them by the outside world, whose persecution forms the next topic (xv. 18-xvi. 3), passing over into the compensations for the bodily absence of Jesus from His afflicted followers (xvi. 4-xvi. 33). This stream of counsel and warning closes with a word of triumph (xvi. 33=xiii. 31b-32), which runs out into a renewed appeal for mutual love among the disciples. Then follows Peter's protest (xiii. 36-38), exactly as in the Synoptic tradition (Matt. xxvi. 31-35) after Christ's mournful anticipation (xvi. 32). The final discourse of xiv. ends in the prayer of xvii. (cf. xiv. 30=xvii. 1 ; xiv. 6 f.=xvii. 2 f. ; xiv. 13= xvii. 4). In the solemn pause before the exit— a pause too short for such a discourse as that of xv. and xvi.—Jesus utters this sublime rhapsody of faith, and then (xviii. 1) leads the disciples out to face the end.' [1]

(e) The Rev. G. Henslow has republished in pamphlet form an article from *The Interpreter* under the

---

[1] *Introduction*, p. 557.

title, *Our Lord's Discourses with His Apostles after His Resurrection.* Among these he includes chapters xiv.-xvii. in this Gospel. On this hypothesis the following considerations may be offered : (i) It is an assumption of which we need proof that such continuous teachings were given, and even could be given, remembered, and recorded under the exceptional conditions of the appearances after the Resurrection. (ii) Even if that possibility be allowed, an analysis of the contents of these chapters would in the writer's opinion forbid the assigning of the whole of these chapters. Chapter xiv. contains teaching altogether appropriate to the Last Supper, and the prayer of xvii. also suits that occasion. (iii) Uncertainty regarding the proper position of xv. and xvi. must be admitted ; and if there were nothing in these chapters to forbid our placing them where this pamphlet does, and the hypothesis itself were credible, the suggestion might be entertained. · (iv) In the sections xv. 1-xvi. 4 nothing absolutely forbids that assumption, but xvi. 5 must be placed in time before xiii. 36 and xiv. 5, and *v.* 18 before xiii. 33. The section on the Spirit might be attached to xv. 26-27, and might possibly belong to the post-resurrection teaching ; but from *v.* 16 onwards we are in a situation before the Passion, and not after the Resurrection.

(*f*) This discussion suggests three considerations of a more general character. (i) This Gospel so often presents Jesus in a polemic and assertive attitude that it is an immeasurable gain to be able to regard this discourse as in substance authentic, and thus to become acquainted with Jesus in His more tender, gracious, consolatory, and attractive aspects. We may claim that the present object of Christian faith was once in historical reality all He now is. (ii) While the discourse would have value ' as the Evangelist's inspired interpretation of his real experience of the indwelling and inworking of the living Christ by His Spirit, just as the apostle Paul's exposition of the Gospel of the grace of God in Christ Jesus,'[1] yet it is for the confirmation of faith to be able to regard that experience as the fulfilment by the living Christ of promises, assurances, and comforts given by the historical Jesus. Could there have been such fulfilment in the experience had there not been the prediction in the history ? (iii) Even had John the son of Zebedee, as presented in the Synoptics, been capable of apprehending, appreciating, and appropriating, and thus preserving and transmitting, such teaching, would he, as the close companion of Peter, not so have influenced him as to make impossible the partial presentation of the teaching and work of Jesus, for which Peter as the source of Mark's Gospel was responsible ? Two close companions could surely not have been the sources of two so divergent streams of tradition.

(g) An attempt must at least be made to give a summary of the teaching in the Upper Room. (i) The witness's interpretation of Jesus' consciousness in xiii. 3 belongs to his theology, and yet has its roots in the soil of Jesus' teaching regarding His relation to God and to His disciples. So eager was the love of Jesus that His disciples should be delivered from the spirit of ambition, rivalry, and faction, which threatened their unity and so imperilled the continuance of His work by them, that, conscious of His dignity as Son of God, and also of the urgent necessity of their conversion (cf. Matt. xviii. 3) before He was

---

[1] *Studies in the Inner Life of Jesus*, pp. 372-373.

taken from them, He stooped to the slave's service, mainly as an example of humility (*vv.* 12-17), even as on a former occasion He set a child before them, but also, as the conversation with Peter shows (*vv.* 6-11), as a symbolic act of the cleansing from sin without which they could not be His disciples, and which He was imparting to them even as by His example He was making them penitent and obedient. If He approved John's baptism, and appointed baptism for His own community, and if He invested Mary's anointing of His body, a token of her devotion, with the meaning of a preparation for His burial (xii. 7), it is not at all incredible that the one act should bear the double sense, especially as it was by His example that the cleansing would be effected. The familiar phrase of Dr. Chalmers, ' the expulsive power of a new affection,' may serve as an illustration. Affection for Him prompted imitation of Him, and imitation meant liberation from their faults of purpose and spirit.

(ii) Whether Jesus did anticipate by a covert allusion, as in the words of *v.* 10, ' but not all,' the express announcement of Judas' betrayal, or not, He had been foreseeing the base act for some time, but at this moment He realized it with intense emotion (*v.* 21). His love had been striving against Judas' hate, and made its last appeal in the choice morsel offered to him (*v.* 26), a token understood only by the beloved disciple, the witness. His words, ' That thou doest, do quickly ' (*v.* 27), express His final judgment on the fixity of Judas' evil purpose : it is not approval, but acquiescence in his deed. Better that the deed should be done with the possibility of reaction after action, penitence after crime, than that the purpose, hindered or delayed, should breed more inward

corruption. Two other reasons for this acquiescence
may be suggested : *first*, Jesus recognized that it
was His Father's will that He should thus be betrayed ;
and *secondly*, as He enjoined, so He Himself practised
non-resistance to evil done to Himself. Only after
the spirit of Jesus had been relieved by the withdrawal of the traitor could the call to mutual love
be given. The two thoughts in the conversation
at the washing of the disciples' feet were resumed :
verses 34 and 35 continued the thought of *vv.* 12-19
when this hindrance had been removed, and xv. 1-8
enforced generally the dependence which Peter was
taught in *vv.* 6-10 ; the idea of cleansing is common
to xiii. 10 and xv. 2, 3.   In *v.* 6 there was surely an
allusion to Judas, who had just been cast forth.

(iii) The common witness of the disciples could
be borne, and their common work could be done, only
as the small company was kept in love, and so the
teaching about love already given was focussed in
the new commandment of such mutual service as
Jesus had given an example of in washing their feet ;
it was to secure such unity that He had loved them
to the uttermost (xiii. 34-35).   What discipleship involved was then set forth in the comparison of the
Vine and its branches : the demand was fruitfulness,
abundant service ; the condition of its fulfilment constant dependence on Him, in whom alone sufficiency
could be found ; the penalty of unfruitfulness severance from Him ; the reward of fidelity confidence
in prayer ; and its still greater result, the honour of
God's name (xv. 1-8).   In this respect the disciple
must be as the Master, who recognized the necessity
of His own death as the condition of His fruitfulness
(xii. 24).   The thought then reverted to the new
commandment.   As Jesus' enjoyment of God's love

depended on His obedience, so also the disciples' joy in His love would be fulfilled only as they fully obeyed. Of His love He had given the surest proof in the sacrifice He was to offer, and now He called them into the most intimate relation of friends, not servants, to whom His confidence would be fully given, and whom He had freely chosen to service, to boldness in prayer, to love (*vv.* 9-17). His love to His disciples and their love for one another suggested by contrast the hatred of the world, to which they would be exposed, even as He had been, because of the difference of His and their purpose and spirit from the world's. The servants would be persecuted as the Master had been, because of the world's unbelief in His mission. Judgment from which there could be no escape must fall, because hatred of Himself was hatred of His Father, and, as groundless, was entirely blameworthy (*vv.* 18-25).

(iv) The verses dealing with the Spirit's functions (*vv.* 26-27) break the continuity of the thought, and will afterwards be discussed along with the other references to the same subject. The thought of the world's hatred is developed in the following chapter in warnings concerning persecutions. These warnings were now given that when the persecutions did fall on the disciples, faith might not falter, because the Master had foreseen, and had before His departure foretold, all that would befall (xvi. 1-4). Although He had spoken of departure, the disciples had remained incurious as to His destination, and yet His words had saddened them ; and so He at once reassured them that separation would be brief (*vv.* 5, 6, 7*a*, and 16). This teaching caused perplexity, which Jesus at once sought to remove by the assurance that their sorrow in contrast to the world's joy would speedily

be changed to joy, even as a woman's in childbirth,
by His return to them in a permanent communion,
in which all perplexity would be removed, all prayer
answered, and joy would abound (*vv.* 17-24). Recognizing that His language *now* must be figurative,
He assured them that *then* in the new revelation of
God there would be no obscurity. That revelation
would inspire such confidence in prayer to God as
Father that they would not need the assurance of
His intercession, as they would have the certainty of
God's favour upon them, because of their relation of
devotion to Himself and recognition of His divine
mission both in His descent to earth and ascent to
heaven (*vv.* 25-28). This declaration evoked from
the disciples a confession of the intelligibility of His
speech, the adequacy of His knowledge, and the
certainty of His coming from God (*vv.* 29-30). How
far was the disciple company capable then and there
of such a confession ? Or how far is the witness
ante-dating the faith of a later time ? Some words
must have evoked the warning that all would forsake
Him and leave Him alone with the Father ; but
looking beyond the immediate present He assured
them that all He had said was spoken in order that
amid the trials awaiting them they might be ever
able to find in Him, the world's conqueror, their sure
peace (*vv.* 31-33).[1]

(v) The declaration of His victory over the world
was fittingly followed by an affirmation of His present
glorification in His death, and His future glorification
in His Resurrection. Yet while He was Himself
sustained by His assurance, He did not and could

---

[1] Credible as this sequence of thought appears, a doubt must
arise about *v.* 32, which sounds like an echo of Mark xiv. 27, a warning
spoken on the way to Gethsemane.

not forget that His glorification involved separation
from His disciples so dear to Him (xiii. 31*b*, 32, 33),
and thus He turned from further speech about Himself
to comfort them.[1] The remedy for distress of soul
is in faith in God and in Himself (xiv. 1).[2] His
destination was but another abode in God's home for
His children, and of this His silence offered assurance.
His purpose was to prepare an abode for them also,
and to return to welcome them there.[3] They were
not ignorant of the mode in which He would reach
that destination (namely, the path of obedience to
God's will which He was now treading). At once
Thomas showed that Jesus was taking too much for
granted in assuming their understanding ; and so He
assured them that in Himself as showing men God's
truth, and imparting to them God's life, and Himself
alone, could men be brought into such relation to God
as would secure them this destination, for so clearly
and fully was the Father revealed in Him that an
understanding of Him would bring such a knowledge
of God as would have the certainty of a vision. Philip's
request for a theophany evoked the declaration of
such an immanence of the Father in the Son, and such
a revelation in word and deed of the Father by the
Son, even in the earthly life, as made any theophany
superfluous (*vv.* 2-11). That revelation would not
be ended in the earthly life, for His return to the
Father would invest Him with such influence and
authority, that through His disciples even that revelation would be transcended, as they by prayer could

---

[1] The warning to Peter (*vv.* 36-38), as has already been shown, does
not belong to this context.

[2] We need not now pause to discuss all the alternatives of interpretation offered by the ambiguous form of πιστεύετε.

[3] The reference might be to the Second Advent, or to each disciple's
death.

command His greater resources to the honour of the
Father in the Son : but the prayer which could so
prevail must be a prayer of obedient love (*vv.* 12-15).[1]
The connexion between love and obedience is now
more fully developed. Obedience was evidence of
a love to Himself which would secure the Father's
love and the Son's, and a fuller manifestation (*v.* 21),
so that they would not be left desolate ; but would
not only know Him as the world could not, but would
find their life in Him the Living One, and in Him
God and man would share a common life (*vv.* 18-20).
In answer to Judas, Jesus showed that only obedient
love could receive such a revelation of, and communication from, God (*vv.* 22-24). His last bequest to His
disciples was the peace characteristic of Himself in
His dependence on and submission to God (*v.* 27 ; cf.
Matt. xi. 27-30). His last appeal was that they should
not sadden His departure by their fears and griefs,
but should in love to Himself try to share His gladness
in returning to His Father, to whom He confessed
His inferiority and subordination (*v.* 28). The very
conception of Sonship in the Godhead involves the
declaration in the words, ' the Father is greater than
I.' His last resolve was that, guiltless as He was
of any share in the world's sin, He would submit to
His Father's will in accepting death (*vv.* 30-31).

(vi) Probably as Jesus and the disciples stood
around the Table, He offered the prayer of xvii., in
form rather a soliloquy towards God than petition.
First, Jesus prayed that God would even in His death
honour Him as the bearer of eternal life to men, so
that He might honour God. As He had honoured
God by fulfilling His vocation on earth, so He desired

---

[1] These verses may belong to the saying about the Spirit, but may
also come between *vv.* 21 and 22, as Judas' question takes up the
thought of *v.* 19.

to return to His pre-existent honour.[1] His work had not been vain, as His divine mission had found a full recognition in the disciples whom the Father had given Him (not by an arbitrary election, but by the drawing of God's Spirit in their enlightening and quickening : cf. vi. 44 ; *vv.* 1-8). *Next,* for a time concentrating His solicitude on His disciples, Jesus, conscious of how great a loss to them His departure must prove, and to how great perils they would be exposed in a hostile world, committed them to the guidance and guardianship of His Father, so that their unity might be preserved, and they might individually, by the dominant influence of the revelation of truth and grace which He had already given them, be delivered from such a loss of faith as Judas had suffered. As they had a mission in the world, even as He had, and as He had devoted Himself to His calling in order that they might be so devoted, He did not desire their withdrawal from the hostile world in which that mission had to be discharged, but only their preservation from the power of evil dominant in that world by their entire devotion and submission to the revelation of God they had received in His teaching (*vv.* 9-19). *Lastly,* extending His interest beyond the circle of His disciples, Jesus prayed on behalf of the whole Christian community that its unity might so reproduce the divine unity as to convince the world of His divine mission. For He had called all its members so to share His relation to His Father, that through their development into this unity it might be made manifest in His divine mission that the Father's love to Him was extended

---

[1] For Paul the Resurrection was more than only a return to the pre-existent state. Cf. Phil. ii. 9-11. *The name above every name* is a higher exaltation than *the form of God* (v. 6).

also to them all. This common sharing in the Father's love, which for Him was eternal reality, He desired for them not only in their present experience, but also in their future destiny with Himself. To the righteous Father the plea was in closing offered that in an unbelieving world He had known God and revealed Him, and His disciples had acknowledged God's revelation in Him of a love which, first of all His, had through Him become theirs also (*vv.* 20-26).

It has been found impossible in this summary to reproduce all the minute details of the discourse, nor did that seem necessary, since we must recognize that we have no *verbatim* report before us, that Jesus' method of speech as the Synoptists reveal it was not of this fashion, and that the witness brooding over what He had heard for many years turned the thoughts over and over again in His mind, and so is responsible for the subtle distinctions and frequent repetitions. It is in the great leading thoughts that we seem to come into touch with the mind of Jesus Himself.

(*h*) It seems most fitting at this stage to consider the passages in which the Spirit's work is set forth, which are scattered throughout the farewell talk, and which, as the previous summary shows, break the context. While we know from the Synoptic Gospels that Jesus did promise the Spirit to the disciples (Matt. x. 20 ; Luke xxiv. 49 ; cf. Acts i. 4), and it was relying on His promise that they awaited the endowment with power from on high, yet the functions assigned to the Spirit in the Fourth Gospel are so different from the Pentecostal manifestations and so harmonious with the more inward type of experience which the Gospel leads us to assign to the witness, that we are led to raise the question whether the teaching about the Spirit found in the

Gospel reproduces Jesus' own words or reflects the witness's own experience, admitting that the experience presupposes the teaching. Even if Jesus did speak with some fulness on the work of the Spirit, it is probable that the report of His words would be coloured by the medium through which it has come to us. This does not lessen the value of the promise by the Master, but adds the confirmation of the fulfilment in the disciple. The teaching may be briefly stated.

(i) In view of His own approaching departure, Jesus by prayer secures for His followers in their great religious and moral need another Counsellor and Helper (ἄλλον παράκλητον); but, unlike Himself, He is to be invisible to the world, while a real inward presence with them; and in this Paraclete Christ Himself will be present with them (xiv. 16-20). The Spirit of Truth or the Holy Spirit—the truth in Jesus being the means, the holiness of the disciple being the end—will be sent in Christ's name, that is, in continuation of the revelation of God in Him; and this revelation will be carried on in two ways, the teaching of Jesus will be recalled, and all such fresh teaching as the position of the disciples may require will be added (v. 26). The revelation of Christ is to be carried on not only by the Spirit in the disciples, but to the world through the disciples. Their task will be, as those who have known the whole course of His ministry, to bear witness to Him; and their witness will be confirmed by the witness of the Spirit (xv. 26-27).

(ii) The condition of the Spirit's coming for His work both in the disciples and to the world is, however, Christ's own departure. The outward relation of the earthly ministry must cease before the inward relation by the Spirit can be begun. It is easier for us to understand this necessity on its subjective side as it concerns the disciples, since we can see how the one phase of experience must follow the other. But Jesus is represented as asserting the necessity on the objective side as it concerns Himself ; and this is not so obvious to us. What it surely means is that the saving act of His death and rising again has to be completed before the salvation in Him can in all its fulness be experienced. But this is not all : the work of the Spirit is conviction, which ' involves the conceptions of authoritative examination, of unquestionable proof, of decisive judgment, of punitive power.' [1] The three moral and religious realities in respect of which the Spirit determines the world's condition are *sin* exposing it, *righteousness* demanding it, and *judgment* executing it. This work, which is here presented objectively as by the Spirit of God in the course of human history, we conceive subjectively as the operation of conscience. The rejection of Christ is the evidence of the world's sin ; the ascension of Christ is the manifestation to the world of the righteousness God approves and rewards ; in the victory of Christ over Satan by His death and rising again the world's judgment is pronounced. The Spirit's work toward the world is to bring home to the human conscience all that Christ means for its salvation from sin, or condemnation in sin. As regards the disciples, however, the Spirit's work is simply to continue and complete the work Christ has begun, but has to leave unfinished because of their immaturity. There are truths He has not been able to teach them, and truths He has taught them which they have not been able as yet to understand. All that His life

[1] Westcott's *The Gospel of St. John*, p. 228.

means has not been disclosed. The Spirit's function will be not to add another revelation, but to bring out the full significance of the revelation already given. This is the dominant thought, but in one clause, ' He shall declare unto you the things that are to come,' there is a going back to the older view of the prophetic function of the Spirit, and that may be an editorial addition. In any case it interrupts the course of the argument. The whole passage (xvi. 7-15) subordinates the Spirit's function to the person and work of Christ. The representation of the Spirit's work, even if it be derived ultimately from Christ, is rooted in the witness's experience. For him his meditation on, as well as memory of, the words and works of Jesus was the work of the Spirit in him ; and so he was unaware of any incongruity between his reminiscences and reflexions, and saw no necessity for distinguishing the one from the other.

(iii) For one whose inner life was of this type, the Spirit of God within him recalling and interpreting the historical reality, an appropriate conception of God was that of Spirit (iv. 24). This is a reflexion arising naturally out of the context ; but it also expresses the distinctive religious conviction and attitude of the witness, his personal qualification for giving us the ' spiritual Gospel.'

(3) THE ARREST, THE TRIALS, AND THE CRUCIFIXION
(xviii., xix.)

(a) In dealing with this portion of the Fourth Gospel we find ourselves on ground common to it and the Synoptics, and are especially confronted with a discrepancy about the day and the hour of the death

of Jesus. (i) Many scholars give the preference to
the view of the Fourth Gospel, that the Lord's Supper
was held on the day prior to the Passover (xiii. 1,
πρὸ δὲ τῆς ἑορτῆς τοῦ πάσχα ; xviii. 28, ἵνα μὴ
μιανθῶσιν ἀλλὰ φάγωσιν τὸ πάσχα) ; and that Jesus
died at the time when the Passover Lamb was being
sacrificed. This seems to have been also Paul's view
(τὸ πάσχα ἡμῶν ἐτύθη Χριστός, 1 Cor. v. 7). It
likewise appears to be the primary tradition in the
Synoptics. According to Mark xiv. 2 (=Matt.
xxvi. 5) the plan of the Jewish rulers was to
take Jesus by craft, and to put Him to death, but
' not on the feast day, lest there be an uproar of
the people.' To the secondary tradition in the
Synoptics is due the identification of the Last
Supper with the Paschal meal ; and to this view
there are several objections. ' Work was going on
(Mark xv. 21 ; Luke xxiii. 56) and arms were being
carried (Mark xiv. 47), both of which, as well as a meeting of the Sanhedrin, were strictly prohibited on the
feast days. Some of the details preserved in the
Synoptic Gospels about what happened on the day
of the Crucifixion and the day after tally, in fact,
with the primary tradition, and are inconsistent
with the special identification of the Last Supper
and the Passover. . . . The Synoptic Gospels are
inconsistent with themselves, and the Fourth Gospel
intervenes in support of the better tradition.' [1]
Dr. Moffatt adds a very important general consideration : ' The recognition of this has important bearings
on the whole question of early Christian tradition,
for if, in one case, the typological significance of an
event is proved to be derived from the event, there is
a probability that in other cases an incident is not

[1] Moffatt's *Introduction*, p. 544.

to be dismissed as unhistorical simply because it lends itself to a religious application or moral.' [1] The evangelists did not invent history to illustrate doctrine, but actual history suggested doctrine to them. Dr. Moffatt also finds a confirmation of the Johannine view in Luke xxii. 15-16, where Jesus expresses His desire to eat the Passover with His disciples, and also confesses the disappointment of His hope. The writer has preferred to set forth the argument in favour of the view of the Fourth Gospel in the words of a scholar who cannot be suspected, as he himself might be, of a bias to overestimate the value of the Gospel historically. He would, however, add one suggestion. As the witness was in close touch with the ruling classes in Jerusalem, is it not possible that he had discovered a plot to arrest Jesus in the night before the Passover, for the arrangement with Judas cannot have been made so hastily, that he let Jesus know, and that he had put his house at the disposal of Jesus for a farewell meal a day earlier than Jesus had Himself hoped ? As he knew all the circumstances, he would retain a more accurate remembrance than the other disciples.

(ii) According to Mark xv. 25, the Crucifixion took place at the ' third hour,' that is, nine in the morning ; but, according to John xix. 14, at the ' sixth hour,' that is, noon, the trial was still going on. Not only has Mark the consistent notes of time (Jesus is brought to Pilate ' straightway in the morning ' (v. 1) ; the Crucifixion takes place at nine o'clock ; and there is darkness from noon till three o'clock (v. 33)) ; but the hour mentioned in the Fourth Gospel does not seem to allow time for all the events which followed before nightfall. Mark's notes of time might be

[1] *Idem*, pp. 544-545.

challenged on the ground that, as the slaughter of the Paschal lambs began at three o'clock, that hour would also be fixed as the time when the sacrifice of Christ was consummated ; but against this argument is the consideration that Mark places the Crucifixion on the day following the Paschal meal, as he identifies the Last Supper with it. The difficulty has been evaded in several ways. A corruption of the text in the Fourth Gospel has been assumed (an ancient solution) ; and John is supposed to have used a different reckoning of time, corresponding to the modern, from midnight to noon, but even Bishop Westcott,[1] who favours this explanation, admits that this mode was unusual, and Dr. Sanday[2] has given it up. Sir Wm. Ramsay appeals to the elasticity of the reckoning of time in the East ; but allowing for this to the utmost, could Mark's third hour follow John's sixth ? With Dr. Sanday we must leave the question open, only adding that while in this instance the Synoptic reckoning seems more probable than the Johannine, yet that does not justify a suspicion of general inaccuracy in the Fourth Gospel.

(b) While it is beyond the purpose of this volume to attempt a minute comparison of the Fourth Gospel with the Synoptics to produce a complete harmony of their contents, we may glance at the omissions and additions in the Fourth Gospel in so far as by these we may learn something of the character of the Gospel and the qualifications of the witness. Bishop Westcott gives a useful summary of these.[3] Without attempting to deal with them all, we may select the most important. (i) Why does the Fourth Gospel omit an account of the Agony in Gethsemane, and pass

---

[1] *The Gospel of St. John*, p. 282.   [2] *Outlines,* p. 147.
[3] *Op. cit.* pp. 249-250.

at once to an account of the Arrest (xviii. 1-3) ?   As
the witness is not ashamed of the humanity of Jesus,
but lays stress on it, we are not justified in saying
that the Agony was doctrinally offensive to him, and
so he passed it over.   It has already been suggested
that xii. 27 sounds like a faint echo of the Synoptic
tradition of the scene of which he was not an eye-
witness.   A reason may now be suggested for his
absence from the Garden at the Agony, and his presence
at the Arrest.   If he was, as has been argued hitherto,
an influential citizen of Jerusalem, connected by
some close relationship, as we shall conclude in discussing *v.* 15, with the high priest, if he was the host
at the Last Supper, and if he alone knew why Judas
had left the board, what more probable than that,
when Jesus went to Gethsemane, he went to the
high priest's house to discover what was being done,
and that he came to Gethsemane with or soon after
the band sent to arrest Jesus ?   Was the young man
mentioned in Mark xiv. 51-52 (generally supposed to
be that evangelist himself) sent by the witness as
host to watch and bring him word of what might
happen in his absence ?   He had not reached the
spot when Judas gave the traitor's kiss (Mark xiv.
44 ; Luke xxii. 48), and so he has not recorded it.
For had he witnessed it, he who was not inclined to
spare the traitor any of his infamy (cf. xii. 6) would
not have passed over the shameful act.   He had
arrived, however, when Jesus made the voluntary
surrender.   While the motive which he assigns in
v. 4 is in accord with his theological attitude, the
effect of Jesus' presence which he records in *v.* 6
need not be regarded as doctrine turned into history ;
for a similar power to overawe a crowd is ascribed
to Jesus by Luke (iv. 30) ; and there are many authentic

instances of such influence exercised by a strong
personality.[1] Jesus' appeal that His disciples should
be spared (*v.* 8) is quite consistent with His character,
even although the reason given for it in *v.* 9 again
betrays the standpoint of the witness or the evangelist.
If intended to indicate Jesus' motive it introduces
an artificiality which we may be sure had no place
in the ' inner life ' of Jesus. The mention of the
name Malchus (*v.* 10) is not a suspicious realistic touch,
but a proof of a more intimate knowledge of the
household of the high priest. The words in which
Jesus rebukes Peter repeat the image of the prayer
in Gethsemane, and so bear the marks of authenticity
(*v.* 11) ; and it is significant that the Fourth Gospel
offers us this close link with the Synoptics.

(ii) Why again does the Fourth Gospel alone record
the private examination before Annas or Caiaphas
(xviii. 12-14, 19-24) and omit any mention of the
public trial recorded by the Synoptists ? We may
here also follow the clue that has led us hitherto.
The witness alone was present as a privileged spectator
at the private examination, while the eleven who
had forsaken Jesus at His arrest and fled made no
attempt to rejoin Him for some time, even if it had been
possible for them to gain admission. When Peter
did venture back, it was only the influence of the
disciple known to the high priest, *i.e.* the witness,
which secured him admission to the outer court (*v.* 16),
not the inner chamber, when the examination was
going on. It is probable that as soon as the witness
learned the intentions of this private conclave regarding Jesus, the confirmation of which by the public

---

[1] The writer's own father, during a strike of his workpeople,
passed unscathed through a mob which had been threatening his
death.

assembly of the Sanhedrin seemed certain, he did not
wait any longer, but made his way to the palace of
Pilate to use what influence he had to convey to the
procurator the truth about the situation. Do not
Pilate's attitude and conversation indicate that he
knew more about Jesus than His accusers were
imparting ; and is not a reasonable explanation the
intervention in some form of the witness ? Can such
an intervention explain Pilate's wife's dream (Matt.
xxvii. 19) ? It must be admitted, however, that the
course of the events is not made quite clear in this
passage. It has been argued in chapter iv. that the
story of Peter's fall is an insertion by the redactor,
and that this has led to other displacements. Making
the changes there suggested, the order of events
becomes clear. Taken to the house of Annas for some
purpose of which we are now ignorant, and of which
the witness may not have had personal knowledge,
as he may not have had so free access to the house
of Annas as of Caiaphas (vv. 13-14), Jesus was sent
bound to Caiaphas, by whom the private examination
was conducted (v. 24). The witness, ' another disciple,'
secured Peter's admission to the court in the palace
of Caiaphas (vv. 15-16),[1] but he himself went with
Jesus into the house, and heard the examination
(vv. 19-23). It is a bare conjecture that Annas had
been more active in securing Jesus' arrest than Caiaphas, and that the captors would therefore go to
him for further directions ; but that to preserve the
appearance of legality, as soon as possible the prisoner
was sent to the high priest himself. A minor point
in this passage demands a brief notice. The description of Caiaphas as ' high priest that same year '

---

[1] The account of Peter's denials (vv. 17-18, 25-27) is not told by
the witness, who was meanwhile in the high priest's house.

(*v.* 13 ; see xi. 49-51) is no proof of ignorance of
Jewish customs, for the words do not represent the
high priesthood as an annual appointment, but
simply mean that for the witness the year of the
death of Jesus stood out from all other years he
remembered.

(iii) Peculiar to the Fourth Gospel is the account
of the first conference of the Jews with Pilate, and
Pilate's private examinations of Jesus (xviii. 28-38*a* ;
xix. 9-11). We may offer the same explanation as
before. At the conference and private examinations
the witness was present as one who had access to the
governor as he had to the high priest. Probably
the language of Jesus has been modified to some
extent by his characteristic phraseology, and his
distinctive view of truth and witness-bearing. The
conversation between Pilate and Jesus does not
appear at all improbable, even if we have not a
verbatim report of it. Pilate was anxious to discover
if Jesus cherished the political ambition charged
against Him. Jesus convinced Pilate that no danger
to the Roman dominion need be feared from Him.
In emphasizing the spirituality of His aims He impressed His judge as a harmless visionary. The
contemptuous, sceptical question, What is truth ?
suits both context and occasion. The theological
interest and standpoint of the witness or the evangelist
is betrayed in *v.* 32. Is it likely that Jesus in speaking
to Pilate would have described His enemies as the
Jews (cf. xiii. 33) ? The account of the Fourth
Gospel covers common ground with the Synoptics
as regards the offer of the release of a prisoner and
the choice of Barabbas rather than Jesus (xviii. 39-40
=Matt. xxvii. 15-17, 20-21=Luke xxiii. 16-21) ; but
differs from the Synoptics in placing a scourging, a

mocking by the soldiers, and the *Ecce Homo* (xix. 1-5) between this choice and the call for crucifixion (*v.* 6). It alone reports the charge of blasphemy made by the chief priests and officers (*v.* 7), when Pilate refused to condemn on the political accusation, and Pilate's attempt to probe the matter to the bottom in the second private interview with Jesus (*vv.* 9-11). Jesus' silence at the beginning of this second interview was a rebuke of the treatment of His previous declarations by Pilate (xviii. 38) ; but it was broken in compassion to remind Pilate, who claimed the authority of judge, that his position involved the obligation of righteous judgment. There is a touch of pity in the declaration that Caiaphas' sin was the more heinous because he was using the Roman judge as his tool, and, in the indirect indication that in consenting to be so used, Pilate himself could not remain guiltless. In all these and other additional details there is nothing that need excite our suspicion, as the witness had sources of information which the Synoptists lacked, and their accounts cannot be taken as the absolute standard of historical accuracy. In the final encounter of Pilate with the Jews (*vv.* 12-16), ending in his weak compliance, the Fourth Gospel is in substantial agreement with the Synoptics, although differing in details. The omission of the second mockery after the condemnation, the impressment of Simon, the lamentations of the women and Jesus' compassionate warning, the repentance of one of the robbers, is no proof of any tendency ; but rather confirms the assumption, which the writer believes all the evidence warrants, that the witness almost entirely confined himself to reporting what he had himself seen and heard ; and this is surely a safer clue to follow in explaining both omissions and

M

additions than the constant ascription of this or that tendency unless the pragmatism is quite obvious.

(c) Without noticing any further details of the narrative, we may concentrate our attention on the words from the Cross reported in this Gospel alone, the last charge, the cry of bodily need, the sigh of relief, or shout of triumph (xix. 26, 27, 28, 30). (i) That the mother of Jesus was committed to the care of the beloved disciple is not in itself improbable : because the brothers of Jesus had remained unbelieving, and the tragedy of the Cross was likely to harden them in unbelief ; because he alone had a home in Jerusalem, to which he could at once take her ; and because he, with his more intimate knowledge of the mind of Jesus, could help and comfort her more than any of the Twelve. If, whenever the charge was given, he led the mother away to his home (v. 27), his absence for a time from the Cross may explain his silence regarding one or two of the sayings recorded elsewhere : e.g. the cry of desolation may have been uttered during his absence, and we need not seek a theological explanation. (ii) Even if he reported the confession of thirst in opposition to the Docetism which he met with in his later years (cf. 1 John i. 1, iv. 2), yet such a cry is altogether probable, as a burning thirst was one of the worst tortures accompanying crucifixion. At first sight v. 28 has a suspicious appearance ; but Marcus Dods gives the true explanation : ' Jesus did not feel thirsty and proclaim it with the intention of fulfilling Scripture —which would be spurious fulfilment—but in His complaint and the response to it John sees a fulfilment of Psalm xix. 22.' [1] This argument from prophecy appears also in vv. 24, 36, and 37, but there is nothing

[1] *Expositor's Greek Testament*, i. p. 858.

in any of the details in which such fulfilment is found
to warrant the assumption that the prophecy made
the history. (iii) Probably the saying, ' It is finished '
(v. 30), is not so much a sigh of relief as a call of
triumph at an accomplished task ; but whatever be
its meaning there is nothing intrinsically improbable.
The witness records the phenomenon in v. 34 as an
evidence of the reality of the death, and gives no
hint whatever of the symbolical meaning which
seems to be assigned in 1 John v. 6, although the
reference there might be to the Baptism and the
Crucifixion. There is no warrant for Westcott's
supposition that this was a supernatural sign : ' As
He hung upon the Cross He was shewn openly to be
the source of a double cleansing and vivifying power,
which followed from His death and life.' [1] A physiological explanation has been offered : ' Dr. Stroud
(*Physical Cause of the Death of Christ*) advocates the
view that our Lord died from rupture of the heart,
and this accounts both for the speedy cessation of
life and for the effusion of blood and water. Previous
literature on the subject will be found in *Critici Sacri*,
and select passages in Burton's *Bampton Lec.*, 468-469.
Without physiological knowledge John records simply
what he saw, and if he had an eye to the Docetae as
Waterland (v. 190) supposes, yet his main purpose
was to certify the real death of Jesus. The symbolic
significance of the blood and water so abundantly
insisted on by the Fathers (see Burton's *B.L.*, 167-172
and Westcott's additional note) is not within John's
horizon.' [2] ' Whether medical evidence,' says Dr.
Strachan,[3] ' can really support the evidence for the

[1] *The Gospel of St. John*, p. 279.
[2] Dods in *The Expositor's Greek Testament*, pp. 859-860.
[3] *Op. cit.* pp. 221-222.

fact on which the Evangelist is reflecting is extremely
doubtful.' He offers two explanations, one taken
from Burkitt's *Gospel History and its Transmission*
(p. 233, note). 'According to 1 John v. 6-8, the
living personality has in it three elements, viz. spirit,
water, blood. From the " water " we are begotten ;
by the " blood " we are sustained ; and the " spirit "
or breath is the immaterial element that enters at birth
and leaves at death. The spirit quitted Jesus when
He died, leaving behind the water and the blood of
a human body, the existence of which was demonstrated
to the onlookers by the spear-thrust of the soldier.'
According to this interpretation, the evangelist is
again concerned to defend the crucifixion of Jesus
against the Docetic theory that only a phantom
Jesus was crucified. The other is that of Westcott
already noted which is pronounced ' entirely fanciful.'
If *v.* 35 were the witness's, we might charge him with
protesting too much ; but we need not regard him
as making an ostentatious display of his own trustworthiness since the verse has already been explained
as an editorial gloss.

(*d*) We must now consider more fully the significance of the statement in xviii. 15, that ' that disciple
was known unto the high priest.' Is it likely that
a Galilaean fisherman would have such acquaintance
with the high priest, and such access to his house ?
Even if, as has been conjectured, John the son of
Zebedee looked after the sale of his father's fish in
Jerusalem, and the high priest was a customer, is
the fishmonger more likely than the fisherman to have
had this privileged position ? During the ministry
of Jesus this John was with Jesus in Galilee, and if
he were identified with the unnamed disciple who
followed Jesus, he was with John the Baptist before

that ; and thus he could not have had so recent a connexion with the high priest's household as the description suggests. It has again and again been pointed out how familiar the witness was with the varied and varying states of opinion and sentiment in Jerusalem ; how well-informed he was of the designs of the priesthood against Jesus. In this discussion it has also been suggested as probable that he was an eye-witness of the private examination before Caiaphas, and also of the private interview of Jesus with Pilate. Here surely is cumulative evidence that he was a person of distinction and influence in Jerusalem. A confirmation of this view may be found in the testimony of Polycrates, bishop of Ephesus, in a letter written to Rome about 190 A.D. that ' John, too, who leaned on the Lord's breast, who had been a priest and worn the high priest's mitre ($\tau\grave{o}$ $\pi\acute{\epsilon}\tau a\lambda o\nu$), both witness ($\mu\acute{a}\rho\tau\nu\varsigma$) and teacher—he sleeps in Ephesus.' [1] Professor Burkitt's comment on this statement is, ' Here it is definitely implied that the Fourth Evangelist was a member of one of the high-priestly families.' [2] According to this writer, the conclusions we may draw about the evangelist are that (1) he had been a Jew of Jerusalem ; (2) he had been (as some evidence in his Gospel indicates—his views of the resurrection and angels) an adherent of the Sadducean party ; (3) he had been a priest, for he describes himself as known unto the high priest (xviii. 15), and Polycrates ascribes to him even high-priestly functions.[3] If it be objected that a disciple of such position would have been expressly mentioned in the Acts of the Apostles, we may recall what has

---

[1] Eusebius' *Ecclesiastical History*, bk. v. c. 24. See Eng. trans. pp. 242-243.

[2] *The Gospel History*, p. 251.   [3] *Op. cit.* pp. 247-251.

been before said about what appears to be the intentional concealment in the Synoptics in regard to the family in Bethany, and we may further observe that, if this Gospel is to be trusted, there were Judaean disciples, and yet in the history of the early Church Judaean disciples do not come into prominence. Was there a reason in some family connexion why the witness did not openly cast in his lot with the primitive community and hold a conspicuous position in it ? Did he hope by avoiding an open breach with the priesthood to continue the exercise of his influence on behalf of the disciples, as has been conjectured he did on behalf of the Master ? Can xii. 42-43 contain a personal confession ? Such questions are worth pondering.

(4) The Resurrection (xx.)

(a) It is not necessary here to discuss the general problem of the evidence of the Resurrection ; we are now concerned with the narrative in this chapter and the light it throws on the question of the authorship, character, and credibility of this Gospel.   (i) In the first division of the chapter (vv. 1-9) the visit of Peter and the other disciple to the tomb to verify Mary Magdalene's report that it was empty is recorded. Matthew xxviii. 1-10, Mark xvi. 1-8, and Luke xxiv. 1-12, also report the discovery of the empty tomb, not only by Mary Magdalene as here, but also by other women ; but in much greater detail than in the Fourth Gospel. Probably the witness mentions the discovery of Mary Magdalene only to introduce the visit to the tomb, in which he had a personal interest. Luke records the visit of Peter alone to the tomb (v. 12) and of no other disciple. The other

disciple's hesitation to enter, the greater boldness of
Peter, the beginning of faith in the Resurrection of
the Lord, the confession of the failure of the disciples
to understand the Scriptures, as they afterwards
understood them, as foretelling the victory over death,
these are all life-like touches which inspire our confidence. The use which Dr. Sanday [1] makes of one
feature of the narrative—the association of the witness
with Peter—as a reason for assigning the Gospel to
John, the son of Zebedee will be discussed fully in
the last chapter.

(ii) Dr. Strachan assigns vv. 2-10 to the redactor.
' Certain reasons for assigning vv. 2-10 to R may be
indicated : (1) Mary speaks as though she had not
come alone. Note that in v. 13 Mary speaks in the
first person singular. (2) In v. 11 Mary stands where
she was in v. 1. (3) What Mary sees in v. 12 is
different from what Peter and John see in vv. 6, 7.
(4) Is it likely that Mary would communicate with
the disciples twice in v. 2 and again with a definite
commission in v. 17. In general it may be said that
R tends to lay more stress on the empty grave than
the Johannine writer. As in xi. 38-44 and in xx.
24-29, he probably has in mind those who could not
rest upon the spiritual experience of others as proof
of the resurrection, but must have some assurance
that the stern and ghastly facts of death and the
grave were surmounted by Jesus.' [2] The reasons
given above seem to the writer altogether unconvincing. The change from the singular (v. 1) to the plural
(v. 2) and back again to the singular (v. 11) is surely
explicable if Mary was joined by other women (Mark
xvi. 1), and then was alone on returning to the tomb

[1] *The Criticism of the Fourth Gospel*, p. 107.
[2] *Op. cit.* p. 223, note.

(*v.* 11).   It need not be assumed that she was standing at the same spot at the times referred to in *v.* 1 and *v.* 11 without any intervening departure and return. Might not the difference of her mental condition account for the difference in what she saw and heard ? Why should she not first announce with dread the empty tomb and then with joy the Risen Lord ?   If the witness is the disciple referred to in *v.* 2, and yet he is not responsible for the narrative in *vv.* 2-10, the redactor seeks to represent as from him a story he got elsewhere.   That Peter and he saw only the empty grave and not the Risen Lord is surely a confirmation of the trustworthiness of the record.   More ground might be found for doubting the authenticity of the narrative in *vv.* 11-18, if it is not the empty grave which is the stumbling-block to our belief. Of *vv.* 2-10 there is a partial support in Luke xxiv. 12, unless that too is to be suspected.

(*b*) In the second division of the chapter (*vv.* 11-18) the appearance to Mary Magdalene is reported. (i) Matthew (xxviii. 9) records an appearance to the women returning from the empty tomb without any special mention of Mary ; but she may have lingered behind at the tomb, or returned to it, and the loving and pitiful Lord, after the word of cheer to the others, may have appeared to comfort her sad heart, as He did to Peter (Luke xxiv. 34 ; 1 Cor. xv. 5) and James (1 Cor. xv. 7).   That this appearance is not mentioned by Paul in 1 Cor. xv. may be explained in two ways : he may not have heard of it ; or he may have omitted the account, as of the appearance to the two disciples on the way to Emmaus (Luke xxiv. 13-35), because he confined his list to those who, as apostles, were commissioned to be witnesses of the Resurrection. Features in the record which may be noted are, the

failure of Mary to recognize Jesus, as of the two on the
way to Emmaus, indicating a change in His appearance,
the recognition by the tones of the voice here, as there
by the movement in the breaking of bread, the prohibi-
tion of her loving touch, signifying that the former
earthly relationship was ended, and a higher heavenly
fellowship was to take its place. The reason why the
witness recorded an appearance which was not shared
by him as were the other two which he reports, may lie
in the interest for him of some of these details. The
declaration of *v.* 17 may have specially appealed to
him as continuing previous declarations which he had
reported (xiii. 33 ; xiv. 2-28 ; xvi. 28). (ii) The
interpretation given by Dr. Strachan of the words
of Jesus in *v.* 17 demands close scrutiny : ' Mary's
mission is to tell the disciples that *Jesus is ascended
to the Father*,' he asserts ; but is it so ? It is the present
tense, 'Αναβάινω, which is used, and Moffatt [1] renders
by the continuous present, ' I am ascending.' It
is a process still continuing during the appearances.
At least this seems as possible a view as what Dr.
Strachan next advances : ' The Ascension, in the
view of the Evangelist, takes place some time between
the events of *vv.* 11-18 and *vv.* 19-29. This is clearly
implied in *vv.* 17-18. As a basis for faith the Resurrection is incomplete without the Ascension. Not
direct from the empty grave, but from the " glory "
with the Father, Jesus returns to reform the tie
that had been broken, and to bestow the Holy
Spirit.' [2] The base is too narrow for such a structure
of speculation.

(*c*) The third division of the chapter (*vv.* 19-23)
contains several features of special interest. (i) In
v. 19 there is an indication that it was necessary to

---

[1] *A New Translation*, p. 143.   [2] *Op. cit.* p. 226.

observe secrecy as to the dwelling and gathering-place
of the disciples. A similar caution is the probable
explanation of the arrangements made to secure both
the guest-chamber for the Last Supper (Mark xiv.
13-14) and the ass for the Entry (xi. 2-4). If in all
three cases the witness himself was the unnamed
friend and helper, may we not here find the clue to
the silence of the Synoptic tradition regarding so
influential a disciple ? He risked much in rendering
the services he did, owing to the greater enmity which
would probably have been turned against him by the
priesthood. His ability to befriend may have depended
on his not coming too much out into the open ; and
gratitude as well as prudence enjoined silence regarding
him.

(ii) Although we must not press the details too
hard, yet the narrative suggests that Jesus appeared
in the midst of the disciples suddenly, the doors
remaining closed. This is one with other indications
that the risen body of Jesus was not subject to ordinary
physical conditions ; and yet it could at will apparently
be made accessible to the sense both of sight (v. 20)
and of touch (v. 27) with proof of identity. Another
token is offered in the corresponding passage in Luke
(xxiv. 41-43). Jesus eats before them. To meet the
objection to so complete a materialisation of the
resurrection body Bernard [1] offers the following argument : ' This ' (proof of identity), he says, ' with a
view to the persons dealt with, could be best done
by taking food. If there be a resurrection of the
body, there is no reason why such a body should not
have the power of taking food without depending
on it. Once cross the boundary of the present sphere
of existence and we are in a realm where we can no

---

[1] Hastings' *Bible Dictionary*, iv. p. 234.

longer say, " this is impossible." Indeed it was the
reality and identity of the risen body which the Lord
had to insist on : the difference was evident, and
spoke for itself.' While admitting the possibility here
mentioned, several considerations forbid confidence.
First of all, why does the witness, who *ex hypothesi*
was present, mention only the proofs of sight, sound,
and touch ? *Secondly*, the intention of the passage
in Luke is ostentatiously apologetic. It is difficult
to believe that the risen body had *flesh and bones*,
even if it had power of manifestation to the various
senses of sight, sound, and touch in proof of its reality.
Thirdly, while in the Appendix to this Gospel it is
not expressly stated that Jesus Himself took food,
He is represented as dividing bread and fish among
His disciples (xxi. 12, 13). This trait may belong
to a late tradition, and we are at least justified in
suspending judgment as to its trustworthiness.

(iii) There is nothing to excite suspicion in the
words ascribed to the Risen Lord. We may admit
the possibility that some of the sayings ' summed up
the Church's confession of faith conceived as uttered
by the lips of the Risen One.' [1] The action and words
in *v.* 22 are to be regarded as symbolically prophetic,
as in Luke (xxiv. 49) a promise is given, which was
fulfilled at Pentecost, unless the witness anticipated
events in his record, as has been conjectured in other
instances. Verse 23 recalls the logion in Matthew
(xvi. 19) ; and for such a declaration the context in
the Fourth Gospel seems more appropriate than that
in the First.

(iv) The possibility of an anticipation of events
by the witness is affirmed as an actuality by Dr.
Strachan : ' Whatever difficulties it may occasion in

---

[1] Bruce in *The Expositor's Greek Testament*, i. 340.

our minds, there is no doubt that the Evangelist here
describes what for him is equivalent to Pentecost
(Acts ii. 1). Luke separates by a definite interval
of time the Ascension and Pentecost (Acts i. 8). In
the thought of the Fourth Evangelist, the gift of
the Holy Spirit is the climax of the Resurrection.
The Cross, Resurrection, Ascension, Pentecost are
all moments in one great event (cf. xii. 31-32). They
are, as it were, telescoped.'[1] The writer is convinced
that we do wrong to the witness in assuming that he
is wilfully departing from the common tradition of
the Church, without trying to discover some explanation which preserves the historical value of his
narrative. If Pentecost was the culmination of a
process of spiritual recovery in the Christian Church
from the loss of faith and hope, due to the death of
Christ, as the certainty that Christ had risen was more
and more realized, is it not reasonable to suppose
that the process may have begun in the Upper Room
with the leaders of the Christian community, and
from them may have spread, until the whole community was reached ? At least this must be recognized
as a possibility.

(*d*) The fourth division (*vv.* 24-29) presents four
points for notice : (i) The representation of the
disposition of Thomas here is quite consistent with
the two other references in this Gospel. He expects
death as the result of the return to Bethany, and yet
he is prepared to run the risk (xi. 16). He cannot
understand how the disciples can be expected to know
the way when they know not whither the Master
is going (xiv. 5). He was despondent, and yet devoted ;
and his absence may have been due to the utter
overthrow of his faith by his grief.

[1] *Op. cit.* p. 228.

(ii) The presence of the disciples in Jerusalem after ' eight days ' demands explanation, in view of the command given to depart into Galilee (Matt. xxviii. 10 ; Mark xvi. 7). Was it the unbelief of the disciples that kept them from instant obedience, and so necessitated the appearance of Jesus on the first occasion to awaken their faith ? Could His loving heart no longer delay in giving them the comfort they needed ? Did they consider the first appearance in Jerusalem as cancelling the command to go to meet Him in Galilee ? We can but ask these questions. At least the narrative does not contain any rebuke or reproach for disobedience.

(iii) The exclamation of Thomas (v. 28) when convinced of the reality of the Risen Lord, whether by touch or by the words uttered, is difficult to accept. ' His faith returns,' says Dr. Dods, ' with a rebound and utters itself in a confession on which the Gospel culminates. The words are not a mere exclamation of surprise.' [1] But even if Thomas fully shared Peter's confession of Jesus as the Messiah, the Son of the Living God, this faith falls short of the recognition of divinity such as is here affirmed. This confession goes beyond the doctrine of the early apostolic preaching. It shows a lack of historic sense when Dr. Dods adds in confirmation, ' In Pliny's letter to Trajan (112 A.D.) he describes the Christians as singing hymns to Christ as God,' for a considerable doctrinal development had intervened. Here again the witness anticipates the development, and puts on the lips of Thomas the doctrine which his Gospel aims at proving.

(iv) Jesus' answer gives no indication that so advanced a confession had been made, proving a faith

---

[1] *The Expositor's Greek Testament,* i. 866.

beyond that any other disciple had reached ; for
surely words of commendation must in that case have
been deserved and bestowed, and not the censures
that Thomas' faith resting on sensible evidence was
inferior to the faith resulting from moral insight and
spiritual discernment regarding His person and work.
The witness, however, does teach a physical and not
only a spiritual resurrection, for he records the empty
grave, and the sensible proofs of some kind of continuity between the buried and the risen body ; and
of both he claims to write as an eye-witness. If
we accept him as at all trustworthy, we must in
forming our conception of the resurrection reckon
with the fact.

(v) This whole passage Dr. Strachan also assigns
to the redactor : ' Not without some hesitation
vv. 24-29 are here assigned to *R*. The following
reasons may be given. It must not, however, be
supposed that by assigning the passage to *R* the
devotional value and psychological truth of it are
in any way minimised. (1) The Gospel naturally
reaches its finale at *vv.* 22-23. (2) The occurrence
described in *vv.* 24-29 is not in the writer's mind in
vv. 22-23 ; otherwise it would mean that Thomas
was excluded from the gift of the Spirit. (3) The
spurious ending to Mark (xvi. 19-20) is evidently
based, at least partially, on John xx. The writer
agrees in assigning the first appearance to Mary ;
then he mentions the Emmaus incident, then an appearance to the eleven. There is no room here for a final
appearance to Thomas.' [1] Not one of these reasons
seems to the writer at all convincing. Verse 29 seems
a very fitting close. If *vv.* 22 and 23 do not describe
Pentecost, the second reason does not hold at all.

[1] *Op. cit.* p. 230, note.

Should the omission in a spurious document cast discredit on a narrative included in an authentic one ? The witness seems to have had a personal interest in Thomas (cf. xi. 16 ; xiv. 5).

(e) A formal conclusion is given to the Gospel by vv. 30-31, which indicate that there has been a selection of the material which has been presented, and that the selection has been made with a distinct doctrinal and practical purpose. It may be due to the witness himself, but on the whole it is more probable that it belongs to the evangelist. But, as has been shown in the course of the previous discussion, the additions or omissions in comparison with the Synoptic records are not to be explained exclusively from this point of view. The witness's own personal presence or absence must be recognized as an explanation of the inclusion or exclusion of some incidents : as for the most part the Gospel is the testimony of an eye-witness who had a distinctive personal interest in what he saw and heard, remembered, reflected on, and then reported. This consideration justifies the conclusion that vv. 30-31 express the evangelist's rather than the witness's intentions. The attempt has been made in the previous discussion to show, wherever it is to be traced, the influence of theology on history, and yet to prove that we must not so exaggerate this influence as on account of it to regard the history as unauthentic. It is in opposition to any such tendency that the writer has had occasion in a number of instances to express his dissent from the opinion of Dr. Strachan. His is one of the most recent works upon the subject, and is likely to reach a very much wider circle of readers than most books on such a subject do. It is a work of very great learning and ability. It represents the critical position with

moderation of tone and evident desire to assert the
spiritual and moral value of the Gospel ; and yet the
impression it leaves is that theology so determines
the choice and the presentation of the material that
any historical character must be denied to the Gospel.
The frequent references to the book show, not de-
preciation, but appreciation of its value. Its main
conclusion the writer's studies have led him most
strenuously to contest, with what success or failure
he must leave it to the readers of this volume to
judge.

(*f*) In the record of the Resurrection there emerge
a few matters of theological interest. (i) Attention
must first of all be called to the evidence regarding
the resurrection-body, personal identity as regards
voice and gesture, transcendence of the physical
limitations of the material organism, capacity to give
at will sensible tokens of reality, and, less certainly
proved, a gradual transition from the natural to the
spiritual body. So far as we allow ourselves to be
guided by the record we cannot assert a merely spiritual
resurrection, an unwarranted use of the word *resurrection*, if only a survival of the body by the soul is
intended : but must assert a physical resurrection
in the sense not of material identity of the buried
and the raised body, but at least of some continuity
in the organ of the spirit corresponding to its un-
changed identity. Paul's statement (1. Cor xv. 50-53)
suggests what the process may have been, although
it may not have been effected ' in a moment, in the
twinkling of an eye.' The subject is not one for
dogmatic affirmations, but still less for dogmatic
negations. Jesus' restraint of Mary's signs of affection
indicates a cessation of the former earthly relationship
of bodily contact, and a transition to the abiding

heavenly relationship of spiritual communion (xx. 13-17).

(ii) While Jesus is represented as distinguishing His relation to the Father from that of the disciples (else He had said ' our '), it is significant that He speaks of the Father as ' my God.' The confession ascribed to Thomas, ' My Lord and my God,' seems to go beyond Jesus' own claim. His teaching had not prepared any of the disciples for such a declaration.

(iii) It has already been argued that we need not regard the witness as antedating Pentecost in his account of the meeting in the Upper Room. It is not impossible that the symbolic prophecy did include (v. 23) a separation of the apostolic company to the function of representing Christ in declaring to men God's forgiveness or judgment ; but we must beware of reading into the words later ecclesiastical pretensions. The possession of the Spirit is the condition for the exercise of this or any other spiritual function in the Church of Christ, and only as the Church is conscious of the gift can it without any arrogance exercise the authority so entrusted. In keeping with this insistence on the spiritual qualifications is Jesus' rebuke of Thomas' desire for an outward sign, though that was granted, in His exaltation of the faith which requires no proofs of sense over the faith that rests on such evidence (v. 29). If the signs of v. 30 are miracles, then the evangelist was mistaken in his method of proof, and inconsistent with the witness's record of what Jesus Himself desired as an acceptable faith.

N

IX

THE JESUS CHRIST OF THE FOURTH GOSPEL

(a) THIS is not intended to be a systematic treatment
of the theology of the Fourth Gospel, as this volume
is concerned with the composition, authorship, and
trustworthiness of the Gospel. All that will be
attempted is a discussion of the characteristics of Jesus
Christ as He is presented in the Gospel. Most of the
teaching will come into view, as here Christ is all,
and in all. In this inquiry we shall also be finding
an answer to the two questions, What did the witness
know of the historical Jesus ? What was his experience of the living Christ ? An adequate Christology
must take account of both. The secondary elements,
due to the evangelist and to the redactor, must be
left out of account, as we want to know not what
was taught in later theological developments, but
what conception was formed by one whose knowledge
was rooted in history and grew in experience. (i) Jesus
appears filled with holy enthusiasm, as one conscious
of fulfilling a vocation, probably that of the suffering
Servant of Yahveh (Isaiah liii.) ; and confident that
He can restore the religion which priests and scribes
are destroying ; can give men such a knowledge of
God as will enable them to worship aright, and can
satisfy man's deepest need. Assured of open communion with God, He exercises a searching insight
into the moral and spiritual condition of men ; and,
guided by that insight, He chooses the followers who

194

can receive His message, demands an entire inward change in the self-satisfied Pharisee, and distrusts the belief which His miracles excite in the multitude. Superior to, and confessed such by His forerunner, He acts independently of human advice in constant and entire dependence on God's guidance. In doing His works of healing, even on the Sabbath, He is but imitating the constant activity of His Father, of whom He has perfect knowledge, by whom He is perfectly loved, and to whom He ever renders perfect obedience.

(ii) As His mission from God is certified by His forerunner, His works, His own self-knowledge, and even the Holy Scriptures, unbelief in Him must be due to an evil choice, the issue of an evil nature. He offers Himself as the full satisfaction of man's need of God, as the Bread from Heaven, the Living Water, and the Light of the World. To those who believe in Him He imparts abounding spiritual power, liberation from the bondage of sin, and deliverance from the grasp of death. Not only will He discharge the function of the Judge of men hereafter, but He is already exercising a present judgment. Resistance of Him reveals a nature from beneath, descent not from Abraham, but from Satan, and so involves final condemnation. Salvation, the possession of the eternal life, is possible only through faith in Him, who is the Door, and this faith God gives. His relation to believers is that of the Good Shepherd watching over, caring for, and even giving His life on behalf of His sheep, and of the Vine to the branches, the source of all their sufficiency for service. Intimacy with Him, dependence on Him, love for Him, and obedience to Him, are the marks of His own sheep, His living branches.

(iii) He anticipates His own death voluntarily

endured, not only as a token of His devotion to His own sheep, and as a proof of His obedience to His Father, but as the necessary condition of His universal spiritual effectiveness among men. He must be lifted up on the Cross from the Grave, to Heaven, to secure eternal life for all men, and to win all to Himself. Not in His words and works only, but also in His sacrifice is He the sustenance of the soul of man. His death is His glorification, but also the world's judgment because of its unbelief, and Satan's over-throw.

(iv) His death leads to His further glorification in His return to the Father ; His recovery of the dignity that He had before the world was, due to the eternal love of the Father for Him. His consciousness of pre-existence is rooted in and springs from His sense of oneness with God, and gains certainty the more His claim is challenged. While His return to God in His death means a temporary separation from His disciples, He anticipates a speedy reunion, not under the former earthly conditions, but in their inward experience of His presence and power in the other Paraclete. The Spirit of Truth, the Holy Spirit, will recall His teaching to them, unfold the meaning hitherto hidden from them, lead them into all truth only to make Him, and God the Father in Him, the better known, and the more real to them, in a relation which will inspire confidence in prayer, and sufficiency for service, and will issue in a human unity of believers corresponding to the divine unity of the Father and the Son.

(v) As He lives, so do those who are joined to Him by faith live the eternal life : as He goes to Heaven, so He prepares an abode for them in Heaven. While on earth they will be persecuted as He has been ;

but as He has conquered the world, so, while they are still in the world, God will keep them from the evil, and amid its trials and sorrows they will share the peace which He has won, and by their witness to Him they will secure the world's acknowledgment of His relation to and mission from God.

(b) It has been impossible to reproduce every detail of the self-witness of Jesus as given in the witness's reminiscences, coloured by his reflexions. All that has been attempted is to convey the total impression of the person and work of Christ as presented by the witness. His reminiscences have often been so coloured by his reflexions that they cannot be distinguished ; at other times reminiscences and reflexions do seem distinguishable. We cannot with confidence separate in all cases these reflexions of the witness from the evangelist's comments, although some instances where we can have already been noted. In what follows an effort is made to show how the presentation has been affected by these secondary elements. (i) It is probable that the disclosures of Messiahship by Jesus, and the confessions of it by others, are antedated. The faith of a later period of the ministry is thrown back to its beginnings.

(ii) The supernaturalness of the knowledge of Jesus is exaggerated, so as to give the impression that omniscience is ascribed to Him. And yet the record itself demands only an insight and foresight corresponding to the moral conscience and religious consciousness of Jesus, which we may call supernatural if we will, but must not treat as a solitary miracle. There is a tendency, too, as in the account of the raising of Lazarus, to emphasize the supernatural power unduly. As regards both, however, the corrective evidence is given, that Jesus did not primarily

base His claims on these signs, but on the relation
to God as Father of which He was conscious, and the
function from God on behalf of man with which He
knew Himself entrusted.

(iii) In several passages the apologetic interest
leads to ascribing to Jesus what cannot be otherwise
described than an artificial pose. For instance, in
vi. 5-6 Jesus' questioning of Philip is represented as
simply a test of him, and not allowed to be a proof
of any anxiety in His own mind ; in xi. 42 a most
unlikely reason for Jesus' thanksgiving for answered
prayer is suggested ; in xii. 30 as unlikely an explanation of the voice is given. These occur in
passages which may belong to the redactor, and not
the witness or the evangelist ; but in a passage which
comes from the witness, the same tendency appears.
In xiv. 29 and elsewhere in the farewell discourse,
Jesus is reported as assigning a motive for His
warnings which seems remote from His dominating
purpose.

(iv) It is probable that there is a disproportion in
the presentation of the teaching of Jesus. While
it is not unlikely that to meet vehement opposition
Jesus was driven to unusual self-assertion, and that
he was also led, as a relief from this strain, to intimate
self-disclosure to a chosen few ; yet is He likely to
have spoken quite so much about His relation to God
as the Gospel reports ? The claim to be perfectly
related as Son to God as Father we may confidently
accept as the self-witness of Jesus ; but, as the names
Father and Son themselves indicate, He makes no
claim to equality as His opponents alleged (v. 18c),
but He acknowledges subordination (xiv. 28), dependence, and obedience.

(v) In the passage in which the evangelist or the

witness develops his own doctrine of the relation of Father and Son (v. 19-29, except *v.* 24), what is confessed first of all is absolute dependence, complete knowledge, and so entire resemblance. If equal honour is claimed for the Son, it is because He can quicken the dead even as does the Father, and the Father hath given Him all judgment. Whether we interpret these functions spiritually or eschatologically, the statement does not go beyond what Jesus in the one case claimed for Himself, and in the other foretold and the Church believed, about Him. And these functions, too, are exercised in dependence on the Father. If we interpret the statements eschatologically, that seems a reason for assigning the passage to the evangelist rather than the witness. The statement about a resurrection of the wicked to judgment has no other parallel in the New Testament, and points to a later development. If the passage, which reads like an expansion of the meaning of the Supper (vi. 51c, 52-57) is not due to the redactor, to whom we may trace most of the chapter, but is a reminiscence or a reflexion of the witness, it does no more than affirm man's absolute dependence by faith on Jesus, especially in His sacrifice, for his spiritual sustenance and satisfaction. Here already theology and religious experience blend together. Still more evident is the personal valuation in the passage (iii. 16-21), in which eternal life is declared to depend on faith in the Son as the gift of God's love ; a contrast is presented between God's intention of salvation for all, and the result of condemnation, due to unbelief, on many ; and the explanation of faith or unbelief is sought in attraction to or aversion from truth and goodness. The severity of the witness's judgment on unbelief is the obverse of the intensity of his personal devotion to Christ, and the absolute value which his personal experience of Christ led him to ascribe.

(vi) While we are justified in distinguishing theological explanations from experimental reflexions, and assigning less significance for to-day to the one than to the other, the witness would make no such psychological analysis, but would ascribe the total reproduction in his consciousness of the historical reality of Jesus to the instruction and the illumination of the Spirit whom Christ promised, and whom the community of believers was confident of having received *not by measure* (iii. 34). An inference as to the inner life of Jesus from his own consciousness of Spirit-filled life would be drawn by him, if the A.V. rendering, ' God giveth not the Spirit by measure unto Him,' were correct. He would represent the relation between the Father and the Son as mediated by the Spirit, the germs of a trinitarian doctrine. Such a doctrine would be far removed from metaphysical abstractions, and would keep close to experimental reality ; but the interpretation cannot be pressed. Apart from it, however, there is abundant evidence for this characteristic of the Gospel. The passages dealing with the Holy Spirit, scattered throughout the farewell discourse, are as significant for the light which they throw on the witness's experience as on the teaching of Jesus ; for here surely reminiscence is developed by reflexion, and the promise expands in the fulfilment. The writer must express his conviction that many scholars have been led astray in their interpretation of the Gospel by seeking in it speculative metaphysics instead of the reality of the experience of Christ Himself, and of Christians. The reflexions no less than the reminiscences disclose the historical reality of the Christ as He lived on earth, and as He no less

lived in one of His disciples. The Johannine interpretation is no less valuable for Christian thought
than the Pauline ; and both are experimental, and
not merely or mainly speculative.

(vii) The Prologue which was intended to commend
the Gospel to contemporary thinkers has been a
stumbling-block to many modern scholars, as they
have tended to interpret the Gospel through it. It
must, however, be regarded as a porch to the temple
of somewhat discordant style. In so far as there is
accord, it is because the Gospel has modified the
borrowed philosophy and not been to any great
extent determined thereby in either its contents or
its method. We must not, however, dismiss it as
of no importance. If Jesus has the absolute value
for the moral and religious life of man for his relation
to God which the Gospel assigns to Him, the metaphysical significance as Word or Logos which the
Prologue assigns is not in contradiction to, but in
consistency with, that valuation. He who reveals
God to man, and redeems man to God, must stand
in a relation to God which demands some such solution.
Theology must find a place for Him in the eternal
nature of God corresponding to His place in the
temporal history of man. To fix His place in the
one or the other it must not neglect but give attention
to the presentation in all its aspects in the Fourth
Gospel of the historical personality of the Incarnate
Word of God.

X

THE AUTHORSHIP OF THE GOSPEL

In the previous discussion of the composition of the Gospel, three sources have been indicated : (1) The Prologue and some Comments in the Gospel have been assigned to the evangelist who was a disciple of the witness, and stood in a similar relation to him as did Mark to Peter. (2) The Appendix and some insertions in the Gospel, having affinity with the Synoptic tradition, have been ascribed to the redactor, whose motives have already been adequately discussed. (3) When these two sources have been separated, there remain the reflexions and the reminiscences of the witness, whom the writer identifies with ' the disciple whom Jesus loved,' but not with John the son of Zebedee. In justifying his conclusion, the writer will not only more fully develop his argument for it, the data of which have already been indicated, but will take fuller account of contrary opinions than has hitherto been done. First of all, the personality of the beloved disciple must be briefly described.

(1) ' The Disciple whom Jesus loved '

(i) He was a Judaean, and probably even a young, rich, and influential citizen of Jerusalem, closely connected with the family of the high priest, if not himself a priest, and an adherent of the Sadducean party. His dominating interest is in the progress of Jesus' self-testimony and the growing unbelief and hate provoked by it in the Jewish leaders and teachers ; and he again and again shows an intimate knowledge of the conflicting currents of opinion among the people and the secret machinations of the hostile party. If, as has been maintained, the sixth chapter is an insertion by the redactor, he had no interest in the Galilaean ministry as Peter had not in the Judaean. Probably he provided both the ass for the triumphal entry and the guest-chamber for the Last Supper, and was also able, owing to his rank and wealth, to offer some protection and hospitality to the company of disciples. A constant companion of Jesus at the beginning of His ministry, but not one of the Twelve in Galilee, he renewed his contact with Jesus only at the visits to Jerusalem. He enjoyed, however, a peculiar intimacy, as did others outside of the apostolic circle, such as the family in Bethany.

(ii) As an appreciative and sympathetic hearer, it is probable that Jesus laid bare to him His inner life as He could not even to the Twelve. The difference of the Synoptic and the Johannine reports is, if not entirely, yet to a large extent, explicable by two circumstances. In His public utterances in Judaea Jesus was urging His claim on the Jewish people through its representatives, the priests and scribes, and He exercised less reserve than in Galilee, for the peril of a mistaken Messianic movement was absent ; and He gave more advanced teaching doctrinally, as He was addressing Himself to a learned class and not the unlearned masses. In His private conversations He was confiding His secrets to a companion who could understand. Owing probably to family influences the witness did not confess Jesus openly, but kept in the background in the early Church, so that he is not mentioned in the Acts of the Apostles and the Pauline letters. But even in his later years he did not reveal his name, and probably it was out of respect to his wishes that the disciple who reported what he had taught did not betray his secret, but gave as a tribute of his affection the description of him as ' the disciple whom Jesus loved,' if that description is not itself a humble self-confession, and a grateful adoration of Christ on the part of the witness. The same silence regarding the family of Bethany is found in the Synoptics, and probably for the same reason. This account is in all particulars based on the data discussed in detail in the preceding pages ; and it offers a consistent, and to the writer at least a convincing, picture. It has served him so well as a clue in the labyrinth of the Gospel that he desires to share with others the help it has brought to him.

(2) The External Evidence

It may be objected that the tradition that John the son of Zebedee was the author bars the way to this account. (i) Dr. Drummond, after an exhaustive and searching discussion of the external evidence for the traditional belief, concludes that ' the attestation is perfectly unanimous in favour of the early date of the Gospel, for in this even the dubious Alogi are supporters of the Catholic view '; but that ' the second point, that the Apostle John was the author, can hardly claim the same degree of confidence.' He admits, however, that ' if the Gospel was issued soon after the apostle's death by some writer who chose to keep himself unknown, and on the ground either of its own title or of internal evidence was pronounced to be John's, and generally accepted as such, the phenomena of the existing attestation would be sufficiently explained ; in other words, we have no testimony which affords us any security against an error of this kind.' [1] It is true that he holds such an error not probable ; but he leaves us with a door not altogether closed, but at least ajar. The authorship by John the son of Zebedee is not a certainty, but only a probability. Dr. Sanday states his aim as follows : ' I propose to defend the traditional view, or (as an alternative) something so near to the traditional view that it will count as the same thing.' [2] The alternative referred to is Delff's theory that the evangelist was not the apostle, the son of Zebedee, but the disciple whom Papias mentions separately and describes as the presbyter. While he inclines still to the traditional view, he admits the possibility of this theory. He too, therefore, allows that we are not shut up to the authorship of John the son of Zebedee.

(ii) His statement of the alternative view to which he refers deserves quotation : ' The hypothesis which ascribes the Gospel to John the Presbyter has taken different forms, some more and some less favourable to the historical truth and authority of the Gospel. From a conservative point of view the most attractive form of the hypothesis is that put forward by the late Dr. Hugo Delff of Husum in Hanover, to some extent adopted and defended by Bousset in his commentary on the Apocalypse, and by one or two others. The theory is that the beloved disciple was not of the number of the Twelve, but that he was a native of Jerusalem, of a priestly family of wealth and standing. We are expressly told that he was " known

---

[1] *An Inquiry into the Character and Authorship of the Fourth Gospel*, pp. 348-349.
[2] *The Criticism of the Fourth Gospel*, p. 3.

to " the high priest (John xviii. 15) ; and he seems
to have had special information as to what went on
at meetings of the Sanhedrin (vii. 45-52 ; xi. 47-53 ;
xii. 10 ff.). These facts are further connected with
the statement by Polycrates, Bishop of Ephesus,
towards the end of the second century, that the John
who lay upon the breast of the Lord " became, or
acted as, priest, and wore the frontlet of gold " (Eus.
H.E. v. 24, 2 ff.). This John is claimed as one of
the "great lights" of the Churches of Asia.' [1] In view
of the account given of the composition of the Gospel
in this volume, the writer is not prepared without
reserve to assent to the identification of the beloved
disciple with John the presbyter ; for it seems to him
as probable (if not more probable) that the evangelist
was John the presbyter, and that the redactor, who
did not distinguish the evangelist and the witness,
was led by the name to assume that the Gospel came
from John the son of Zebedee. To this we must
return.

(iii) In support of the view that John the presbyter
may be distinguished from the apostle John the son
of Zebedee, the statement of Papias may be quoted :
' If then, any one came, who had been a follower of
the elders, I questioned him in regard to the words
of the elders—what Andrew or what Peter said, or
what was said by Philip, or by Thomas, or by James,
or by John, or by Matthew, or by any other of the
disciples of the Lord, and what things Ariston, and
the presbyter John, the disciples of the Lord, say.' [2]
Eusebius draws the obvious inference that two persons,
bearing the same name John, are here referred to,

---

[1] *The Criticism of the Fourth Gospel,* p. 17.
[2] Quoted by Eusebius, *H.E.* iii. c. 39, Eng. trans. by McGiffert,
p. 171.

although, in accordance with the fixed tradition of
his time, he identifies the first with the evangelist,
and conjectures that the second may have seen the
Revelation, if it was not the first. He also refers
in confirmation of his view to the statement that
there were two tombs in Ephesus, each of which is
called John's (attested also by Dionysius of Alexandria
and Jerome).   Even if we lay stress on the difference
of tense, εἶπεν and λέγουσιν, it is surely too subtle
an explanation that not two persons but two methods
of reporting are referred to here, the one written,
the other oral.

(iv) The early martyrdom of John the son of
Zebedee is accepted by a number of scholars as a
probable fact on the evidence of the De Boor Frag-
ment,[1] an epitome of the Chronicle of Philip of Side
(about 430 A.D.), and the ' Papias tradition ' as given
by Georgius Monachus or Hamartolos, a writer of
the ninth century. (a) The first statement runs thus :
' Papias in his second book says that John the Divine
and James his brother were slain by Jews.' [2] The
second is fuller : ' Papias, the bishop of Hierapolis,
having become an eye-witness of this one, declares
in the second book of the Oracles of the Lord that
John was put to death by the Jews, having evidently
fulfilled with his brother the prediction of Christ
concerning him, and his own confession and assent
in regard to this.' [3]

(b) The first statement does not necessarily involve
that the martyrdoms of the two brothers were con-
temporaneous. The author of the second in the same
paragraph excludes that inference in the words :

[1] It is so called from its discoverer, and was first published in
Texte und Untersuchungen, v. 2, p. 170, in 1888.
[2] Quoted by Burkitt, *The Gospel History*, p. 252.
[3] Quoted by Drummond, *An Inquiry*, p. 228.

' After Domitian, Narva reigned one year ; and he, having recalled John from the island, dismissed him to live in Ephesus.' This prolongs John's life till A.D. 96-98 at least. It is of course possible that here there is a confusion of John the son of Zebedee and John the elder. Burkitt states that ' the statement is historically of importance, not because these late chroniclers had independent knowledge of the facts, but because they base their information on Papias.' [1] But Papias may have been misunderstood. For there is evidence that Georgius misunderstood Origen when he appealed to him ' as saying in his commentary on Matthew that " John hath suffered martyrdom," ' for when we go to the original we find that Origen saw in the exile to Patmos and what was suffered there a sufficient fulfilment of Christ's words regarding the cup that he and his brother should drink.[2]

(c) To the trustworthiness of this statement Dr. Sanday objects on the one hand ' that this statement appears in no other early authority, and especially that no hint of it is found in Eusebius,' and on the other that ' the common tradition of the Church did not ascribe to St. John a violent death.' [3] A suspense of judgment seems here necessary. If the son of Zebedee was his brother's companion in an early martyrdom, and the fact was not generally known, one can understand that another John, living in Ephesus, and also bearing witness as a disciple of Jesus, might be confused with him. But even if this early martyrdom is not proved, the identity of the son of Zebedee with the John of Ephesus is not established.

[1] *Op. cit.* p. 252.
[2] *The Fourth Gospel in the Light of Modern Scholarship*, by A. T. Robertson in *Constructive Quarterly*, v. pp. 675-676.
[3] *Op. cit.* p. 107.

After the end of Acts we have certain historical evidence only about Peter.

(v) Although Dr. Drummond and Dr. Sanday admit the possibility of the confusion of the author of the Fourth Gospel, especially if his name were known to be John, with the son of Zebedee, yet some writers on the external evidence assume that this possibility need not be taken into account.

(a) In the article by Dr. A. T. Robertson, referred to in a previous page, a number of unproved assumptions are made, to which attention may be called. Authorship by John the son of Zebedee is not necessary for the historical trustworthiness of the Gospel, nor for its genuineness, nor for its sufficiently early date for us to treat it as a first-hand literary source of the life of Jesus. If it was written, as is here maintained, by a disciple who was present wherever the presence of the beloved disciple is asserted, who had better sources of information about Jewish conditions than a Galilaean fisherman was likely to have, who says so little (if anything) about the Galilaean ministry, and so much about the Judaean because he was, not a Galilaean but a Judaean, and because he was with Jesus in the one, and not the other, the value of the Gospel is in all respects enhanced. To insist on the authorship of the son of Zebedee is not to strengthen, but rather to weaken the position. What in this argument is being defended is not the character of the Gospel, but the infallibility of a tradition in the Church.

(b) What the real issue is should at the outset be made clear. We need not concern ourselves at all for our present purpose with all the external evidence for the use of the Gospel as Holy Scripture, or for the authorship by a John. What is the conclusive

evidence that this John was the son of Zebedee ?
The ascription of it by later writers to John the apostle
is not conclusive evidence.   Is the author so described
as to exclude any other possibility ?   If Irenaeus
claims as a disciple of Polycarp to have heard ' the
accounts which he gave of his intercourse with John
and others who had seen the Lord,' and describes the
author of the Gospel as the disciple of the Lord who
also lay on his breast (*Ad. Haer.* iii. 1), that statement
is quite consistent with the authorship which is here
assigned.   Even if Polycarp told Irenaeus all he knew
about John, what proof is there that he stated anything
to fix the identity of his teacher with the son of
Zebedee ?   Even if he made such a statement it
might have been an assumption on his part.   For
it has already been shown that the writer of the
Gospel desired for some reason to conceal his identity.
The tradition that John lived to an old age in Ephesus
has no relevance as it may refer to the other John,
and not the apostle as was simply assumed in later
times.

(*c*) The objections Dr. Robertson offers to the
alternative which even Dr. Sanday is prepared to
entertain are adequately met in the view here advocated.   The Synoptic record is incomplete as
regards the Judaean ministry : and as it is almost
entirely confined to the Galilaean, there was no
occasion to mention a Judaean disciple.   Why the
beloved disciple is not mentioned in Acts, and yet
appears in the Fourth Gospel as a companion of Peter,
has already been explained.   On the one hand he did
not wish openly to identify himself with the Galilaean
circle of disciples ; and yet on the other hand he acted
as host and helper to them so far as his desire for
concealment allowed.   John the son of Zebedee appears

in public with Peter in the record in Acts ; the beloved
disciple goes in private with Peter to the sepulchre
(John xx. 3).   If he was the host at the Last Supper,
and got admission for Peter to the high priest's house,
he may have continued Peter's host.   If he did not
go from the Upper Room to Gethsemane, but to the
high priest's house to find out what was being plotted
as has been suggested, and sent as his messenger to
Gethsemane John Mark, with whom the young man
who fled naked is usually identified, a personal link
is found with Peter.   The exhaustive discussion about
the use of the term disciple which follows in a later
section will sustain the conclusion that, as the witness
had no occasion to mention the sons of Zebedee, his
silence regarding them is no proof that he had any
feeling against them, if he was not one of them.   The
mention of them in the Appendix has already been
fully dealt with in a previous chapter.   The defence
of the Gospel by Dr. Robertson against other conclusions of modern scholarship need not for our present
purpose be further considered.

(vi) It is clear that what is of crucial importance
in respect of the external evidence is the testimony
of Irenaeus, and to that a series of articles by the Rev.
Dr. H. A. A. Kennedy has been recently devoted.[1]
For our purpose it is necessary to discover whether
he establishes the identity assumed in the tradition.

(a) The close connexion of Irenaeus with Polycarp
need not be doubted, and Dr. Kennedy's proof of the
fact may be accepted.   The statement of Irenaeus
already quoted in a previous page does not give any
decisive evidence of the identity of the John ' who
had seen the Lord,' and who had been one of ' the

---

[1] *Irenaeus and the Fourth Gospel*, in *Expository Times*, xxix.
pp. 103 ff., 168 ff., 235 ff., 312 ff.

eye-witnesses of the Word of Life.' This last phrase
makes it clear that he is referring to the author of
the Fourth Gospel; but proves nothing as to his
identity with John the son of Zebedee. Irenaeus
may also have been acquainted with Papias, whom
he describes as ' the hearer of John, and a companion
of Polycarp,' and includes in ' the elders who saw
John, the disciple of the Lord.' [1] But these statements
again tell us nothing as to who this John was. If
he gives no indication that he understood Papias
as claiming an acquaintance with two Johns, as the
passage from Papias already discussed most obviously
means, that proves nothing for or against the truth
of that statement. With other Church leaders who
had listened to the disciples of the apostles he may
also have had contact, as also Pothinus may have
been for him a link with a much older generation;
but these conjectures prove nothing about the
identity of the author of the Gospel.

(b) What Eusebius tells us about Polycarp in
connexion with the controversy about the Passover
does not make his testimony any more decisive of the
question before us. ' What he had always observed
with John, the disciple of our Lord and the other
apostles, with whom he had associated,' [2] for we are
not entitled to assume that the word apostle was
restricted to the Twelve, even if it was indeed used
by Polycarp himself, whatever meaning Eusebius
himself put upon it. Have we a right to impose the
narrower sense of the term even when Irenaeus uses
it in his statement that ' Polycarp was not only
instructed by apostles, and conversed with many
who had seen Christ, but was also, by apostles in

[1] *Ad. Haer.* v. c. 33 [34], Eng. trans. ii. pp. 146-147.
[2] *H.E.* v. 24. 16, Eng. trans. p. 244.

Asia, appointed bishop of the Church in Smyrna.' [1]
Even if Irenaeus restricted the title to the Twelve,
may not Polycarp have used the term in the sense
we find in the New Testament, a sense applicable
to the beloved disciple as his person is represented
in this volume ? Is there any kind of evidence
whatever that Polycarp came into contact with any
of the Twelve, except the son of Zebedee, if the John
he mentioned is indeed he ? To assume that the
mention of apostles justifies the identification of this
John with the son of Zebedee is going far beyond
the evidence.

(c) The same consideration applies to Irenaeus'
further statement about the elders, ' those who were
conversant in Asia with John, the disciple of the
Lord [affirming] that John conveyed to them that
information. Some of them, moreover, saw not only
John, but the other apostles also, and heard the
very same account of them, and bear testimony as
to the [validity of] the statement.' [2] The statement
regarding our Lord's age, for which so imposing an
array of witnesses is claimed, happens to be altogether
incorrect. Does this warrant our treating Irenaeus
in all other appeals he makes to tradition as entirely
trustworthy ? The remark of Harvey quoted in the
translation as a footnote deserves reproduction :
' The reader may here perceive the unsatisfactory
character of tradition where a mere fact is concerned.
From reasonings founded upon the evangelical history,
as well as from a preponderance of external testimony,
it is most certain that our Lord's ministry extended
but little over three years : yet here Irenaeus states
that it included more than ten years, and appeals

---

[1] *Ad. Haer.* iii. 3-4, Eng. trans. i. pp. 262-263.
[2] *Idem,* ii. 22. 5, Eng. trans. i. p. 201.

to a tradition derived, as he says, from those who
had conversed with one apostle.' If, as Dr. Kennedy
concludes, Irenaeus is here altogether dependent on
Papias, his claim to a connection with elders who
saw John and the other apostles loses its force.
Dr. Kennedy himself recognizes that in regard to the
elders, to whom Irenaeus has various references, ' it
must be noted, however, that he quotes nothing from
this source which has a bearing on John of Asia in
his connexion with the Fourth Gospel.' Polycarp
and Papias alone remain as links with this John,
Polycarp certainly, Papias probably.

(d) John is usually described as *the disciple of the
Lord*. This is pressed by Dr. Kennedy into a proof
that he was an apostle by this conjecture : ' Apparently the term " disciple of the Lord " was a
favourite second-century description of members of
the Twelve, for Papias in the famous paragraph
examined above applies the phrase to them. The
same terminology is found in other writers of the
period. It need scarcely be pointed out that this
reflects the usage of the four Gospels, in which ἀπό-
στολος as compared with μαθητής is extremely rare
(only once each in Mark and Matthew).' [1] Because an
apostle can be called a disciple, does it follow that
every disciple must be an apostle, or even every
apostle one of the Twelve ? If the appeal is to be
to the New Testament, does not the New Testament
use both terms in a wider sense ? That second-century
writers assumed that this John was one of the Twelve
does not prove that he was unless evidence can be
produced that they were warranted in this assumption.
The second link in the chain of argument forged by

[1] *Irenaeus and the Fourth Gospel*, in *Expository Times*, xxix.
p. 236.

Dr. Kennedy that Irenaeus reckoned this John among the apostles is not a bit strong. The instance just given of Irenaeus' appeal to apostolic authority should make us pause in claiming infallibility for him, or even ordinary care, especially where, as in controversy, he had to make out as strong a case as he could against the heretics. That the Valentinians appealed to John, the disciple of the Lord, the third link of argument for reasons already given is no proof that this John was the son of Zebedee. The reference to the Ephesian residence of the author of the Fourth Gospel, already mentioned, contributes nothing decisive, nor does the statement of Polycrates, already referred to.

(e) Dr. Kennedy's conclusion from this statement must, however, be explicitly disproved. 'This "great luminary" of Asia is by two influential witnesses placed in the innermost circle of Jesus' disciples, which all readers of the Synoptics in the second century knew to consist of Peter, James, and John.'[1] In the first place it will be shown in the next section that the Synoptic representation of the disciples around Jesus, on which second-century opinion depended, was incomplete, as applying to the ministry in Galilee mainly. Secondly, natural as was the inference that the beloved disciple was John the son of Zebedee, it cannot now, in view of the considerations there advanced, be accepted as conclusive evidence.

(f) As the statement of Papias regarding the two Johns, and the statement regarding the early martyrdom of John have already been discussed, Dr. Kennedy's references to them may be passed over; but his defence of the accuracy of Irenaeus demands fuller notice. It is not necessary to assume that ' Irenaeus was a credulous, unreliable man, of singularly in-

[1] *Op. cit.* p. 238.

accurate memory,' [1] to admit the possibility that
he assumed the John, of whom Polycarp spoke to
him, to be the son of Zebedee without evidence from
Polycarp to that effect. If the witness of the Fourth
Gospel chose to conceal his identity under the de-
scriptive phrase, ' the disciple whom Jesus loved,'
or the evangelist was instructed so to conceal it, when
the Gospel was published, are we not entitled to
assume the possibility that he was very reticent
regarding his past life even to his followers in Ephesus,
and that Polycarp had nothing definite to tell Irenaeus ?
Is every scholar to-day familiar with the biography
of his teacher, even when *Who's Who* exists to lighten
the inquiry ?   That he spoke as an eye-witness would
give such assurance that inquiry would not be made,
and identity would be assumed.   Further, is it not
to transfer our methods of historical inquiry to an
age which knew them not to suppose that Irenaeus
questioned Polycarp, or Polycarp John, regarding
his identity with the son of Zebedee ?   The fact that
Irenaeus ' stood in the main current of the life of the
Church ' [2] does not warrant our assuming that he had
other sources of information which did supply the
lack in what Polycarp told him about John.   What
might have been borne to him along these main
currents would have been such traditions as we have
already examined, and been led to regard as inconclusive evidence.   If, as has been argued, the redactor
added the Appendix with a view to identifying the
beloved disciple with the son of Zebedee, and felt
warranted only in doing it in a tentative way, it is
this sort of conjecture that might have come to
Irenaeus.   That a usually accurate and careful scholar
may sometimes make a mistake is a fact that must

[1] *Op. cit.* p. 312.   [2] *Idem,* p. 313.

be admitted. Two instances have come under the
writer's own personal observation, a confusion between
the two Sabatiers in the one case, and the two
Schmiedels in the other. We may admit Irenaeus'
general trustworthiness without insisting on his infallibility. If the external evidence alone is to be
regarded, there seems to be no doubt to the writer
that, as Dr. Kennedy holds, the evidence of Irenaeus
must be preferred to any other. But in his view the
internal evidence has a claim greater than the external ;
and he has no doubt that this conclusively proves
that John the son of Zebedee was not the author of
the Fourth Gospel. The doubt that the external
evidence leaves allows us to turn from it to the
internal.

(vii) The external evidence, however, may throw
some light on the composition of the Gospel. (i) A
conjecture has already been offered on a previous
page, that this John of Ephesus may have been
the evangelist, not the witness, and that the name
may have led the redactor to identify the beloved
disciple (the witness) with John the son of Zebedee.
In Chapter I. Dr. Stanton has been quoted as holding
the view that it was unlikely that the witness himself
would assimilate the teaching of Philo as the evangelist
may have done. To this subject we may now return.
While Dr. Stanton accepts the external evidence
about the residence and activity of John the son of
Zebedee ' in Asia in his latter years ' [1]—a conclusion
which the writer has for the reasons given not accepted
—and regards him as the witness behind the Gospel,
he does not follow the tradition as to the authorship
of the Fourth Gospel. ' The authorship of the Fourth
Gospel by the Apostle John, though included in the

[1] *The Gospels as Historical Documents*, iii. p. 279.

second-century tradition about him, cannot be regarded
as therefore established. For the writing of the
Gospel would be a work performed in private, of
which few could have direct knowledge, while from
the first there would be a general disposition to magnify
the apostle's connexion with the book if he had, or
could be supposed to have had, any at all. For these
reasons also the statement by a later hand at xxi. 24,
in regard to the contents of the preceding work cannot
be taken as decisive, at least to the full extent of what
it declares.' [1] While he thinks it improbable that a
man of the mature age of the apostle John could have
undergone so marked a development, as the Gospel
shows, he thinks a much younger man, who as a boy
had sometimes seen and heard Jesus, would answer
the claim of the Gospel that the evangelist was one
' who had " seen the glory " of the incarnate Son of
God,' [2] and would also be capable of so great a change
of mental outlook. He denies that the expressions
used can refer to spiritual vision. ' One can, however,
understand,' he writes, ' that the claim in question
might be made by a youth or boy, younger by some
years than the Apostle John even if the latter was
the youngest of the Twelve, but who could remember
having sometimes himself seen and heard Jesus, and
who had derived a sense of knowledge, which was
at least almost immediate, of the Divine revelation
made in the Lord, by intimate association with His
personal disciples very soon after His departure.' ' It
fits in with this view of the writer that the acquaintance with Palestinian localities shown in the Fourth
Gospel suggests that the writer had at some time lived
there. He may have gone to Asia before John did,
and at all events probably he did so at an age when

[1] *Op. cit.* pp. 279-280.　　[2] *Idem*, p. 281.

his mind was more supple, and it is more natural to attribute to him the capacity for producing the Fourth Gospel in the last decade of the first century, earlier than which it is difficult to place its composition.'[1] If this be a description of the evangelist which can command our assent, and if we may identify him with John the elder, surely it becomes much more intelligible how by honest inference without any deliberate invention the authorship of the Gospel came to be assigned to John the son of Zebedee. In the considerations advanced by Dr. Stanton against the identification of the evangelist with John the son of Zebedee, we may find confirmation of the distinction made on other grounds between the evangelist and the witness. The witness was not so assimilated to the Ephesian environment as was the evangelist ; he was probably dead before the end of the second century.

(ii) This identification of the evangelist with John the elder offers us the advantage that we do not set tradition aside altogether, and can see why it went astray where it did. Dr. Bacon, however, is entirely opposed to it : ' As regards John the Elder and his supposed connexion with the author of the " Johannine " Epistles and Gospel, we emphatically reject the idea that he has any connexion of the kind.' He pronounces *irrational* any attempt ' which seeks to connect the Fourth Gospel with him,' on the ground that ' the traditions actually traceable to him are the very opposite pole from the doctrine of these writings. They represent a crude millenarianism of the most pronounced type, utterly irreconcilable with the highly spiritualized eschatology.'[2] To meet this

[1] *Op. cit.* pp. 281-282.
[2] *The Fourth Gospel in Research and Debate*, pp. 452-453.

objection the distinction which on other grounds we
have been led to make between the evangelist and the
witness comes to our aid. The older eschatology is
found in the passage v. 19-29, which is more probably
to be assigned to the evangelist; and one of the
differences in the theology of the Epistles and the
Gospel as a whole is that the First Epistle does give
a place to the common apostolic hope of a speedy
outward appearance of the Lord, as the Gospel except
in a few additions does not. If we recall the fluctua-
tions in Paul's eschatology we need not deny the
possibility that the Elder's ' crude millenarianism '
may have been modified, but not suppressed, by the
more ' spiritualized eschatology ' of the witness. The
probability, or at least the possibility of the identification cannot be regarded as altogether excluded
by Dr. Bacon's summary rejection of it ; critical
scholars can sometimes be too dogmatic.

(iii) Regarding the redactor, as to whose activity
the writer finds himself in general agreement with
Dr. Bacon, his words may be quoted in this connexion :
' For the author of the Appendix and recaster of the
Gospel, who adjusted the Asiatic or Pauline tradition
to the Petrine of Syria and Rome, we have no de-
signation save the title Redactor. This editor (R)
gave to the Gospel its authoritative currency by his
not unnatural identification of " the disciple whom
Jesus loved " with the son of Zebedee, and by ascribing
to him the writing and testimony. R was a contemporary of Papias, Polycarp, and Justin, probably a
Roman. He doubtless believed with Papias and
Justin that " John the Apostle " had been " in the
Spirit " in the island of Patmos, whence he had
addressed letters to the churches of Asia. What more
natural than to attribute to John the anonymous

Gospel also ? ' [1] If the Gospel was not anonymous, but came from another John, such ascription would be still more natural. Having considered what is relevant as regards external evidence to the present purpose, attention may now be fixed on the internal evidence as it bears on the identity of ' the disciple whom Jesus loved.'

(3) The Internal Evidence

(i) It will be necessary first of all to examine the grounds on which the authorship of John the son of Zebedee is maintained.

(a) The writer can go with Bishop Westcott [2] entirely in the first three steps of his argument, i.e. that the author was a Jew, a Jew of Palestine, and an eye-witness (although of course referring to the witness and possibly also the evangelist) ; but the next step that he was an apostle rests on the assumption that the Twelve alone stood in so intimate relations to Jesus as the author of the Fourth Gospel appears to stand, whereas it has been shown in the previous discussion that the Twelve formed Jesus' constant companions in Galilee, but that in Judaea there were other disciples who came in close contact with Him also. ' It is not on the face of it certain,' says Dr. Sanday,[3] ' that " the disciple whom Jesus loved " must have been one of the Twelve.' But it is only by assuming this as certain that Bishop Westcott is justified by the method of exclusion in taking his last step to John as the author.

(a) In order to show that this assumption is invalid, it is worth while examining in detail the passages in

---

[1] Op. cit. p. 454.   [2] St. John, Introduction.
[3] The Criticism of the Fourth Gospel, p. 98.

the Fourth Gospel in which mention is made of the disciples, so as to prove that the reference need not be to the Galilaean disciples in all cases, and that in some cases it may be to Judaean disciples only. In John i. 35-37 the disciples of John the Baptist are spoken of, and they transfer their allegiance to Jesus, the names mentioned being Andrew, Simon Peter, Philip, Nathanael ; the unnamed follower (*v.* 40) was probably *the beloved disciple*. Probably all these were with Jesus at Cana on the first visit (ii. 2, 11, 12). If, as is probable, iii. 22-30 follows ii. 12, the Galilaean disciples may have left Capernaum with Him, and come to Judaea when He for a time exercised a ministry of repentance like the Baptist's. But when He went up to Jerusalem for the feast (ii. 13) no disciples are mentioned. The disciples referred to in *vv.* 17, 22 may have been Judaeans, including the beloved disciple. In Judaea a number of disciples had been won, and baptized not by Jesus Himself, but by His disciples (iv. 2). On the journey through Samaria He is accompanied by disciples, but as no names are mentioned, there is no evidence that any of the Twelve were included (iv. 8, 27, 31, 33) ; but it is likely that the beloved disciple was one, as much of the story reads like that of an eye-witness. Does not *v.* 45 even suggest that the Galilaeans were with Jesus only at the feasts, although not as disciples in close associa-tion ? There is no mention of disciples in the account of the second visit to Cana. It was probably sub-sequent to it, when Jesus began His public ministry in Galilee, that the company of Twelve was formed. Till then disciples had come and gone. When the Fourth Gospel deals with the work in Galilee in vi., not only is there frequent mention of the disciples (*vv.* 3, 8, 12, 16, 22, 24, 60, 61, 66), but some of the

Twelve are mentioned by name, *e.g.* Philip (*vv.* 5, 7), Andrew (*v.* 8), Simon Peter (*v.* 68), Judas (*v.* 71). Reason has been shown in a previous chapter why this account is not to be assigned to the witness. In the story in v. which should follow vi. no disciples are mentioned. Probably Jesus went up alone, and desired to attract no attention, although His intention was frustrated by the garrulity or treachery of the man He had cured (*v.* 13). The taunt in vii. 3 refers to Judaean disciples. The disciples mentioned in viii. 31 have just been won to Jesus' cause. The question in ix. 2 was put more probably by Judaean than Galilaean disciples, as it is probable that the blind beggar was a familiar sight to the questioners, and may even have been a subject of dispute among them. If so, the question was not casual, but intended to settle a difference of opinion. There is nothing to determine whether the disciples mentioned in xi. included all the Twelve. Thomas alone is mentioned by name (*v.* 16). Had Peter been present, would he not have been the spokesman ? Further, had he been present, the silence of Mark regarding the miracle is more difficult to explain. The beloved disciple was probably not with Jesus beyond Jordan, but remained in Jerusalem, and got at second hand the story in xi. 1-16. His presence at Bethany is more probable. That the Twelve as well as other disciples were present in Jerusalem in the week of the Passion is certain ; but that does not prove that they were with Jesus at previous feasts, and the beloved disciple may have been with Him when the Twelve were not. The evidence does not support the assumption that the Twelve were always with Jesus, but rather the conclusion that they were not usually with Him in Jerusalem until the last week, and that there Judaean

disciples (including the beloved disciple) took their
places. This conclusion would afford a satisfactory
explanation of the silence of the Synoptics regarding
the visits to Jerusalem, and the silence of the Fourth
Gospel regarding the public ministry in Galilee.

(β) This conclusion is confirmed by an examination
of the references to any of the disciples by name.
Simon Peter is mentioned in i. 40, 41, 42, 44, and in
vi. 68. He is very frequently mentioned in xiii.,
xviii., xx., and xxi. He is not once alluded to in the
record of the visits to Jerusalem prior to the last.
Ready and even hasty as he was for speech and action
at all times, is it at all likely that, if he had been present
at all, on any of the occasions, there would not have
been some reason for referring to him ? This does
seem a case in which silence warrants our inferring
absence. Of the other apostles Andrew is mentioned
in i. 40, 44 ; vi. 8 ; and xii. 22. Philip is associated
with him on each of these occasions (i. 43-44, 45, 46,
48 ; vi. 5, 7 ; xii. 21, 22) ; and he is also reported as
having asked Jesus to show the Father (xiv. 8-9).
Nathanael was a friend of Philip's, and was brought
to Jesus by him (i. 45, 49). He is not again mentioned
until we reach the Appendix to the Gospel (xxi. 2).
Thomas is first mentioned as proposing the return
to Judaea if need be to die with Jesus (xi. 16). It is
he who confesses his ignorance of Jesus' goal and the
way to it (xiv. 5). He is solitary among the Twelve
by his absence from the Upper Room when Jesus
appeared to the disciples, and his disbelief of the
testimony of others (xx. 24) ; but on the second appearance his unbelief was turned to faith (vv. 26-29).
In the Appendix also his name is given (xxi. 2). The
Appendix reports names mentioned in the Gospel,
and adds ' the sons of Zebedee' (v. 2), regarding whom

the Gospel is altogether silent, and ' two other of his
disciples.' The reasons for this have already been
discussed in dealing with the Appendix. Of Judas
Iscariot necessarily frequent mention is made, but
always in connexion with the betrayal (vi. 71 ; xii. 4 ;
xiii. 2, 26, 30 ; xviii. 2, 5). Another Judas, not
Iscariot, is once mentioned as asking a question in
the Upper Room (xiv. 22). Neither James of Alphaeus
nor Matthew is referred to in this Gospel. The dis-
tribution of the names in the Gospel offers conclusive
evidence that the Twelve were not with Jesus in Jerusalem, except on the last visit.

(γ) Let us look at the references to the disciple,
who is assumed as the eye-witness of what the Fourth
Gospel records, to discover if that necessitates or
justifies the identification with John the son of Zebedee.
It is an inference, but a legitimate inference, that he
was one of the two disciples (Andrew being the other)
who left the Baptist for Jesus (i. 37). It is a conjecture that the rest of the Gospel does not offer any
ground for, that this unnamed disciple was the son
of Zebedee, John, and that he brought his brother
James, after Andrew had brought Simon (the word
first in *v.* 41). If he is not to be identified with John
the son of Zebedee, although the Appendix leaves
open the identification, room is left for him by the
mention of the two unnamed disciples (xxi. 2) ; but
in view of the character of the Appendix, no stress
can be laid on any evidence it offers. He, too, may
be identified with the disciple who was known to the
high priest, and who secured Peter's admission to
the high priest's palace (xviii. 15, 16). At the Last
Supper he is described as ' the disciple whom Jesus
loved ' (xiii. 23), and so also when the mother of Jesus
is entrusted to him (xix. 26) and when he is Peter's

P

companion to the tomb (xx. 2, 4, 8 ; cf. xxi. 7, 20,
23). If he was the master of the house, his position
at the Last Supper is explained. Why he was made
guardian of Jesus' mother has already been shown.
As Peter's host, his being with Peter at the tomb is
also explained. The Appendix refers to his position
at the Supper (v. 20) and claims that he is the witness
for the things recorded (v. 24). Not one of these
references represents him as in the position with Peter
and James in which John is presented to us in the
Synoptics. These three intimates of Jesus were
with him when He withdrew from the other disciples
in Gethsemane (Matt. xxvi. 37). If the beloved
disciple was John, why does the Fourth Gospel pass
over that sacred experience ? There is nothing in
all these references that shuts us up to the conclusion
that the beloved disciple was one of the three intimates,
even one of the Twelve, even a companion of Jesus
in Galilee. Thus Bishop Westcott's last link is not
only severed ; it does not exist at all.

(b) Dr. Sanday uses in favour of the authorship
of the Gospel by the son of Zebedee the argument
that the Fourth Gospel represents Peter and the
beloved disciple as holding the same relation to one
another as Peter and John the son of Zebedee in the
Book of Acts ; and it is more natural and obvious
' to regard the later relation as the direct continuation of the earlier ' than to suppose ' two pairs who
would be too much the doubles of each other.' This
argument demands close examination in detail. His
interpretation of xx. 2 is that ' they lodged together
in Jerusalem.' [1] But if the beloved disciple was
Peter's host, this verse does not bear the significance
Dr. Sanday finds in it. The details with which the

---

[1] *The Criticism of the Fourth Gospel*, pp. 102-107.

meetings in the Upper Room on two successive ' first days of the week ' are recorded, as compared with the less definite account in Luke xxiv. 33, suggest that he was on both occasions the host as he had been at the Last Supper (xx. 19-29). That at a later date Peter went to the house of Mary cannot be quoted in disproof, as amid persecution the believers would move from place to place (Acts xii. 12). Dr. Sanday's further statement, that xxi. 20 shows that ' they each take an affectionate interest in the other,' loses its force if the Appendix is a much later addition to the Gospel of much lower credibility. If the beloved disciple was a disciple of John the Baptist's with Andrew, Peter's brother (i. 40), this connexion does not necessarily indicate the close association assumed. On two other occasions, at the Last Supper and at the high priest's palace, is he brought together with Peter, but in the one case the position at the table of each, and in the other the willingness to do a good turn to any follower of Jesus, are an adequate explanation. The writer at least cannot find any adequate proof of the special friendship Dr. Sanday assumes. In view of the prominence of John the son of Zebedee alongside of Peter in the Synoptics and Acts, it is impossible to understand why the identity is so carefully concealed in the Fourth Gospel. Elsewhere the reason for that concealment has been indicated, if the beloved disciple was what the writer holds him to have been.

(c) The writer is, however, in entire accord with Bishop Westcott and Dr. Sanday in insisting that in the Gospel we are dealing with an eye-witness, and it is hoped that throughout this discussion the evidence for this conclusion has been strengthened. He is inclined to insist that the reason for the addition

or the omission of an incident is not altogether, or
even mainly, to be found in the witness's pragmatism ;
but, where that is not obvious and needs to be discovered by strained ingenuity, in his presence or
absence from the scene.   If we set aside the insertions
of the redactor, and the additions of the evangelist,
in what remains we may assume that the witness is
recording what he saw and heard, and the reflexions
which his reminiscences inspired.   The view of Dr. E. F.
Scott, that ' apart from its allegorical value, the
picturesque detail in John's narrative can be set down,
not to the accurate memory of the eye-witness, but
to the fine instinct of the literary artist,' appears not
only intellectually improbable, but even morally
offensive, as the witness seems far too serious and
sincere to stoop to any devices such as are suggested
in the following sentence : ' All the more that the
prevailing tenor of his work was abstract and medi-
tative, he felt the need of relieving it with touches
of livelier colour.' [1]   What we meet with in the Gospel
is reality and not realism.   The intensity of religious
faith excludes the artifices of literary culture.   The
writer must confess that he has found not only Dr.
Scott's but other books written from the same standpoint too ingenious and altogether unconvincing.

(d) It seems to be altogether more difficult to
maintain the general historical credibility of the
Gospel, if we assume that a Galilaean disciple who
was Jesus' companion throughout His whole ministry
there was so indifferent to and ignorant of the course
and characteristics of the ministry, as the witness in
the Fourth Gospel shows himself to be, and that a
fisherman of Galilee had a dominating interest in,
and an intimate knowledge of, not only the Judaean

[1] *The Fourth Gospel : its Purpose and Theology*, p. 19.

ministry, but of all the local and temporary conditions
of it such as the Fourth Gospel displays. To preserve
a tradition, the defenders of the authorship by the
son of Zebedee weaken the defence of the historical
value of the Gospel. All the reasons offered in the
previous discussion for regarding the witness as a
disciple of Jerusalem are reasons against the traditional
authorship, as has been shown at each point. The
capacity and character of the witness who in loving
intimacy with Jesus could appreciate His higher
teaching, as the Twelve could not, do not correspond
with the impression of the son of Zebedee which the
Synoptics leave upon us. ' Them [John and James]
he surnamed Boanerges, which is, sons of thunder '
(Mark iii. 17).   It was John who forbade the disciple
who did not follow to use His name in exorcisms,
and who with his brother desired to call down fire
on the inhospitable Samaritan village (Luke ix. 49-56).
The two brothers, James and John, with their mother,
plotted to get a favoured place in the Kingdom (Matt.
xx. 20-28).   The beloved disciple was not this manner
of man. If it be urged that in a long life he was
much changed, so that the fiery zealot became the
thoughtful and tender interpreter of the heart of
God in Christ, it has to be pointed out that the thoughtful and tender intimacy he enjoyed with Jesus was
not in his old age, but at the very time with which
the Synoptics deal.   To have received and remembered
what He afterwards recorded he must have been other
than the son of Zebedee was.   He must have already
been as companion what he proved as witness, appreciative of and sympathetic with that ' inner life ' of Jesus
which he has unveiled for us, and for which, as the
Synoptic Gospels testify, the company of the Twelve
was so unintelligent and insensitive.   The questions

in the Upper Room show how dull these disciples were, and the records before us give no evidence that the son of Zebedee was any way more fit than his comrades. The writer is firmly convinced that no internal evidence can be produced for, and all the internal evidence is opposed to, the authorship of the Fourth Gospel by John the son of Zebedee. It is only an undue deference to the tradition about the authorship, which is by no means convincing on the one hand, and a baseless assumption that only among the Twelve could a disciple be found who could produce such a Gospel on the other hand, that have led so many scholars so persistently to maintain this traditional view, despite the difficulties in regard to the historical value of the Gospel which such a view involves.

(ii) Can we identify the witness with any of the persons whose names are mentioned in the New Testament ? To this question we must now address ourselves.

(a) Dr. Swete [1] has suggested that the beloved disciple may be identified with the rich young ruler. Some support is lent to the identification by two facts, *first*, that he asked a question concerning eternal life, and *second*, that Jesus is said to have loved him when He looked upon him (Mark x. 17, 21). For *first*, the conception of eternal life dominates the Fourth Gospel, and not that of the Kingdom of God as in the Synoptics ; and *second*, the witness is described as ' the disciple whom Jesus loved.' If this be his own description, it may be a sorrowful confession ; ' still loved though afraid openly to acknowledge the loving Master.' The objection to the identification is that it is towards the close of the ministry that

[1] *Journal of Theological Studies,* July 1916.

the Synoptic record places the coming of the rich
young ruler to Jesus, and the Fourth Gospel contains
the reminiscences of a disciple from the beginning.
The objection, however, is not insuperable. He may
have been a companion before the public ministry
began. He may, however, have avoided openly
identifying himself with the disciples of Jesus on His
visits to Jerusalem. Overcome by his aspiration to
find from the lips of Jesus the answer to his question,
he may have forgotten his prudence for a moment
in this act of homage. Jesus, anxious to bring the
waverer to decision in an open confession, may have
desired by his severe demand to loose the bonds that
bound him. Is Jesus' attitude to him, or his to Jesus,
not more intelligible if there were some previous
connexion ? Would Jesus have given the call to
become one of His followers at so great a cost to a
stranger, had He had no ground in previous knowledge
for expecting that it would be heard and answered.
Although the open confession may have been delayed
for years, and the silence of the Synoptists regarding
the identity of the rich young ruler may have been due
to his own desire to remain a secret disciple ; yet
at last, if only in distant Ephesus, and not in Jerusalem itself, the confession may have been made.
May he not include himself among those to whom
reference is made in xii. 42-43, an utterance of con-
trition ? Was the memory of the ' great refusal ' too
painful to be explicitly recorded, and was the confession made thus indirectly ? This identification
must, however, remain only a plausible conjecture.

(b) Another conjecture has been put forward by
the Rev. B. Grey Griffith, Cardiff [1]: ' The phrase
" The disciple whom Jesus loved " (ὃν ἠγάπα ὁ Ἰησοῦς)

_____
[1] *The Expository Times*, xxxii. p. 379.

does not occur till we come to the 13th chapter, and
then is found several times to the end of the Gospel.
Some one has come into the story who carries the
title. Either he was not in the story before, or he
has received a new name. But a similar phrase is
found in chapter 11, " He whom thou lovest is sick "
(Κύριε, ἴδε ὃν φιλεῖς ἀσθενεῖ). No name is mentioned,
no name is needed. Jesus recognizes the reference to
Lazarus, who evidently is known as the one who is
loved by Jesus. This is the word used of the household at Bethany, but used of none other. John 11. 5,
Ἠγάπα δὲ ὁ Ἰησοῦς τὴν Μάρθαν καὶ τὴν ἀδελφὴν
αὐτῆς καὶ τὸν Λάζαρον. It is true that in the first
intimation concerning Lazarus the word used is
φιλεῖς, but this is the word also used in chap. 20. 2
about this " other disciple." The two words are
evidently used interchangeably. If we were reading
without any previous notions and had marked the
passage in chap. 11. 5, " and Jesus loved Martha . . .
and Lazarus," and then had come across the phrase
in chap. 13, " The disciple whom Jesus loved," we
should, I think, immediately connect the two. *It
is Lazarus who has come into the story.* Can he fill
the picture ? ' The following reasons are given.
(1) Like his sister Mary (John xii. 16) he ' lives in
the atmosphere of " understanding." ' (2) He meets
what all the allusions require. (3) As one who had
been raised from the dead, the empty grave is enough
for him ; he needs no appearance to believe (xx. 2).
(4) ' It was said that he would not see death. This
is just what we should expect, namely, that Lazarus
who had been raised should not again have to face
death.' The last reason loses its force if the view
of the Appendix given in this volume holds. None
of the other reasons is conclusive. He sets aside the

objection that Lazarus cannot have been at the Last
Supper by insisting that he had become one of Jesus'
intimates, so that 'his absence would have been
remarkable.' He had 'been introduced into the
company.' The objection from xxi. 24 falls to the
ground with the view taken of the Appendix, and the
argument offered against it can be passed over.

(c) Rev. F. Warburton Lewis combines the two
conjectures. He holds that 'the points mentioned
by Mr. Grey Griffith are capable of even more emphasis
than he has placed upon them,' but dissents from
him in not identifying 'another disciple' of xviii. 15
with the beloved disciple, and takes xxi. 24 as referring
to the whole Gospel. He regards the Gospel as 'the
work of Lazarus issued (and perhaps edited) by the
apostle John or that other John beloved of critics.'
The story of the beloved disciple he states begins
'in Mark 10. 21—Jesus loved him at sight—the young
ruler was Lazarus.'[1] Some of the reasons for identifying the beloved disciple with the rich young ruler
on the one hand, and with Lazarus on the other,
lend plausibility to identification of the one with the
other ; but there is no real evidence.

(d) To the identification with Lazarus the Rev. H.
Rigg offers 'some formidable objections.'[2] (1) The
danger to Lazarus indicated in John xii. 10, 11 makes
it unlikely that he would 'move about so freely in
the court and palace during the Lord's trial.' (2) He
was not a companion of Jesus in Gethsemane, as we
might have expected him to be if he was so intimate
with Jesus as Mr. Griffith represents him as being.
(3) An argument should not be based on an emotional
utterance of the sisters. Why did they not use the
recognized title, 'the disciple whom thou lovest,' if

[1] *The Expository Times*, xxxiii. p. 42.   [2] *Op. cit.* pp. 232-233.

it did belong to their brother ?   (4) Why is Lazarus
not mentioned with Mary in Acts i. 13, 14, if he was
looking after her ?   These objections are not so formidable as their author thinks. Persons in peril
have been known to take risks. A good reason has
been given why the beloved disciple was not at Gethsemane, and for Lazarus' absence there might have
been a like reason. There is some force in the difference
of phrase to which attention is called. That her
guardian must always be with Mary is a groundless
assumption.   Mr. Rigg's is inconclusive reasoning.

(e) There seem to be two objections to the identification with Lazarus. The first is this : why, when
the name is elsewhere withheld, should it be given
only in chapter xi. ?   Why should Lazarus, if the
author, so mystify us ? The second is that the
narrative in xi. is from the standpoint of an observer,
and not of the experient. If the author had himself
been recalled from the grave, would there be no trace
of that experience in his record ? For our interpretation and estimate of the Gospel neither of these identi-
fications is of any importance, and the arguments
are in neither case conclusive. There the matter may
rest.

(iii) The third question to which we may address
ourselves is this, what does an examination of the
Gospel prove regarding its composition ? (a) In the
preceding discussion the following conclusions have
been reached, and may here be recalled : (1) The
Appendix with certain other passages which have
affinity with the Synoptic records have been assigned
to a redactor. (2) The Prologue with some passages
the theology of which is akin to that of the Prologue
have been ascribed to the evangelist, who may be
regarded as having the same relation to the witness,

'the beloved disciple,' as Mark had to Peter in the composition of the Second Gospel. He may have been John the Elder. (3) The bulk of the Gospel may be traced back to the witness, although doubtless the evangelist did not simply *record verbatim* what he had heard from his teacher, but gave a local and contemporary colouring to the stream of tradition. What the witness taught included his reflexions as well as his reminiscences ; and only in a few places can we be certain of the transition from the one to the other. We can sometimes, however, detect the *ipsissima verba* of Jesus, and can follow the workings of the mind of the witness as memory passed into meditation. Some of the reminiscences are given in their appropriate context, and others seem out of place where they are now found, and for them we can often conjecture a more fitting framework, such as iii. 12-15, vi. 62, which would be in a more suitable environment after xii. 31-32, and vi. 53-57, which, if it is authentic, can find a place only in connexion with the Last Supper. If the evangelist had to depend on notes of the witness's public teaching or private talk, we can easily understand how reminiscences might not always have been given in strict chronological order. It is probable that the reflexions of the witness were for the most part experimental, and that the explanations of a more speculative character are to be traced to the evangelist. Much of the difficulty and failure to appreciate properly the value of the Gospel arises from the neglect of this distinction, which we may perhaps express in this way. When the relation of Christ to the believer is the subject of meditation we are in the region of experience. When, however, the relation of the Son to the Father is being expounded we are in the region of speculation. In

his experimental reflexions the witness had no intention
of adding his own private interpretations to the
teaching of Jesus ; but as he meditated on what
he remembered, he became conscious of the Master's
presence and of the enlightening and quickening of
His spirit to bring all things to his remembrance, and
thereby to guide him into all the truth. Accordingly
he was not aware of any incongruity between his
reminiscences and his reflexions ; he was not conscious
of any offence against historical veracity when he
presented both, blended together, as his testimony
to the truth and grace of the only-begotten and well-
beloved Son, in whom his reporter, the evangelist,
also saw the Word become flesh. He doubtless did
not distinguish his experience in and his doctrine
about Christ ; but we, with our more accurate
epistemological method,cannot avoid doing so. There
are many portions of the Fourth Gospel in which
the most spiritual Christian piety finds itself at home
as nowhere else even in the New Testament. The
witness has in his reflexions interpreted as no other
has done what Christ is to and does for the intensely
devout soul. If in the report of the discourse in the
Upper Room we cannot always claim to possess
historical testimony, we have experimental evidence
regarding the work and worth of Christ for the spiritual
life. This element in the Fourth Gospel belongs
surely to the revelation of God in Christ, and has
permanent and universal value. ' The Spirit,' says
Dr. Strachan, ' has revealed to the Evangelist (*i.e.* the
Witness) the whole truth about Jesus, and under His
guidance and in fulfilment of His promise he has
given us the narrative and the teaching in the form
in which we have them.' [1]   We can provoke only con-

---

[1] *The Fourth Gospel,* p. 186.

tradiction if we make a like claim for the entire Christology of the Gospel. There is a self-witness of Jesus going beyond, and yet consistent with, and even necessary to complete the Synoptic representation, which we may accept as authentic. Jesus' consciousness of a unique sonship in entire dependence on, constant communion with, and perfect submission to God as Father we may accept as belonging to the historical reality to which the Gospel bears testimony. But in the more speculative explanations, as in the comments of the evangelist, there goes a tendency to over-emphasize the supernaturalness of Jesus' knowledge and power, which does not invent its illustrations, but imposes an interpretation on facts which these contradict. We can easily detect the instances of this tendency —and they do not lower the value of the Gospels, historically or spiritually.

(b) It is in an interest vital to Christian thought and life that the investigation resulting in these conclusions has been undertaken. The writer cannot agree with Dr. Drummond that we ' may well withhold our hands from the seamless robe,' [1] for it does seem to him to matter whether we have only speculative or even experimental interpretation of the historical testimony. While the Gospel does not hold the two apart, the experimental interest is primary. The writer cannot understand how it can be of no interest to Christian piety whether Jesus was or was not as the Gospel represents Him, whether He spoke, did, and suffered as He is represented. It is because he is convinced that the view of the authorship and composition of the Gospel here advanced removes objections to and affords reasons for the credibility of the Gospel as both historical

[1] *The Character and Authorship of the Fourth Gospel*, p. 41.

testimony and doctrinal interpretation that he has risked this adventure of literary and historical criticism, although his work lies usually in another field.

(c) It would be quite impossible to discuss all the views of the composition of the Gospel which have been advanced in recent years. With the view of Dr. Bacon on the one hand and of Dr. Stanton on the other, the view here presented has points of contact. So frequent reference has been made in the detailed discussion to Dr. Strachan's book that reasons for dissenting from its general position may here be given. Dr. Strachan sees also ' the hand of an editor ' in (1) ' the chronological scheme of chapters i.-xii., according to which the narrative of the ministry is arranged according to cycles of Jewish feasts ; (2) the very evident heightening of the miraculous element of chapter xi., superimposed on what is evidently in its original form a simple narrative of raising from the dead.' ' As regards (1),' he continues, ' his motive may be conjectured to be a desire to represent Jesus as consistently keeping the national feasts.' [1] The writer himself can see no adequate reason for assigning the chronological scheme to an editor. For he has tried to show the historic probability of a ministry of Jesus in Jerusalem just at the feasts, when the witness as a Jerusalemite was in close contact with Him, and so could give the account of one present. As regards the story of Lazarus its difficulties have been recognized, and it would be assuredly a relief if we could assign the heightening of the effect to another than the witness. For (2) the editorial activity in xi. Dr. Strachan finds ' an eschatological motive,' namely, ' that the Parousia is delayed, and many who expected to be alive at His coming are

[1] *The Expositor*, 8th series, vol. vii. p. 256.

dead.' If there be such a motive, would it not affect the witness no less in his old age than any disciple ? 'The same motive,' he says, 'prompts the editorial additions in such passages as vi. 39*b*, 40*b*, 44*b* (ἀναστήσω . . . τῇ ἐσχάτῃ ἡμέρᾳ), xiv. 1 ff. (which seems to me to have a very close connexion with the thought of xxi. 23).' As regards xiv. 1, the writer feels no need for any such assumption. In the other passages he is prepared to recognize an editorial addition (*i.e.* the evangelist's). The passage v. 21-29, which Dr. Strachan finds 'essentially true to the consciousness of the Fourth Evangelist as well as to the thought of Jesus,' [1] the writer has assigned to the evangelist rather than the witness. These are comparatively secondary matters. The one crucial issue Dr. Strachan raises is that regarding the chronology, and here the writer must altogether dissent from his view. The value of the Gospel lies in this, that the witness can report, what the Synoptics omit, the repeated ministry of Jesus in Jerusalem. The credibility of the Gospel as a historical record is, therefore, seriously affected if we ascribe the chronological framework to an editor of a later time, and not to the witness himself.

(4) CHARACTERISTICS OF THE GOSPEL

Although in the previous discussion it has been necessary to call attention to characteristics of the Gospel, it will be convenient to bring together what has been elsewhere referred to in a closing statement.

(i) It must be frankly and fully conceded that the Fourth Gospel is not as nearly objective history as are the Synoptics, although its contents may for the

---

[1] *Op. cit.* p. 258.

most part be traced to an eye-witness. Fact is coloured
by faith, record by doctrine. The miracles are signs,
proofs of what Jesus is. The discourses are not at
all in the manner or language of the Synoptic utterances, although there are sayings of Jesus in the
Fourth Gospel like those in the Synoptics. The
witness has reproduced the thought of Jesus in his
own speech, and the evangelist may have further
modified the language. He is not only translating
from Aramaic to Greek,[1] but from Jerusalem to
Ephesus, from the Judaic to the Hellenistic environment, from the fourth to the last decade of the first
century, from what he had once heard to what that
truth now meant to him. There is no good reason
for doubting that when Jesus had a receptive and
responsive hearer He could and did speak more plainly
about the deeper things than was possible with the
Galilaean multitude or even the circle of His Galilaean
disciples, and that in Judaea the controversy with
Jewish rulers and teachers assumed a persistence
and vehemence which were absent from the Galilaean
ministry ; and yet we must admit that these aspects
were emphasized beyond the historical probability
by the influence of the witness's environment when,
after the lapse of so many years, he tried to convey
to others what he himself had received from Jesus.
That in his own public teaching in reproducing what
he had learned he may have been influenced as regards
form by the *diatribe*, or discourse of the Greek philo-
sophical teachers, cannot be denied. And yet, making
all due allowance for all these changes, surely reminiscences were preserved, and developed by the Spirit
of Truth in the reflexions of the witness, which warrant

---

[1] This was written before Dr. Burney's *The Aramaic Origin of the
Fourth Gospel* appeared.

our feeling that we are really getting closer to the very
mind and heart of the Christ of our faith than we do
in the Synoptics.

(ii) There is good reason for holding that the chronological scheme is not imposed upon it by a later
editor, but that there was a succession of short
ministries of Jesus in Jerusalem at the great feasts
in which He repeated the attempt to win the nation
from unbelief to faith. We must recognize the
incompleteness of the Synoptic representation, and
gratefully accept the Fourth Gospel as complementary
to them, and as giving us a more intelligible and
credible conception of the course of the ministry of
Jesus as has already been shown. Bishop Westcott
and Dr. Sanday have called attention to the precision
of the Gospel in many details of time, place, and
person. The varying currents of public opinion and
popular sentiment are reproduced for us with striking
fidelity. There was a real drama enacted of the
struggle of faith with unbelief, of truth with error,
and grace with sin. Substantially the Gospel brings
us into living touch with historical reality. It must
be conceded, however, that the present as experienced
constantly affected the past as remembered. The
confession of the Messiahship is obviously ante-dated,
and so also other features in the gradual development
of the disciples. The occasion for sayings of Jesus
is mentioned, but the story is not completed ; as for
instance the request of the Greeks to see Jesus is
followed by His teaching about His death, and the
Greeks disappear from the scene altogether. The
story has interest only as the occasion for doctrine.
What is so dominant an interest in the Synoptics, and
cannot have been confined to Galilee in contrast to
Judaea—eschatology—has almost quite vanished, and

Q

its outward expectations have been transformed into inner experiences of the soul. The traces of the older eschatology which appear are probably due to the evangelist rather than the witness, as the hope of the Second Advent is also found in the First Epistle (ii. 18, iii. 12). It is possible, however, that in the mind of the witness even as in the mind of Paul the old and the new elements lay side by side, without any contradiction being perceived, as it appears to us now.

(iii) These characteristics become more intelligible when we recall the purpose of the Gospel, which is stated in xx. 31: 'These are written, that ye may believe that Jesus is the Christ, the Son of God ; and that believing, ye may have life in His name.' Even if this statement is due to the evangelist, and not the witness, it corresponds very closely with the contents of the Gospel. The purpose, as thus stated, does not necessarily impose an unhistorical character on the Gospel. Not only did Jesus claim to be the Messiah according to the Synoptic record, but even in the Synoptics He does claim the unique relationship to God as Son. And a study of the Gospels justifies the assertion that for Jesus the sonship was the more original and essential element in His own self-consciousness. It must be admitted, however, that the evangelist, if not the witness, imposes His own Christology on the self-witness of Jesus. While in the Synoptics the religious good is the Kingdom of God, yet even there eternal life appears as an end to be sought. The rich young ruler desires to inherit eternal life (Mark x. 17), and so does the lawyer (Luke x. 25). Faith is emphasized no less in the Synoptics ; but the faith of the Fourth Gospel, though not intellectualist, yet does emphasize the recognition of the truth about the person of Jesus as the Synoptics do not. The miracles and discourses are reported with this definite purpose in view. It is the religious and theological, and not the biographical interest which dominates. While the witness could and did remember the hearers who gathered around Jesus Himself, and again and again showed just how they thought and felt ; yet there is also present to his or the evangelist's mind another audience, the Christian community in Ephesus at the end of the first century, members of which had doubtless come to him with their doubts and difficulties. Not only had these Christians been taught and trained in the Pauline Gospel ; but their own intellectual environment was exercising a constant influence upon them. An objectively historical account of the works, words, and person of Jesus would not have answered just the questions which they asked. The eschatological hopes had to be replaced by an assurance of eternal life (and consequent immortality) in Christ. The docetism which was becoming a dominant tendency among speculative thinkers had to be resisted by an assertion of the reality of the complete incarnation of God in Jesus. As for every age so for this, the relation of historical fact to religious faith had to be explained ; the identity of the historical Jesus and the living Christ had to be asserted. For the witness reflexion had already so transformed reminiscence that the answer to all these questions could be found in his report.

(iv) While in interpreting the Gospel we must constantly take due account of the environment of the hearers or readers to whom the record was adapted, yet we must not, therefore, ignore the original historical situation assumed.

(a) It is essential that we should understand what

Hellenism was, the channel in which Jewish and
Greek thought met and blended their currents.
But there is another danger which we must also avoid.
Because undoubtedly the hearers of the witness, and
possibly he himself, were influenced by Hellenism,
we must not be too ready to assign to that influence
everything in the Gospel that has any resemblance
to the ideas current in it. It seems a necessary and
legitimate canon of criticism that we need not at
once and altogether refer to the environment, (1) whatever can be properly explained by probable developments of the teaching of Jesus to a more receptive
and responsive hearer than the multitude or even
the Twelve, or to a circle of theologically-trained
opponents in controversy ; (2) whatever can be
accounted for by psychological insight as the unfolding
in the mind of the witness by his reflexions on the
truth which he remembered ; (3) whatever can be
regarded as personal experience of the present Christ
in the working of His Spirit in the witness.

(b) Since scholars of eminence have found it possible
to believe that in substance the teaching of Jesus in
Jerusalem was as it is represented in the Fourth
Gospel, it does not betray unpardonable ignorance
to suggest that we should not confine ourselves to
the probable situation in Ephesus, and ignore what
was possible in Jerusalem. Interesting and important
as is the account which Dr. Strachan gives of the
Hellenistic Environment of the Gospel in Ephesus,[1] it
does seem to the writer that in his exposition he
unduly sets aside these considerations. ' Detached
from the Temple worship at Jerusalem,' he says,[2] ' the
Jews had *synagogues* everywhere, which were centres
of Jewish influence, and thought, and of proselytising

---

[1] *The Fourth Gospel*, pp. 22-53.   [2] *Idem*, p. 25.

zeal. Vast numbers, mostly Asiatic Greeks, must
have adopted the Jewish faith, whilst retaining their
Greek forms of thought. The earliest preachers of
the Christian Gospel found in these synagogue communities a starting-point for their message that the
Messiah had come in Jesus. In this situation, and
not in the more restricted area of controversy depicted
in the Synoptic Gospels, is to be found the key to the
strongly-marked Jewish controversial element in the
Fourth Gospel. In this Gospel the Judaism portrayed
belongs rather to the Synagogue than to the Temple,
and it is constantly opposed in fierce polemic.' Again
and again in this volume has it been found necessary
to insist on the incompleteness of the Synoptic record.
To limit the range of controversy possible in the
earthly ministry of Jesus to the Synoptic representation is to apply an arbitrary standard. It is probable
that Jesus asserted His authority against that of the
Jewish rulers and teachers in Jerusalem as was not
necessary in Galilee; and that He was consequently
involved in controversies there for which there was
no occasion elsewhere. Jerusalem was not so exclusively dominated by the Temple that the ideas
of the scribes to which currency was given in the
synagogues were altogether absent from it. Unless
we can prove that an objection or difficulty was
impossible in Jerusalem during Jesus' ministry, we
are not entitled to dismiss it as only of later date
in Ephesus. In support of this contention Canon
Box,[1] who has the highest qualifications to speak
with authority on matters Jewish, may be cited.
Regarding the statement in John ix. 13-16 he writes :
' It would be unsafe to ignore the evidence of the

---

[1] The writer regrets that he cannot now give the exact reference
for this statement.

Fourth Gospel on this point, as everything suggests
that the tradition behind it regarding contemporary
Jewish life and conditions is extraordinarily good.'
He adds a quotation in a note from Dr. J. Abraham's
Studies in Pharisaism and the Gospels, p. 12 : ' My
own general impression, without asserting an early
date for the Fourth Gospel, is that the Gospel enshrines
a genuine tradition of an aspect of Jesus' teaching
which has not found a place in the Synoptics.'   These
two statements justify the position taken in this
volume that we need not look to Ephesus at the end
of the first century only, but may look mainly to
Jerusalem in the time of Jesus for the conditions of
the controversy, recorded in the Fourth Gospel, while
granting that the environment of later years may
have affected the record of that controversy.

(*c*) It is really a question of balance or proportion,
to which factor in the complex process of the composition of the Gospel we shall assign the greater potency.
Dr. Strachan states, for instance : ' He takes actual
points such as the Sabbath, or the question of descent
from Abraham, that must have emerged in the actual
ministry of Jesus, and so treats them as to make
the issue intelligible to his readers.'   He does seem,
however, to overstate when he continues : ' The points
discussed in these controversies always pass over into
such questions as the equality of Jesus with God
(v. 18 ff.).' [1]   In regard to such an affirmation some
considerations must be offered.   *First,* there is only
this one passage which speaks without qualification
of the equality with God.   *Secondly,* the witness does
not place the claim upon the lips of Jesus, but represents it as the inference drawn by His fanatical opponents from His claim to work as did the Father.

[1] *Op. cit.* p. 26.

Thirdly, even if the witness agreed with the opponents in their inference, elsewhere he reports Jesus as stating that the Father is greater (xiv. 28), and in the passage which immediately follows (*vv.* 19-29), which probably belongs to the evangelist rather than the witness, the dependence of the Son on the Father in the discharge of all His functions is taught (*vv.* 20, 22, 23, 26), as throughout the Gospel. Is it incredible that in Jerusalem such an inference from Jesus' teaching might have been honestly or dishonestly drawn ?

(*d*) There is a tendency here betrayed that besets the scholar to read more into a situation than is necessarily involved in it, just because he is so familiar with later developments of thought. Dr. Strachan himself concedes : ' The fact, therefore, that Jesus is represented as engaged in controversy with Hellenist Jews in Jerusalem cannot be regarded as in itself a breach of historical probability.' But even this statement involves an unproved assumption. Even if the kind of opposition met with was probable in Ephesus at the end of the century, can it be proved that it was impossible in Jerusalem in the ministry of Jesus from *Palestinian Jews* ? The writer is quite willing to be corrected if he is wrong, but he wants evidence, and not assumptions. Because in Justin Martyr's *Dialogue with Trypho the Jew* similar subjects are discussed as in the Gospel, how does that prove the fact that ' the Judaism of the Gospel is the Judaism of a later age ' ? [1] The question : ' How can this man give us his flesh to eat ? ' is in the preceding discussion recognized as certainly not belonging to the historical context in which it appears. The writer cannot, however, see why the question : ' Art thou greater than our father Jacob ? ' could be asked

[1] *Op. cit.* p. 27.

only by Hellenist Jews, and not as it is reported.
So again as regards the witness's dealing with Judas,
if Judas was his only fellow-countryman as a Judaean,
had he not himself interest enough to explain all he
states ? It may seem an ungracious, as it is to the
writer an ungrateful task, to criticise in detail a
scholar of such merits ; but what is involved is a
very serious issue. Shall we go on the assumption
on which he seems to go, that the discourses are for
the most part unhistorical even as regards their
substance, because dealing almost entirely with the
situation in Ephesus at the end of the century or on
the assumption, for which the writer is convinced
there is justification, that they are largely historical,
although the form has often been affected by the
influences of a later time ?

(e) The same kind of criticism must be applied to
some of the illustrations given of the influence of
Stoicism. Is it really necessary to explain with
reference to the *apathy* of Stoicism the three sayings
of Jesus (ii. 4 ; vii. 3 ff. ; xi. 3-7) ? [1] Is there not a
Synoptic parallel (Mark iii. 31-35) ? And are the
sayings not quite appropriate in their historical
setting ? There seems to be almost a lack of fine
feeling in suggesting that the fact ' Jesus wept ' is
recorded in correction of this same apathy. The
attempt to find some such explanation in the environment gives an artificiality to the Gospel which detracts
from its attractiveness and appeal. Had love's
meticulous care nothing to do with the preservation
of such details ? Again, had not the witness's own
experience of life in Christ much more to do with
giving its mystic character to the teaching of Jesus
as here recorded than any influence the mystery

[1] *Op. cit.* p. 35.

religions might exert ; and further, even, must we assume that there was nothing in the actual teaching of Jesus to one who could understand as the Galilaean disciples could not, which afforded full justification for the mysticism of the Fourth Gospel ? Does not the personal relationship of discipleship as presented in the Synoptics point towards such inward communion as the witness experienced and represented as having been promised by Jesus ? Is not the promise of continued presence in Matt. xxviii. 20 a confirmation of the teaching of the Fourth Gospel ? Even if we regard the saying as not from the lips even of the Risen Lord, but as the reflexion of the experience of the Apostolic Church, that such a statement should have found its way into such a writing as is the First Gospel is surely an indication that in the common Christian experience there was an element, it may be only rudimentary in most cases, but of which the Johannine and Pauline mysticisms are full typical developments. May not Jesus Himself have willed and promised before His departure the relation to His own after- wards experienced ? Was Dr. Dale under an illusion when he claimed for himself and other Christians ' fellowship with the living Christ.' Only if such communion be a vain imagination is it necessary to trace the Johannine or the Pauline mysticism to the mystery religions. Has Christianity nothing distinctive and original, its own alone ? Profoundly grateful as we must be to all scholars who out of the fulness of their learning show us all the possibilities of the influence of the environment on the contents of the Gospel, possibilities must not at once be regarded as probabilities, and still less as necessities. What Dr. Strachan has written must be read with great interest by all students of the Fourth Gospel ; but all his instances of the action of the environment in determining the character of the Gospel must be closely scrutinized ; and it will be found, in the judgment of the writer, that they do not all carry conviction. Reminiscences of the historical Jesus, unfolded in reflexions in communion with the living Christ by the enlightening of His Spirit, endow this spiritual organism of the Fourth Gospel with an inherent vitality which makes it less dependent on the environment than modern scholarship generally represents it as being. It is more historical and experimental in its content than this representation allows. This at least is the conviction which has grown upon the writer as he has continued his study ; and has constrained him to write this volume.

(5) 'THE ARAMAIC ORIGIN OF THE FOURTH GOSPEL'

The MS. of this volume had been completed when Dr. Burney's *The Aramaic Origin of the Fourth Gospel* appeared : and what follows has been added to show the bearing of his argument on the conclusions of this volume. It is in many respects a confirmation of what has been advanced, and not in necessary contradiction with the main theses, although if his contention be regarded as proven, some modifications of statement may be necessary.

(*a*) What the writer has contended for in the preceding pages, *i.e.* that the historical situation to be assumed is Judaean and not Ephesian, as Dr. Strachan has maintained, here finds support. That the witness, the evangelist, and the redactor have each contributed to the Gospel as it now is, is a conclusion from the internal evidence of the Gospel itself which the linguistic argument need not disprove, as it has been

already conceded that both the witness and the
evangelist were Judaeans, and so spoke Aramaic ;
and even if the redactor were Greek, it would not pass
his wit to imitate as closely as he could the style of the
book before him. Dr. Burney's argument aims at
proving that the Gospel is a Greek translation of an
Aramaic document. It is for those who have a knowledge of Aramiac, such as the writer does not possess,
to decide whether this is the only conclusion possible,
or the evidence allows for the assumption that the Greek
Gospel itself was composed by a writer (or writers)
who was more at home in the use of Aramaic. The
witness may have been reported by the evangelist
in Aramaic, and when the evangelist wrote the Gospel
in Greek as an Aramaic speaker himself, and as influenced by his teacher, the similarity of style may
have been without any conscious imitation produced.
There seems on linguistic grounds no insuperable
difficulty in adjusting the conclusions of this volume
to this new theory, if it should commend itself to those
who are competent to give a judgment upon it, as the
writer does not pretend to be.

(b) Dr. Stanton, while maintaining that the ultimate
source of the contents of the Gospel must have been
John the son of Zebedee, concedes that the evangelist
himself was a much younger man, who as a boy had
seen Jesus, and so would speak of himself as also
an eye-witness, but who was capable of the intellectual
development which the acceptance of the Logos
doctrine required, as the son of Zebedee at his advanced
age could not be. Dr. Burney does not feel bound
by the external evidence as does Dr. Stanton to suppose
that the John mentioned in the tradition was the son
of Zebedee, but feels free to identify him with John
the elder. He makes what seems to the writer a very

important contribution in regard to the evidence of
Irenaeus—on which so much stress is laid. He shows
that while Irenaeus describes Matthew, Peter, and
Paul as apostles he never once so describes John, but
only as disciple.[1] This description he maintains
that Irenaeus derived from Papias, who distinguished
Aristion and John the presbyter as simply disciples,
and not apostles as well, as were those whom he had
just mentioned. ' On the basis of these facts we
conclude without hesitation that by "John the disciple
of the Lord " Irenaeus means John the presbyter,
and that when he refers to Papias as ὁ Ἰωάννου μὲν
ἀκουστής, he is at any rate as correct as Eusebius when
he says ὁ νῦν δὲ ἡμῖν δηλούμενος Παπίας . . . τοῦ πρεσ-
βυτέρου Ἰωάννου αὐτήκοον ἑαυτόν φησι γενέσθαι. It is
Eusebius who, jumping to the conclusion that John
the apostle (mentioned sixth by Papias in his list of
seven apostles) must be the evangelist (σαφῶς δηλῶν
τὸν εὐαγγελιστήν), attaches to Irenaeus the charge of
misconstruing Papias's evidence which has stuck to
him ever since. In reality Irenaeus appears to be
an impeccable witness as to the early Asian tradition
in regard to John ; and he completes our evidence
that John the evangelist and disciple of the Lord,
who survived to old age at Ephesus, was not the son
of Zebedee, but the presbyter.' [2] ' All that Papias
claims to have learned (or to have endeavoured to
learn) by word of mouth about the apostolic son of
Zebedee is what others said that the presbyters said
that he said : and so far is he from attaching any special
prominence to him that he mentions him only sixth
in a list of seven of the apostles.' [3] Tradition need
not block our way, if so understood, to determine the
question on internal evidence.

[1] *Op. cit.* p. 139.   [2] *Idem*, pp. 141-142.   [3] *Idem*, pp. 135-136.

(c) While agreeing with Dr. Stanton in regard to the youth of the witness and evangelist, for he does not distinguish them, Dr. Burney has not the same reason for so doing, since he assumes for the Logos idea a Palestinian origin and not the adoption and adaptation of it by the evangelist when he passed into a Gentile environment. The summary of his argument as based on i. 14 may be quoted. ' In καὶ ὁ λόγος σὰρξ ἐγένετο we have the Mēmrā ; in καὶ ἐσκήνωσεν ἐν ἡμῖν the Shᵉkīntā ; in καὶ ἐθεασάμεθα τὴν δόξαν αὐτοῦ the Yᵉkārā. This is evidence that, so far from his owing his λόγος doctrine to an Alexandrian source, he is soaked through and through with the Palestinian Jewish thought which is represented by the Targums. Nor would the teaching of the Prologue need time for its development. Any disciple of our Lord who had heard the Targumic rendering of the O.T. in the synagogue, and who was capable of recognizing a superhuman power shining through the Master's Personality in His mighty acts, of detecting the Divine voice in His teaching, and at length of apprehending that in His Presence on earth God had come to dwell among men, could hardly fail to draw the inference that here was the grand fulfilment of O.T. conception so familiar to him through the Aramaic paraphrase.' [1] On the grounds that ' nearly every verse of the Prologue yields evidence pointing to an Aramaic original,' ' the simplicity of the construction,' and ' the many cases of parallelism,' he concludes that ' the Prologue seems to take the form of a hymn written in eleven parallel couplets, with comments introduced here and there by the writer.' [2] Without pronouncing any opinion on the linguistic question, the case does not

[1] *Op. cit.* p. 39.   [2] *Idem*, p. 40.

seem to the writer quite as simple as to Dr. Burney.
Reason has been shown for distinguishing the theology
of the evangelist as it has been affected by the Logos-
doctrine, and the theology of the witness, where the
Son-conception dominates, and it seems impossible
to exclude from the Gospel altogether the influence
of the Gentile environment. The similarity between
John and Paul which Dr. Burney recognizes strengthens
the second consideration, for who can deny that Paul,
Hebrew of the Hebrews as he was, was influenced
in his theology by that Gentile environment ? The
two extremes of the position held by Dr. Strachan,
and of that taken by Dr. Burney, must be avoided,
and the two streams of influence must be carefully
traced. The fact that Dr. Burney can accept the
possibility that ' the author of the apocalypse is one
with the author of the Fourth Gospel and Epistles,'
without himself recognizing that the ' criteria of
theological thought ' [1] forbid such an identification,
raises the doubt of the soundness of his judgment on so
complex a question as the origin of the Logos-doctrine.
Even if the seeds of the doctrine are in the Targums,
the development of the doctrine as we find it in the
Prologue seems to demand some time in a Gentile
environment under the influence of Greek thought.

(d) The account Dr. Burney gives of the author
of the Gospel agrees in many particulars with that
given in this volume of the witness. He represents
him as a young disciple, and ignores the considerations
already offered for regarding the witness as a man
of influence and authority, the householder who
offered the use of his ass and his upper-room. That
a young disciple such as Dr. Burney describes him
' should have been present at the Last Supper,' and

[1] *Op. cit.* p. 152.

had ' a place next his Lord,' does not appear ' only
natural,' [1] as it would if he were the host on the
occasion. With this qualification all he says of the
author of the Gospel can be applied to the witness,
who it has been shown can be distinguished from the
evangelist, a younger contemporary. The resemblance
of the witness to Paul has been well set out. ' Similarity of social position, a common Rabbinic training,
common ideals and pride of race and enthusiasm for
Judaism in its higher developments.' ' We seem
here,' he says, ' to find explained the remarkable
double attitude towards the Jews which characterizes
both the Christian converts ' [2]—antagonism and attachment. ' It was precisely the grasp of Judaism from
the inside only possible to a trained Rabbinic scholar
which emphasized the sense of its privileges and
opened out the vista of its lofty possibilities in the
light of the teaching of Him who was seen to be both
its supreme exponent and its ultimate goal ; while
at the same time strengthening the recoil from those
its professed teachers and practitioners who resolutely
shut their ears to and resisted the Truth, and would
not come to Him that they might have life. Such
scholars were St. Paul and the Fourth Evangelist.' [3]
It is not necessary to discuss the statement regarding
the author in detail. The writer welcomes the confirmation it at many points offers to the considerations
he has himself advanced.

(e) The age of the author is assumed by Dr. Burney
to have been about twenty at the Crucifixion—an
age which seems too young for some of the evidence
—and his age when the Gospel was composed sixty-five
or seventy at most. The Gospel is accordingly
dated A.D. 75-80, at least a decade earlier than that

[1] *Op. cit.* p. 144.   [2] *Idem,* p. 145.   [3] *Idem,* pp. 145-146.

commonly assumed. While that might be the date
when the evangelist wrote the record of the witness's
teaching, the writer must regard this date as too early
for the completed Gospel. Dr. Burney does not
attempt to place it earlier, because ' there seem to
be no indications pointing to a date prior to the
destruction of Jerusalem in A.D. 70 ' : and ' there
are a number of indications which suggest a certain
remoteness, both in time and place, from the scenes
described, and also seem to imply that the author
was not writing, at least primarily, *for Jews,* but for
a larger circle of Christians.' While not written in
Palestine, the ' theory of an Aramaic original seems
to demand that it should have originated in an Aramaic-
speaking country. Thus Syria is indicated, and if
Syria, then Antioch.' [1] The two facts on which
Dr. Burney rests his conclusion are : (1) the traces
of Johannine theology in the Ignatian Epistles, showing
a knowledge of the Gospel, possibly even in the original
Aramaic ; and (2) the dependence of Ignatius on the
Odes and Psalms of Solomon, which Dr. Rendel Harris
and Mingana assign to Antioch in the first century.
' It is noteworthy,' he adds, ' that a great part of the
connexions with the thought of the Gospel, both in
Ignatius' letters and in the Odes, are with the Last
Discourses.' [2]

(*f*) From the standpoint of this volume what is
important is to ascertain whether this connexion is
with every part of the Gospel or only with what has
been assigned to the witness. The parallel between
Ode vii. 4 and John i. 14, 12 does not appear close
enough to compel us to recognize any dependence,
neither that between Ode xviii. 4-6 and John i. 1, 5,
nor yet those between Odes xxxvi. 3, xli. 11 and

[1] *Op. cit.* p. 129.   [2] *Idem,* p. 132.

John i. 9, 11.[1] The mention of the Word, or even
the comparison of it with light, does not seem an adequate proof. The same conclusion holds as regards
the connexion of the Prologue with the Ignatian
Epistles. Εἰς ἕνα ὄντα in *Magnesians* 7 need not be
derived from John i. 18, ὁ ὢν εἰς τὸν κόλπον τοῦ πατρός ;
even such a statement in the next verse, ὅς ἐστιν αὐτοῦ
λόγος ἀπὸ σιγῆς προελθών has probably connexion
with other circles of thought than the Prologue.[2]
In the preceding discussion John v. 19 has been assigned to the evangelist. The clause in *Magnesians* 7
can be derived from John viii. 28.[3] *Romans* 7 has a
likeness to John vi. 32, 33, 55. While the narrative
framework of vi. has been assigned to the redactor,
it has been recognized that he has used sayings that do
belong to the witness's report. This same explanation
applies to the connexion of Ode xli. 11 with John vi.
33, 37.[4] Accordingly if we allow the connexion
of the Ignatian Epistles and the Odes with the
Fourth Gospel, that connexion may be restricted to
the reports of the witness, and we may base on that
fact the origin of this part of the Gospel only in
Antioch.

(*g*) The evidence does not forbid the assumption
that this part of the Gospel was taken by the evangelist
to Ephesus, so that the Gospel assumed its present
form there as has generally been held. The change
of place would throw the witness altogether into the
background, and lead first to the ascription of the
whole Gospel to the evangelist, and at last, if his
name was John, to the identification with John the
son of Zebedee, at which an attempt is made in the
Appendix. It is for scholars familiar with Aramaic

---

[1] *Op. cit.* pp. 167-168.　　[2] *Idem*, p. 156.
[3] *Idem*, pp. 155-157.　　[4] *Idem*, p. 168.

to test Dr. Burney's hypothesis linguistically. On the side of literary and theological criticism it seems to call for qualification, such as has been indicated. While in many respects it confirms the conclusions of this volume, it does not necessarily contradict any of them. Accordingly the writer has not felt under an obligation to reconsider the question, but sends forth this result of many years' occupation with the problem of the Gospel, with a due sense of its imperfections, in the hope that it will contribute to a firmer assurance regarding the historical as well as the theological and ethical value of the Gospel, as he holds strongly the conviction that Christian faith has its unshaken foundation, not in religious ideas and moral ideals, but in historical facts, in the historical personality, by whom God is revealed, and man redeemed, the Son who makes the Father known that men may find eternal life in Him.

INDEX

(1) GENERAL

ABRAHAM, 246.
Allegory, 121.
Andrew, 43, 56, 73, 80.
Antichrist, 27.
Antioch, 256.
Apocalyptic, 26.
Appendix, xv, xvi, xvii, xxi, 30-37, 202, 234, 257.
Aramaic (Origin), 250-258.
Ascension, 185.
Atonement, 26.

BACON, xvi, xxi, 36, 39, 55, 59, 66, 154, 219, 238.
Baldensperger, 1.
Bennett, 27.
Bernard, 186.
Beyschlag, 126.
Blass, 39.
Bousset, 205.
Box, 245.
Bruce, 126, 134, 187.
Burkitt, 180, 181, 207.
Burney, 6, 240, 250-258.
Burton, 110, 111, 179.

CHALMERS, 159.
Charles, 24.
Chastand, 47, 49, 50.
Christology, 5, 8, 21, 27, 46, 102, 123, 139, 189, 194-201, 242.
Chronology, xv, 60, 61-65, 118, 170, 238, 255.
Chrysostom, 68.
Colossians, 7.
Comments, xxi. 14-29, 87, 93, 202.
Controversy, 104, 117, 157, 198.

DALE, 249.
Death, 58, 123, 128, 195, 199.
De Boor, 207.
Dedication (Feast), 118-124.
Delff, 204.
Dionysius, 207.
' Disciple whom Jesus loved,' xvi, xxii, 32, 35, 145, 202-204, 222, 225.
Disciples, 44, 130, 221-224.
Displacements, 2, 40, 41, 43, 76, 101, 143.
Docetism, 178-180, 243.
Dods, 2, 13, 16, 108, 178, 179, 189.
Drummond, 204, 207, 209, 237.
Dualism, 53, 94.

ESCHATOLOGY, 22, 35, 120, 163, 199, 219, 238.
Eternal Life, 93, 196, 242.
Eucharist, 50, 199.
Eusebius, 181, 206, 208, 212, 252.
Evangelist (the), xxi, 2, 4, 7, 14-29, 39, 40, 43, 61, 75, 87, 93, 104, 128, 132, 191, 194, 199, 206, 217-219, 234, 242, 250, 251, 257.
Excommunication, 119.
Experience, 23, 93, 158, 199.

FORBES, 128.
Foreknowledge, 18.

GARDNER, xviii.
Georgius Monachus, 207.
Glory (the), 66, 140-193.
Griffith, 231.
Grubb, 124.

259

(2) SCRIPTURE REFERENCES